Storm Applied

Storm Applied

Strategies for real-time event processing

SEAN T. ALLEN
MATTHEW JANKOWSKI
PETER PATHIRANA

MANNING
SHELTER ISLAND

For online information and ordering of this and other Manning books, please visit
www.manning.com. The publisher offers discounts on this book when ordered in quantity.
For more information, please contact

> Special Sales Department
> Manning Publications Co.
> 20 Baldwin Road
> PO Box 761
> Shelter Island, NY 11964
> Email: orders@manning.com

Manning Publications Co.
20 Baldwin Road
PO Box 761
Shelter Island, NY 11964

Development editor: Dan Maharry
Technical development editor Aaron Colcord
Copyeditor: Elizabeth Welch
Proofreader: Melody Dolab
Technical proofreader: Michael Rose
Typesetter: Dennis Dalinnik
Cover designer: Marija Tudor

ISBN: 9781617291890
Printed in the United States of America
1 2 3 4 5 6 7 8 9 10 – EBM – 20 19 18 17 16 15

brief contents

contents

foreword

"Backend rewrites are always hard."

That's how ours began, with a simple statement from my brilliant and trusted colleague, Keith Bourgoin. We had been working on the original web analytics backend behind Parse.ly for over a year. We called it "PTrack".

Parse.ly uses Python, so we built our systems atop comfortable distributed computing tools that were handy in that community, such as *multiprocessing* and *celery*. Despite our mastery of these, it seemed like every three months, we'd double the amount of traffic we had to handle and hit some other limitation of those systems. There had to be a better way.

So, we started the much-feared backend rewrite. This new scheme to process our data would use small Python processes that communicated via ZeroMQ. We jokingly called it "PTrack3000," referring to the "Python3000" name given to the future version of Python by the language's creator, when it was still a far-off pipe dream.

By using ZeroMQ, we thought we could squeeze more messages per second out of each process and keep the system operationally simple. But what this setup gained in operational ease and performance, it lost in data reliability.

Then, something magical happened. BackType, a startup whose progress we had tracked in the popular press,[1] was acquired by Twitter. One of the first orders of business upon being acquired was to publicly release its stream processing framework, Storm, to the world.

---

[1] This article, "Secrets of BackType's Data Engineers" (2011), was passed around my team for a while before Storm was released: http://readwrite.com/2011/01/12/secrets-of-backtypes-data-engineers.

My colleague Keith studied the documentation and code in detail, and realized: Storm was exactly what we needed!

It even used ZeroMQ internally (at the time) and layered on other tooling for easy parallel processing, hassle-free operations, and an extremely clever data reliability model. Though it was written in Java, it included some documentation and examples for making other languages, like Python, play nicely with the framework. So, with much glee, "PTrack9000!" (exclamation point required) was born: a new Parse.ly analytics backend powered by Storm.

Nathan Marz, Storm's original creator, spent some time cultivating the community via conferences, blog posts, and user forums.[2] But in those early days of the project, you had to scrape tiny morsels of Storm knowledge from the vast web.

Oh, how I wish *Storm Applied*, the book you're currently reading, had already been written in 2011. Although Storm's documentation on its design rationale was very strong, there were no practical guides on making use of Storm (especially in a production setting) when we adopted it. Frustratingly, despite a surge of popularity over the next three years, there were still no good books on the subject through the end of 2014!

No one had put in the significant effort required to detail how Storm components worked, how Storm code should be written, how to tune topology performance, and how to operate these clusters in the real world. That is, until now. Sean, Matthew, and Peter decided to write *Storm Applied* by leveraging their hard-earned production experience at TheLadders, and it shows. This will, no doubt, become the definitive practitioner's guide for Storm users everywhere.

Through their clear prose, illuminating diagrams, and practical code examples, you'll gain as much Storm knowledge in a few short days as it took my team several years to acquire. You will save yourself many stressful firefights, head-scratching moments, and painful code re-architectures.

I'm convinced that with the newfound understanding provided by this book, the next time a colleague turns to you and says, "Backend rewrites are always hard," you'll be able to respond with confidence: "Not this time."

Happy hacking!

ANDREW MONTALENTI
COFOUNDER & CTO, PARSE.LY[3]
CREATOR OF *STREAMPARSE*, A PYTHON PACKAGE FOR STORM[4]

---

[2] Nathan Marz wrote this blog post about his early efforts at evangelizing the project in "History of Apache Storm and lessons learned" (2014): http://nathanmarz.com/blog/history-of-apache-storm-and-lessons-learned.html.

[3] Parse.ly's web analytics system for digital storytellers is powered by Storm: http://parse.ly.

[4] To use Storm with Python, you can find the streamparse project on Github: https://github.com/Parsely/streamparse.

preface

At TheLadders, we've been using Storm since it was introduced to the world (version 0.5.x). In those early days, we implemented solutions with Storm that supported non-critical business processes. Our Storm cluster ran uninterrupted for a long time and "just worked." Little attention was paid to this cluster, as it never really had any problems. It wasn't until we started identifying more business cases where Storm was a good fit that we started to experience problems. Contention for resources in production, not having a great understanding of how things were working under the covers, sub-optimal performance, and a lack of visibility into the overall health of the system were all issues we struggled with.

This prompted us to focus a lot of time and effort on learning much of what we present in this book. We started with gaining a solid understanding of the fundamentals of Storm, which included reading (and rereading many times) the existing Storm documentation, while also digging into the source code. We then identified some "best practices" for how we liked to design solutions using Storm. We added better monitoring, which enabled us to troubleshoot and tune our solutions in a much more efficient manner.

While the documentation for the fundamentals of Storm was readily available online, we felt there was a lack of documentation for best practices in terms of dealing with Storm in a production environment. We wrote a couple of blog posts based on our experiences with Storm, and when Manning asked us to write a book about Storm, we jumped at the opportunity. We knew we had a lot of knowledge we wanted to share with the world. We hoped to help others avoid the frustrations and pitfalls we had gone through.

While we knew that we wanted to share our hard-won experiences with running a production Storm cluster—tuning, debugging, and troubleshooting—what we really wanted was to impart a solid grasp of the fundamentals of Storm. We also wanted to illustrate how flexible Storm is, and how it can be used across a wide range of use cases. We knew ours were just a small sampling of the many use cases among the many companies leveraging Storm.

The result of this is *Storm Applied*. We've tried to identify as many different types of use cases as possible to illustrate how Storm can be used in many scenarios. We cover the core concepts of Storm in hopes of laying a solid foundation before diving into tuning, debugging, and troubleshooting Storm in production. We hope this format works for everyone, from the beginner just getting started with Storm, to the experienced developer who has run into some of the same troubles we have.

This book has been the definition of teamwork, from everyone who helped us at Manning to our colleagues at TheLadders, who very patiently and politely allowed us to test our ideas early on.

We hope you are able to find this book useful, no matter your experience level with Storm. We have enjoyed writing it and continue to learn more about Storm every day.

acknowledgments

We would like to thank all of our coworkers at TheLadders who provided feedback. In many ways, this is your book. It's everything we would want to teach you about Storm to get you creating awesome stuff on our cluster.

We'd also like to thank everyone at Manning who was a part of the creation of this book. The team there is amazing, and we've learned so much about writing as a result of their knowledge and hard work. We'd especially like to thank our editor, Dan Maharry, who was with us from the first chapter to the last, and who got to experience all our first-time author growing pains, mistakes, and frustrations for months on end.

Thank you to all of the technical reviewers who invested a good amount of their personal time in helping to make this book better: Antonios Tsaltas, Eugene Dvorkin, Gavin Whyte, Gianluca Righetto, Ioamis Polyzos, John Guthrie, Jon Miller, Kasper Madsen, Lars Francke, Lokesh Kumar, Lorcon Coyle, Mahmoud Alnahlawi, Massimo Ilario, Michael Noll, Muthusamy Manigandan, Rodrigo Abreau, Romit Singhai, Satish Devarapalli, Shay Elkin, Sorbo Bagchi, and Tanguy Leroux. We'd like to single out Michael Rose who consistently provided amazing feedback that led to him becoming the primary technical reviewer.

To everyone who has contributed to the creation of Storm: without you, we wouldn't have anything to tune all day and write about all night! We enjoy working with Storm and look forward to the evolution of Storm in the years to come.

We would like to thank Andrew Montalenti for writing a review of the early manuscript in MEAP (Manning Early Access Program) that gave us a good amount of inspiration and helped us push through to the end. And that foreword you wrote: pretty much perfect. We couldn't have asked for anything more.

And lastly, Eleanor Roosevelt, whose famously misquoted inspirational words, "America is all about speed. Hot, nasty, badass speed," kept us going through the dark times when we were learning Storm.

Oh, and all the little people. If there is one thing we've learned from watching awards shows, it's that you have to thank the little people.

SEAN ALLEN

Thanks to Chas Emerick, for not making the argument forcefully enough that I probably didn't want to write a book. If you had made it better, no one would be reading this now. Stephanie, for telling me to keep going every time that I contemplated quitting. Kathy Sierra, for a couple of inspiring Twitter conversations that reshaped my thoughts on how to write a book. Matt Chesler and Doug Grove, without whom chapter 7 would look rather different. Everyone who came and asked questions during the multiple talks I did at TheLadders; you helped me to hone the contents of chapter 8. Tom Santero, for reviewing the finer points of my distributed systems scribbling. And Matt, for doing so many of the things required for writing a book that I didn't like doing.

MATTHEW JANKOWSKI

First and foremost, I would like to thank my wife, Megan. You are a constant source of motivation, have endless patience, and showed unwavering support no matter how often writing this book took time away from family. Without you, this book wouldn't get completed. To my daughter, Rylan, who was born during the writing of this book: I would like to thank you for being a source of inspiration, even though you may not realize it yet. To all my family, friends, and coworkers: thank you for your endless support and advice. Sean and Peter: thank you for agreeing to join me on this journey when this book was just a glimmer of an idea. It has indeed been a long journey, but a rewarding one at that.

about this book

With big data applications becoming more and more popular, tools for handling streams of data in real time are becoming more important. Apache Storm is a tool that can be used for processing unbounded streams of data.

Storm Applied isn't necessarily a book for beginners only or for experts only. Although understanding big data technologies and distributed systems certainly helps, we don't necessarily see these as requirements for readers of this book. We try to cater to both the novice and expert. The initial goal was to present some "best practices" for dealing with Storm in a production environment. But in order to truly understand how to deal with Storm in production, a solid understanding of the fundamentals is necessary. So this book contains material we feel is valuable for engineers with all levels of experience.

If you are new to Storm, we suggest starting with chapter 1 and reading through chapter 4 before you do anything else. These chapters lay the foundation for understanding the concepts in the chapters that follow. If you are experienced with Storm, we hope the content in the later chapters proves useful. After all, developing solutions with Storm is only the start. Maintaining these solutions in a production environment is where we spend a good percentage of our time with Storm.

Another goal of this book is to illustrate how Storm can be used across a wide range of use cases. We've carefully crafted these use cases to illustrate certain points. We hope the contrived nature of some of the use cases doesn't get in the way of the points we are trying to make. We attempted to choose use cases with varying levels of requirements around speed and reliability in the hopes that at least one of these cases may be relatable to a situation you have with Storm.

The goal of this book is to focus on Storm and how it works. We realize Storm can be used with many different technologies: various message queue implementations, database implementations, and so on. We were careful when choosing what technologies to introduce in each of our use case implementations. We didn't want to introduce too many, which would take the focus away from Storm and what we are trying to teach you with Storm. As a result, you will see that each implementation uses Java. We could have easily used a different language for each use case, but again, we felt this would take away from the core lessons we're trying to teach. (We actually use Scala for many of the topologies we write.)

Roadmap

Chapter 1 introduces big data and where Storm falls within the big data picture. The goal of this chapter is to provide you with an idea of when and why you would want to use Storm. This chapter identifies some key properties of big data applications, the various types of tools used to process big data, and where Storm falls within the gamut of these tools.

Chapter 2 covers the core concepts in Storm within the context of a use case for counting commits made to a GitHub repository. This chapter lays the foundation for being able to speak in Storm-specific terminology. In this chapter we introduce you to your first bit of code for building Storm projects. The concepts introduced in this chapter will be referenced throughout the book.

Chapter 3 covers best practices for designing Storm topologies, showing you how to decompose a problem to fit Storm constructs within the context of a social heat map application. This chapter also discusses working with unreliable data sources and external services. In this chapter we introduce the first bits of parallelism that will be the core topic of later chapters. This chapter concludes with a higher-level discussion of the different ways to approach topology design.

Chapter 4 discusses Storm's ability to guarantee messages are processed within the context of a credit card authorization system. We identify how Storm is able to provide these guarantees, while implementing a solution that provides varying degrees of reliability. This chapter concludes with a discussion of replay semantics and how you can achieve varying degrees of reliability in your Storm topologies.

Chapter 5 covers the Storm cluster in detail. We discuss the various components of the Storm cluster, how a Storm cluster provides fault tolerance, and how to install a Storm cluster. We then discuss how to deploy and run your topologies on a Storm cluster in production. The remainder of the chapter is devoted to explaining the various parts of the Storm UI, as the Storm UI is frequently referenced in the chapters that follow.

Chapter 6 presents a repeatable process for tuning a Storm topology within the context of a flash sales use case. We also discuss latency in dealing with external systems and how this can affect your topologies. We end the chapter with a discussion of Storm's metrics-collecting API and how to build your own custom metrics.

Chapter 7 covers various types of contention that may occur in a Storm cluster where you have many topologies running at once. We discuss contention for resources within a single topology, contention for system resources between topologies, and contention for system resources between Storm and other processes, such as the OS. This chapter is meant to get you to be mindful of the big picture for your Storm cluster.

Chapter 8 provides you with a deeper understanding of Storm so you can debug unique problems you may come across on your own. We dive under the covers of one of Storm's central units of parallelization, executors. We also discuss many of the internal buffers Storm uses, how those buffers may overflow, and tuning those buffers. We end the chapter with a discussion of Storm's debug log-out.

Chapter 9 covers Trident, the high-level abstraction that sits on top of Storm, within the context of developing an internet radio application. We explain why Trident is useful and when you might want to use it. We compare a regular Storm topology with a Trident topology in order to illustrate the difference between the two. This chapter also touches on Storm's distributed remote procedure calls (DRPC) component and how it can be used to query state in a topology. This chapter ends with a complete Trident topology implementation and how this implementation might be scaled.

Code downloads and conventions

The source code for the example application in this book can be found at https://github.com/Storm-Applied. We have provided source code for the following chapters:

- Chapter 2, GitHub commit count
- Chapter 3, social heat map
- Chapter 4, credit card authorization
- Chapter 6, flash sale recommender
- Chapter 9, internet radio play-log statistics

Much of the source code is shown in numbered listings. These listings are meant to provide complete segments of code. Some listings are annotated to help highlight or explain certain parts of the code. In other places throughout the text, code fragments are used when necessary. `Courier typeface` is used to denote code for Java, XML, and JSON. In both the listings and fragments, we make use of a **bold code font** to help identify key parts of the code that are being explained in the text.

Software requirements

The software requirements include the following:

- The solutions were developed against Storm 0.9.3.
- All solutions were written in Java 6.
- The solutions were compiled and packaged with Maven 3.2.0.

Author Online

Purchase of *Storm Applied* includes free access to a private web forum run by Manning Publications where you can make comments about the book, ask technical questions, and receive help from the authors and other users. To access the forum and subscribe to it, point your web browser to www.manning.com/StormApplied. This Author Online (AO) page provides information on how to get on the forum once you're registered, what kind of help is available, and the rules of conduct on the forum.

Manning's commitment to our readers is to provide a venue where a meaningful dialog among individual readers and between readers and the authors can take place. It's not a commitment to any specific amount of participation on the part of the authors, whose contribution to the AO remains voluntary (and unpaid). We suggest you try asking the authors some challenging questions, lest their interest stray!

The AO forum and the archives of previous discussions will be accessible from the publisher's website as long as the book is in print.

about the cover illustration

The figure on the cover of *Storm Applied* is captioned "Man from Konavle, Dalmatia, Croatia." The illustration is taken from a reproduction of an album of traditional Croatian costumes from the mid-nineteenth century by Nikola Arsenovic, published by the Ethnographic Museum in Split, Croatia, in 2003. The illustrations were obtained from a helpful librarian at the Ethnographic Museum in Split, itself situated in the Roman core of the medieval center of the town: the ruins of Emperor Diocletian's retirement palace from around AD 304. The book includes finely colored illustrations of figures from different regions of Croatia, accompanied by descriptions of the costumes and of everyday life.

Konavle is a small region located southeast of Dubrovnik, Croatia. It is a narrow strip of land picturesquely tucked in between Snijeznica Mountain and the Adriatic Sea, on the border with Montenegro. The figure on the cover is carrying a musket on his back and has a pistol, dagger, and scabbard tucked into his wide colorful belt. From his vigilant posture and the fierce look on his face, it would seem that he is guarding the border or on the lookout for poachers. The most interesting parts of his costume are the bright red socks decorated with an intricate black design, which is typical for this region of Dalmatia.

Dress codes and lifestyles have changed over the last 200 years, and the diversity by region, so rich at the time, has faded away. It is now hard to tell apart the inhabitants of different continents, let alone of different hamlets or towns separated by only a few miles. Perhaps we have traded cultural diversity for a more varied personal life—certainly for a more varied and fast-paced technological life.

Manning celebrates the inventiveness and initiative of the computer business with book covers based on the rich diversity of regional life of two centuries ago, brought back to life by illustrations from old books and collections like this one.

Introducing Storm 1

Apache Storm is a distributed, real-time computational framework that makes processing unbounded streams of data easy. Storm can be integrated with your existing queuing and persistence technologies, consuming streams of data and processing/transforming these streams in many ways.

Still following us? Some of you are probably feeling smart because you know what that means. Others are searching for the proper animated GIF to express your level of frustration. There's a lot in that description, so if you don't grasp what all of it means right now, don't worry. We've devoted the remainder of this chapter to clarifying exactly what we mean.

To appreciate what Storm is and when it should be used, you need to understand where Storm falls within the big data landscape. What technologies can it be

1

used with? What technologies can it replace? Being able to answer questions like these requires some context.

1.1   *What is big data?*

To talk about big data and where Storm fits within the big data landscape, we need to have a shared understanding of what "big data" means. There are a lot of definitions of big data floating around. Each has its own unique take. Here's ours.

1.1.1   *The four Vs of big data*

Big data is best understood by considering four different properties: volume, velocity, variety, and veracity.[1]

VOLUME

Volume is the most obvious property of big data—and the first that comes to most people's minds when they hear the term. Data is constantly being generated every day from a multitude of sources: data generated by people via social media, data generated by software itself (website tracking, application logs, and so on), and user-generated data, such as Wikipedia, only scratch the surface of sources of data.

When people think volume, companies such as Google, Facebook, and Twitter come to mind. Sure, all deal with enormous amounts of data, and we're certain you can name others, but what about companies that don't have that volume of data? There are many other companies that, by definition of volume alone, don't have big data, yet these companies use Storm. Why? This is where the second V, velocity, comes into play.

VELOCITY

Velocity deals with the pace at which data flows into a system, both in terms of the amount of data and the fact that it's a continuous flow of data. The amount of data (maybe just a series of links on your website that a visitor is clicking on) might be relatively small, but the rate at which it's flowing into your system could be rather high. Velocity matters. It doesn't matter how much data you have if you aren't processing it fast enough to provide value. It could be a couple terabytes; it could be 5 million URLs making up a much smaller volume of data. All that matters is whether you can extract meaning from this data before it goes stale.

So far we have volume and velocity, which deal with the amount of data and the pace at which it flows into a system. In many cases, data will also come from multiple sources, which leads us to the next V: variety.

VARIETY

For variety, let's step back and look at extracting meaning from data. Often, that can involve taking data from several sources and putting them together into something that tells a story. When you start, though, you might have some data in Google Analytics, maybe some in an append-only log, and perhaps some more in a relational database. You need to bring all of these together and shape them into something

---

[1] http://en.wikipedia.org/wiki/Big_data

you can work with to drill down and extract meaningful answers from questions such as the following:

Q: *Who are my best customers?*

A: *Coyotes in New Mexico.*

Q: *What do they usually purchase?*

A: *Some paint but mostly large heavy items.*

Q: *Can I look at each of these customers individually and find items others have liked and market those items to them?*

A: *That depends on how quickly you can turn your variety of data into something you can use and operate on.*

As if we didn't have enough to worry about with large volumes of data entering our system at a quick pace from a variety of sources, we also have to worry about how accurate that data entering our system is. The final V deals with this: veracity.

VERACITY

Veracity involves the accuracy of incoming and outgoing data. Sometimes, we need our data to be extremely accurate. Other times, a "close enough" estimate is all we need. Many algorithms that allow for high fidelity estimates while maintaining low computational demands (like hyperloglog) are often used with big data. For example, determining the exact mean page view time for a hugely successful website is probably not required; a close-enough estimate will do. These trade-offs between accuracy and resources are common features of big data systems.

With the properties of volume, velocity, variety, and veracity defined, we've established some general boundaries around what big data is. Our next step is to explore the various types of tools available for processing data within these boundaries.

1.1.2 Big data tools

Many tools exist that address the various characteristics of big data (volume, velocity, variety, and veracity). Within a given big data ecosystem, different tools can be used in isolation or together for different purposes:

- *Data processing*—These tools are used to perform some form of calculation and extract intelligence out of a data set.
- *Data transfer*—These tools are used to gather and ingest data into the data processing systems (or transfer data in between different components of the system). They come in many forms but most common is a message bus (or a queue). Examples include Kafka, Flume, Scribe, and Scoop.
- *Data storage*—These tools are used to store the data sets during various stages of processing. They may include distributed filesystems such as Hadoop Distributed File System (HDFS) or GlusterFS as well as NoSQL data stores such as Cassandra.

We're going to focus on data processing tools because Storm is a data-processing tool. To understand Storm, you need to understand a variety of data-processing tools. They

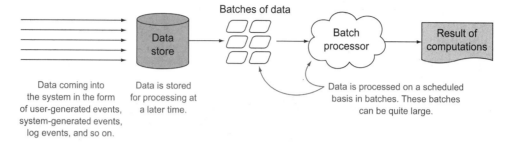

Figure 1.1   **A batch processor and how data flows into it**

fall into two primary classes: batch processing and stream processing. More recently, a hybrid between the two has emerged: micro-batch processing within a stream.

BATCH PROCESSING

Consider for a moment a single datum: a unique click on a website. Now imagine hundreds of thousands of other clicks that are happening over the same time period. All of those clicks together form a batch—a collection of data points to be processed together. Figure 1.1 provides an overview of how data flows into a batch-oriented tool.

Processing a website's log files to extract information about the behavior of visitors is an excellent example of a batch-processing problem. We have a fixed pool of data that we will process to get a result. What's important to note here is that the tool acts on a batch of data. That batch could be a small segment of data, or it could be the entire data set. When working on a batch of data, you have the ability to derive a big picture overview of that entire batch instead of a single data point. The earlier example of learning about visitor behavior can't be done on a single data point basis; you need to have some context based on the other data points (that is, other URLs visited). In other words, batch processing allows you to join, merge, or aggregate different data points together. This is why batch processing is quite often used for machine learning algorithms.

Another characteristic of a batch process is that its results are usually not available until the entire batch has completed processing. The results for earlier data points don't become available until the entire process is done. The larger your batch, the more merging, aggregating, and joining you can do, but this comes at a cost. The larger your batch, the longer you have to wait to get useful information from it. If immediacy of answers is important, stream processing might be a better solution.

STREAM PROCESSING

A stream processor acts on an unbounded stream of data instead of a batch of data points. Figure 1.2 illustrates how data flows into a stream-processing system.

A stream processor is continually ingesting new data (a "stream"). The need for stream processing usually follows a need for immediacy in the availability of results. This isn't always the case and is definitely not a mandate for stream processing. That's why we have an unbounded stream of data being fed into the stream processor. This

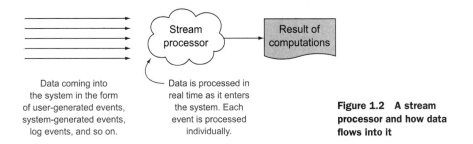

Data coming into the system in the form of user-generated events, system-generated events, log events, and so on.

Data is processed in real time as it enters the system. Each event is processed individually.

Figure 1.2   A stream processor and how data flows into it

stream of data is usually directed from its origin by way of a message bus into the stream processor so that results can be obtained while the data is still hot, so to speak. Unlike a batch process, there's no well-defined beginning or end to the data points flowing through this stream; it's continuous.

These systems achieve that immediacy by working on a single data point at a time. Numerous data points are flowing through the stream, and when you work on one data point at a time and you're doing it in parallel, it's quite easy to achieve sub-second-level latency in between the data being created and the results being available. Think of doing sentiment analysis on a stream of tweets. To achieve that, you don't need to join or relate any incoming tweet with other tweets occurring at the same time, so you can work on a single tweet at a time. Sure, you may need some contextual data by way of a training set that's created using historical tweets. But because this training set doesn't need to be made up of current tweets as they're happening, expensive aggregations with current data can be avoided and you can continue operating on a single tweet at a time. So in a stream-processing application, unlike a batch system, you'll have results available per data point as each completes processing.

But stream processing isn't limited to working on one data point at a time. One of the most well-known examples of this is Twitter's "trending topics." Trending topics are calculated over a sliding window of time by considering the tweets within each window of time. Trends can be observed by comparing the top subjects of tweets from the current window to the previous windows. Obviously, this adds a level of latency over working on a single data point at a time due to working over a batch of tweets within a time frame (because each tweet can't be considered as completed processing until the time window it falls into elapses). Similarly, other forms of buffering, joins, merges, or aggregations may add latency during stream processing. There's always a trade-off between the introduced latency and the achievable accuracy in this kind of aggregation. A larger time window (or more data in a join, merge, or aggregate operation) may determine the accuracy of the results in certain algorithms—at the cost of latency. Usually in streaming systems, we stay within processing latencies of milliseconds, seconds, or a matter of minutes at most. Use cases that go beyond that are more suitable for batch processing.

We just considered two use cases for tweets with streaming systems. The amount of data in the form of tweets flowing through Twitter's system is immense, and Twitter needs to be able to tell users what everyone in their area is talking about right now. Think about that for a moment. Not only does Twitter have the requirement of operating at high volume, but it also needs to operate with high velocity (that is, low latency). Twitter has a massive, never-ending stream of tweets coming in and it must be able to extract, in real time, what people are talking about. That's a serious feat of engineering. In fact, chapter 3 is built around a use case that's similar to this idea of trending topics.

MICRO-BATCH PROCESSING WITHIN A STREAM

Tools have emerged in the last couple of years built just for use with examples like trending topics. These micro-batching tools are similar to stream-processing tools in that they both work with an unbounded stream of data. But unlike a stream processor that allows you access to every data point within it, a micro-batch processor groups the incoming data into batches in some fashion and gives you a batch at a time. This approach makes micro-batching frameworks unsuitable for working on single-data-point-at-a-time kinds of problems. You're also giving up the associated super-low latency in processing one data point at a time. But they make working with batches of data within a stream a bit easier.

1.2   *How Storm fits into the big data picture*

So where does Storm fit within all of this? Going back to our original definition, we said this:

> Storm is a distributed, real-time computational framework that makes processing unbounded streams of data easy.

Storm is a stream-processing tool, plain and simple. It'll run indefinitely, listening to a stream of data and doing "something" any time it receives data from the stream. Storm is also a distributed system; it allows machines to be easily added in order to process as much data in real-time as we can. In addition, Storm comes with a framework called Trident that lets you perform micro-batching within a stream.

What is real-time?

When we use the term *real-time* throughout this book, what exactly do we mean? Well, technically speaking, *near real-time* is more accurate. In software systems, real-time constraints are defined to set operational deadlines for how long it takes a system to respond to a particular event. Normally, this latency is along the order of milliseconds (or at least sub-second level), with no perceivable delay to the end user. Within the context of Storm, both real-time (sub-second level) and near real-time (a matter of seconds or few minutes depending on the use case) latencies are possible.

And what about the second sentence in our initial definition?

> Storm can be integrated with your existing queuing and persistence technologies, consuming streams of data and processing/transforming these streams in many ways.

As we'll show you throughout the book, Storm is extremely flexible in that the source of a stream can be anything—usually this means a queuing system, but Storm doesn't put limits on where your stream comes from (we'll use Kafka and RabbitMQ for several of our use cases). The same thing goes for the result of a stream transformation produced by Storm. We've seen many cases where the result is persisted to a database somewhere for later access. But the result may also be pushed onto a separate queue for another system (maybe even another Storm topology) to process.

The point is that you can plug Storm into your existing architecture, and this book will provide use cases illustrating how you can do so. Figure 1.3 shows a hypothetical scenario for analyzing a stream of tweets.

This high-level hypothetical solution is exactly that: hypothetical. We wanted to show you where Storm could fall within a system and how the coexistence of batch- and stream-processing tools is possible.

What about the different technologies that can be used with Storm? Figure 1.4 sheds some light on this question. The figure shows a small sampling of some of the technologies that can be used in this architecture. It illustrates how flexible Storm is in terms of the technologies it can work with as well as where it can be plugged into a system.

For our queuing system, we could choose from a number of technologies, including Kafka, Kestrel, and RabbitMQ. The same thing goes for our database choice: Redis, Cassandra, Riak, and MySQL only scratch the surface in terms of options. And look at that—we've even managed to include a Hadoop cluster in our solution for performing the required batch computation for our "Top Daily Topics" report.

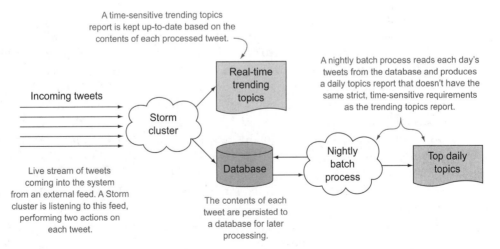

Figure 1.3   Example of how Storm may be used within a system

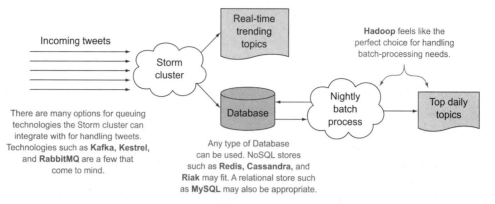

Figure 1.4   How Storm can be used with other technologies

Hopefully you're starting to gain a clearer understanding of where Storm fits and what it can be used with. A wide range of technologies, including Hadoop, can work with Storm within a system. Wait, did we just tell you Storm can work with Hadoop?

1.2.1   *Storm vs. the usual suspects*

In many conversations between engineers, Storm and Hadoop often come up in the same sentence. Instead of starting with the tools, we'll begin with the kind of problems you'll likely encounter and show you the tools that fit best by considering each tool's characteristics. Most likely you'll end up picking more than one, because no single tool is appropriate for all problems. In fact, tools might even be used in conjunction given the right circumstances.

The following descriptions of the various big data tools and the comparison with Storm are intended to draw attention to some of the ways in which they're uniquely different from Storm. But don't use this information alone to pick one tool over another.

APACHE HADOOP

Hadoop used to be synonymous with batch-processing systems. But with the release of Hadoop v2, it's more than a batch-processing system—it's a platform for big data applications. Its batch-processing component is called Hadoop MapReduce. It also comes with a job scheduler and cluster resource manager called YARN. The other main component is the Hadoop distributed filesystem, HDFS. Many other big data tools are being built that take advantage of YARN for managing the cluster and HDFS as a data storage back end. In the remainder of this book, whenever we refer to Hadoop we're talking about its MapReduce component, and we'll refer to YARN and HDFS explicitly.

Figure 1.5 shows how data is fed into Hadoop for batch processing. The data store is the distributed filesystem, HDFS. Once the batches of data related to the problem at hand are identified, the MapReduce process runs over each batch. When a Map-Reduce process runs, it moves the code over to the nodes where the data resides. This is usually a characteristic needed for batch jobs. Batch jobs are known to work on very

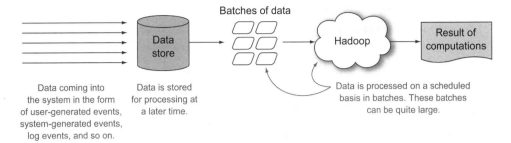

Figure 1.5   **Hadoop and how data flows into it**

large data sets (from terabytes to petabytes isn't unheard of), and in those cases, it's easier to move the code over to the data nodes within the distributed filesystem and execute the code on those nodes, and thus achieve substantial scale in efficiency thanks to that data locality.

STORM

Storm, as a general framework for doing real-time computation, allows you to run incremental functions over data in a fashion that Hadoop can't. Figure 1.6 shows how data is fed into Storm.

Storm falls into the stream-processing tool category that we discussed earlier. It maintains all the characteristics of that category, including low latency and fast processing. In fact, it doesn't get any speedier than this.

Whereas Hadoop moves the code to the data, Storm moves the data to the code. This behavior makes more sense in a stream-processing system, because the data set isn't known beforehand, unlike in a batch job. Also, the data set is continuously flowing through the code.

Additionally, Storm provides invaluable, guaranteed message processing with a well-defined framework of what to do when failures occur. Storm comes with its own cluster resource management system, but there has been unofficial work by Yahoo to get Storm running on Hadoop v2's YARN resource manager so that resources can be shared with a Hadoop cluster.

APACHE SPARK

Spark falls into the same line of batch-processing tools as Hadoop MapReduce. It also runs on Hadoop's YARN resource manager. What's interesting about Spark is that it

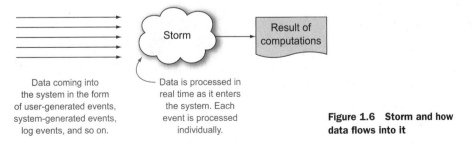

Figure 1.6   **Storm and how data flows into it**

allows caching of intermediate (or final) results in memory (with overflow to disk as needed). This ability can be highly useful for processes that run repeatedly over the same data sets and can make use of the previous calculations in an algorithmically meaningful manner.

SPARK STREAMING

Spark Streaming works an unbounded stream of data like Storm does. But it's different from Storm in the sense that Spark Streaming doesn't belong in the stream-processing category of tools we discussed earlier; instead, it falls into the micro-batch-processing tools category. Spark Streaming is built on top of Spark, and it needs to represent the incoming flow of data within a stream as a batch in order to operate. In this sense, it's comparable to Storm's Trident framework rather than Storm itself. So Spark Streaming won't be able to support the low latencies supported by the one-at-a-time semantics of Storm, but it should be comparable to Trident in terms of performance.

Spark's caching mechanism is also available with Spark Streaming. If you need caching, you'll have to maintain your own in-memory caches within your Storm components (which isn't hard at all and is quite common), but Storm doesn't provide any built-in support for doing so.

APACHE SAMZA

Samza is a young stream-processing system from the team at LinkedIn that can be directly compared with Storm. Yet you'll notice some differences. Whereas Storm and Spark/Spark Streaming can run under their own resource managers as well as under YARN, Samza is built to run on the YARN system specifically.

Samza has a parallelism model that's simple and easy to reason about; Storm has a parallelism model that lets you fine-tune the parallelism at a much more granular level. In Samza, each step in the workflow of your job is an independent entity, and you connect each of those entities using Kafka. In Storm, all the steps are connected by an internal system (usually Netty or ZeroMQ), resulting in much lower latency. Samza has the advantage of having a Kafka queue in between that can act as a checkpoint as well as allow multiple independent consumers access to that queue.

As we alluded to earlier, it's not just about making trade-offs between these various tools and choosing one. Most likely, you can use a batch-processing tool along with a stream-processing tool. In fact, using a batch-oriented system with a stream-oriented one is the subject of *Big Data* (Manning, 2015) by Nathan Marz, the original author of Storm.

1.3   *Why you'd want to use Storm*

Now that we've explained where Storm fits in the big data landscape, let's discuss why you'd want to use Storm. As we'll demonstrate throughout this book, Storm has fundamental properties that make it an attractive option:

- It can be applied to a wide variety of use cases.
- It works well with a multitude of technologies.

- It's scalable. Storm makes it easy to break down work over a series of threads, over a series of JVMs, or over a series of machines—all this without having to change your code to scale in that fashion (you only change some configuration).
- It guarantees that it will process every piece of input you give it at least once.
- It's very robust—you might even call it fault-tolerant. There are four major components within Storm, and at various times, we've had to kill off any of the four while continuing to process data.
- It's programming-language agnostic. If you can run it on the JVM, you can run it easily on Storm. Even if you can't run it on the JVM, if you can call it from a *nix command line, you can probably use it with Storm (although in this book, we'll confine ourselves to the JVM and specifically to Java).

We think you'll agree that sounds impressive. Storm has become our go-to toolkit not just for scaling, but also for fault tolerance and guaranteed message processing. We have a variety of Storm topologies (a chunk of Storm code that performs a given task) that could easily run as a Python script on a single machine. But if that script crashes, it doesn't compare to Storm in terms of recoverability; Storm will restart and pick up work from our point of crash. No 3 a.m. pager-duty alerts, no 9 a.m. explanations to the VP of engineering why something died. One of the great things about Storm is you come for the fault tolerance and stay for the easy scaling.

Armed with this knowledge, you can now move on to the core concepts in Storm. A good grasp of these concepts will serve as the foundation for everything else we discuss in this book.

1.4 Summary

In this chapter, you learned that

- Storm is a stream-processing tool that runs indefinitely, listening to a stream of data and performing some type of processing on that stream of data. Storm can be integrated with many existing technologies, making it a viable solution for many stream-processing needs.
- Big data is best defined by thinking of it in terms of its four main properties: volume (amount of data), velocity (speed of data flowing into a system), variety (different types of data), and veracity (accuracy of the data).
- There are three main types of tools for processing big data: batch processing, stream processing, and micro-batch processing within a stream.
- Some of the benefits of Storm include its scalability, its ability to process each message at least once, its robustness, and its ability to be developed with any programming language.

Core Storm concepts

2

This chapter covers

- Core Storm concepts and terminology
- Basic code for your first Storm project

The core concepts in Storm are simple once you understand them, but this understanding can be hard to come by. Encountering a description of "executors" and "tasks" on your first day can be hard to understand. There are just too many concepts you need to hold in your head at one time. In this book, we'll introduce concepts in a progressive fashion and try to minimize the number of concepts you need to think about at one time. This approach will often mean that an explanation isn't entirely "true," but it'll be accurate enough at that point in your journey. As you slowly pick up on different pieces of the puzzle, we'll point out where our earlier definitions can be expanded on.

2.1 Problem definition: GitHub commit count dashboard

Let's begin by doing work in a domain that should be familiar: source control in GitHub. Most developers are familiar with GitHub, having used it for a personal project, for work, or for interacting with other open source projects.

Let's say we want to implement a dashboard that shows a running count of the most active developers against any repository. This count has some real-time requirements

12

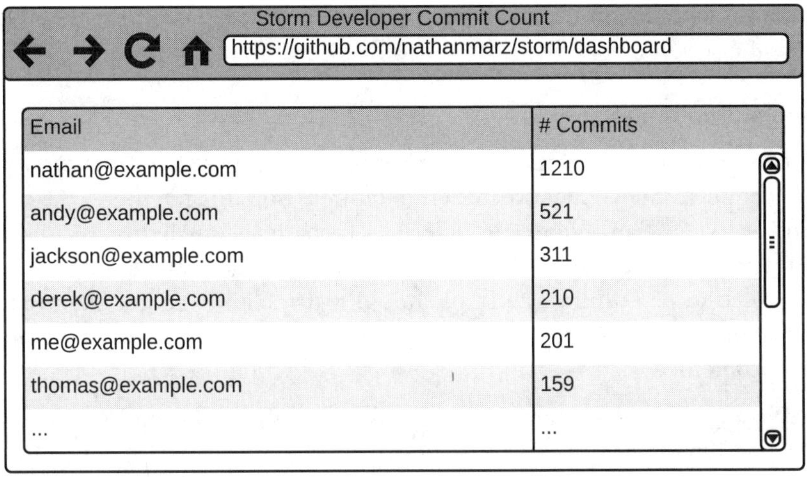

Figure 2.1   Mock-up of dashboard for a running count of changes made to a repository

in that it must be updated immediately after any change is made to the repository. The dashboard being requested by GitHub may look something like figure 2.1.

The dashboard is quite simple. It contains a listing of the email of every developer who has made a commit to the repository along with a running total of the number of commits each has made. Before we dive into how we'd design a solution with Storm, let's break down the problem a bit further in terms of the data that'll be used.

2.1.1   Data: starting and ending points

For our scenario, we'll say GitHub provides a live feed of commits being made to any repository. Each commit comes into the feed as a single string that contains the commit ID, followed by a space, followed by the email of the developer who made the commit. The following listing shows a sampling of 10 individual commits in the feed.

Listing 2.1   Sample commit data for the GitHub commit feed

```
b20ea50 nathan@example.com
064874b andy@example.com
28e4f8e andy@example.com
9a3e07f andy@example.com
cbb9cd1 nathan@example.com
0f663d2 jackson@example.com
0a4b984 nathan@example.com
1915ca4 derek@example.com
```

This feed gives us a starting point for our data. We'll need to go from this live feed to a UI displaying a running count of commits per email address. For the sake of simplicity, let's say all we need to do is maintain an in-memory map with email address as the key and number of commits as the value. The map may look something like this in code:

```
Map<String, Integer> countsByEmail = new HashMap<String, Integer>();
```

Now that we've defined the data, the next step is to define the steps we need to take to make sure our in-memory map correctly reflects the commit data.

2.1.2 *Breaking down the problem*

We know we want to go from a feed of commit messages to an in-memory map of emails/commit counts, but we haven't defined how to get there. At this point, breaking down the problem into a series of smaller steps helps. We define these steps in terms of components that accept input, perform a calculation on that input, and produce some output. The steps should provide a way to get from our starting point to our desired ending point. We've come up with the following components for this problem:

1 A component that reads from the live feed of commits and produces a single commit message
2 A component that accepts a single commit message, extracts the developer's email from that commit, and produces an email
3 A component that accepts the developer's email and updates an in-memory map where the key is the email and the value is the number of commits for that email

In this chapter we break down the problem into several components. In the next chapter, we'll go over how to think about mapping a problem onto the Storm domain in much greater detail. But before we get ahead of ourselves, take a look at figure 2.2, which illustrates the components, the input they accept, and the output they produce.

Figure 2.2 shows our basic solution for going from a live feed of commits to something that stores the commit counts for each email. We have three components, each with a singular purpose. Now that we have a well-formed idea of how we want to solve this problem, let's frame our solution within the context of Storm.

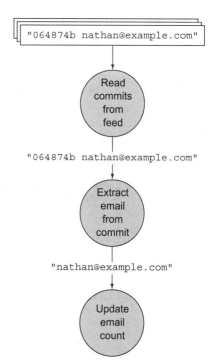

Figure 2.2 The commit count problem broken down into a series of steps with defined inputs and outputs

2.2 *Basic Storm concepts*

To help you understand the core concepts in Storm, we'll go over the common terminology used in Storm. We'll do this within the context of our sample design. Let's begin with the most basic component in Storm: the topology.

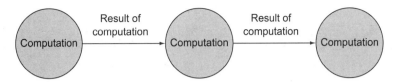

Figure 2.3   A topology is a graph with nodes representing computations and edges representing results of computations.

2.2.1   Topology

Let's take a step back from our example in order to understand what a topology is. Think of a simple linear graph with some nodes connected by directed edges. Now imagine that each one of those nodes represents a single process or computation and each edge represents the result of one computation being passed as input to the next computation. Figure 2.3 illustrates this more clearly.

A Storm topology is a graph of computation where the nodes represent some individual computations and the edges represent the data being passed between nodes. We then feed data into this graph of computation in order to achieve some goal. What does this mean exactly? Let's go back to our dashboard example to show you what we're talking about.

Looking at the modular breakdown of our problem, we're able to identify each of the components from our definition of a topology. Figure 2.4 illustrates this correlation; there's a lot to take in here, so take your time.

Each concept we mentioned in the definition of a topology can be found in our design. The actual topology consists of the nodes and edges. This topology is then driven by the continuous live feed of commits. Our design fits quite well within the framework of Storm. Now that you understand what a topology is, we'll dive into the individual components that make up a topology.

2.2.2   Tuple

The nodes in our topology send data between one another in the form of tuples. A *tuple* is an ordered list of values, where each value is assigned a name. A node can create and then (optionally) send tuples to any number of nodes in the graph. The process of sending a tuple to be handled by any number of nodes is called *emitting* a tuple.

It's important to note that just because each value in a tuple has a name, doesn't mean a tuple is a list of name-value pairs. A list of name-value pairs implies there may be a map behind the scenes and that the name is actually a part of the tuple. Neither of these statements is true. A tuple is an ordered list of values and Storm provides mechanisms for assigning names to the values within this list; we'll get into how these names are assigned later in this chapter.

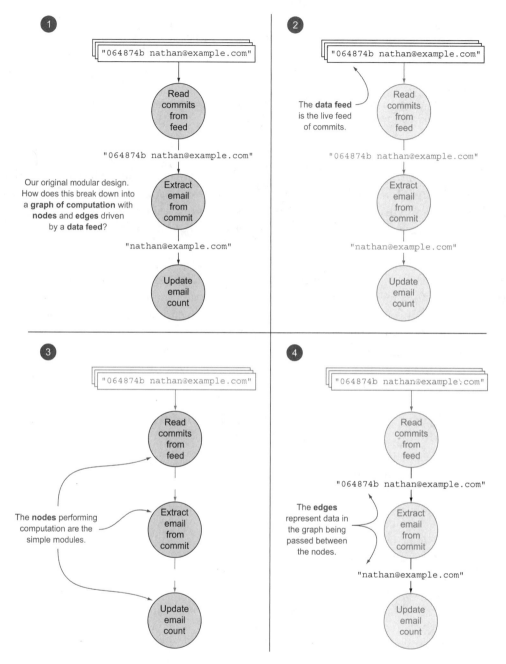

Figure 2.4   Design mapped to the definition of a Storm topology

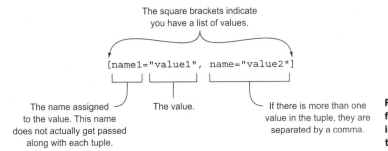

The square brackets indicate
you have a list of values.

`[name1="value1", name="value2"]`

The name assigned
to the value. This name
does not actually get passed
along with each tuple.

The value.

If there is more than one
value in the tuple, they are
separated by a comma.

**Figure 2.5   Format
for displaying tuples
in figures throughout
the book**

When we display tuples in figures throughout the rest of the book, the names associated with the values are important, so we've settled on a convention that includes both the name and value (figure 2.5).

With the standard format for displaying tuples in hand, let's identify the two types of tuples in our topology:

- The commit message containing the commit ID and developer email
- The developer email

We need to assign each of these a name, so we'll go with "commit" and "email" for now (more details on how this is done in code later). Figure 2.6 provides an illustration of where the tuples are flowing in our topology.

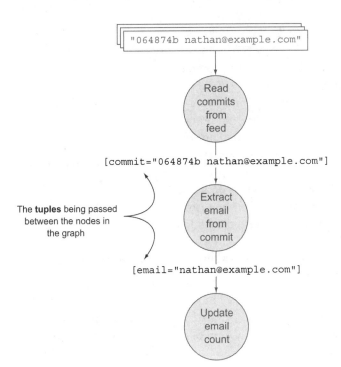

**Figure 2.6   Two types of
tuples in the topology: one
for the commit message and
another for the email**

The types of the values within a tuple are dynamic and don't need to be declared. But Storm does need to know how to serialize these values so it can send the tuple between nodes in the topology. Storm already knows how to serialize primitive types but will require custom serializers for any custom type you define and can fall back to standard Java serialization when a custom serializer isn't present.

We'll get to the code for all of this soon, but for now the important thing is to understand the terminology and relationships between concepts. With an understanding of tuples in hand, we can move on to the core abstraction in Storm: the stream.

2.2.3   *Stream*

According to the Storm wiki, a stream is an "unbounded sequence of tuples." This is a great explanation of what a stream is, with maybe one addition. *A stream* is an unbounded sequence of tuples between two nodes in the topology. A topology can contain any number of streams. Other than the very first node in the topology that reads from the data feed, nodes can accept one or more streams as input. Nodes will then normally perform some computation or transformation on the input tuples and emit new tuples, thus creating a new output stream. These output streams then act as input streams for other nodes, and so on.

There are two streams in our GitHub commit count topology. The first stream starts with the node that continuously reads commits from a feed. This node emits a tuple with the commit to another node that extracts the email. The second stream starts with the node that extracts the email from the commit. This node transforms its input stream (containing commits) by emitting a new stream containing only emails. The resulting output stream serves as input into the node that updates the in-memory map. You can see these streams in figure 2.7.

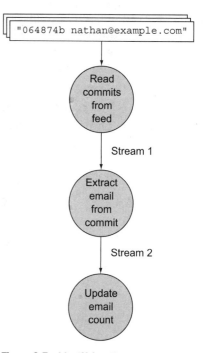

Figure 2.7   **Identifying the two streams in our topology**

Our Storm GitHub scenario is an example of a simple chained stream (multiple streams chained together).

COMPLEX STREAMS

Streams may not always be as straightforward as those in our topology. Take the example in figure 2.8. This figure shows a topology with four different streams. The first node emits a tuple that's consumed by two different nodes; this results in two separate streams. Each of those nodes then emits tuples to their own new output stream.

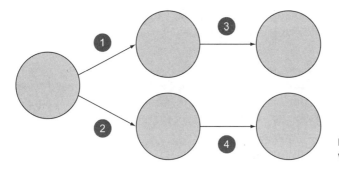

Figure 2.8 Topology with four streams

The combinations are endless with regard to the number of streams that may be created, split, and then joined again. The examples later in this book will delve into the more complex chains of streams and why it's beneficial to design a topology in such a way. For now, we'll continue with our straightforward example and move on to the source of a stream for a topology.

2.2.4 Spout

A *spout* is the source of a stream in the topology. Spouts normally read data from an external data source and emit tuples into the topology. Spouts can listen to message queues for incoming messages, listen to a database for changes, or listen to any other source of a feed of data. In our example, the spout is listening to the real-time feed of commits being made to the Storm repository (figure 2.9).

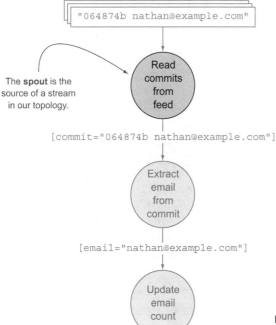

Figure 2.9 A spout reads from the feed of commit messages.

Spouts don't perform any processing; they simply act as a source of streams, reading from a data source and emitting tuples to the next type of node in a topology: the bolt.

2.2.5   *Bolt*

Unlike a spout, whose sole purpose is to listen to a stream of data, a *bolt* accepts a tuple from its input stream, performs some computation or transformation—filtering, aggregation, or a join, perhaps—on that tuple, and then optionally emits a new tuple (or tuples) to its output stream(s).

The bolts in our example are as follows:

- *A bolt that extracts the developer's email from the commit*—This bolt accepts a tuple containing a commit with a commit ID and email from its input stream. It transforms that input stream and emits a new tuple containing only the email address to its output stream.
- *A bolt that updates the map of emails to commit counts*—This bolt accepts a tuple containing an email address from its input stream. Because this bolt updates an in-memory map and doesn't emit a new tuple, it doesn't produce an output stream.

Both of these bolts are shown in figure 2.10.

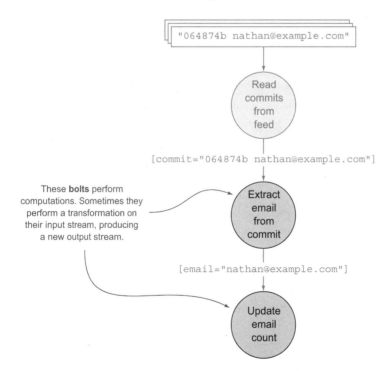

Figure 2.10   Bolts perform processing on the commit messages and associated emails within those messages.

The bolts in our example are extremely simple. As you move along in the book, you'll create bolts that do much more complex transformations, sometimes even reading from multiple input streams and producing multiple output streams. We're getting ahead of ourselves here, though. First you need to understand how bolts and spouts work in practice.

HOW BOLTS AND SPOUTS WORK UNDER THE COVERS

In figures 2.9 and 2.10, both the spout and bolts were shown as single components. This is true from a logical standpoint. But when it comes to how spouts and bolts work in reality, there's a little more to it. In a running topology, there are normally numerous instances of each type of spout/bolt performing computations in parallel. See figure 2.11, where the bolt for extracting the email from the commit and the bolt for updating the email count are each running across three different instances. Notice how a single instance of one bolt is emitting a tuple to a single instance of another bolt.

Figure 2.11 shows just one possible scenario of how the tuples would be sent between instances of the two bolts. In reality, the picture is more like figure 2.12, where each bolt instance on the left is emitting tuples to several different bolt instances on the right.

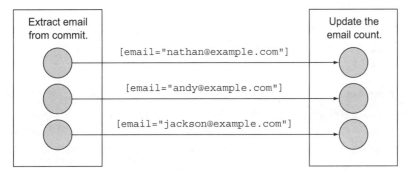

Figure 2.11 There are normally multiple instances of a particular bolt emitting tuples to multiple instances of another bolt.

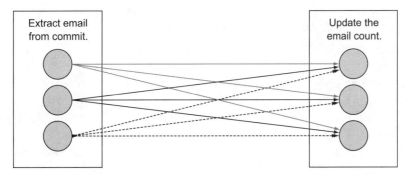

Figure 2.12 Individual instances of a bolt can emit to any number of instances of another bolt.

Understanding the breakdown of spout and bolt instances is extremely important, so let's pause for a moment and summarize what you know before diving into our final concept:

- A *topology* consists of *nodes* and *edges.*
- *Nodes* represent either *spouts* or *bolts.*
- *Edges* represent *streams of tuples* between these spouts and bolts.
- A *tuple* is an ordered list of values, where each value is assigned a name.
- A *stream* is an unbounded sequence of tuples between a spout and a bolt or between two bolts.
- A *spout* is the source of a stream in a topology, usually listening to some sort of live feed of data.
- A *bolt* accepts a stream of tuples from a spout or another bolt, typically performing some sort of computation or transformation on these input tuples. The bolt can then optionally emit new tuples that serve as the input stream to another bolt in the topology.
- Each spout and bolt will have one or many individual instances that perform all of this processing in parallel.

That's quite a bit of material, so be sure to let this sink in before you move on. Ready? Good. Before we get into actual code, let's tackle one more important concept: stream grouping.

2.2.6 *Stream grouping*

You know by now that a stream is an unbounded sequence of tuples between a spout and bolt or two bolts. A stream grouping defines how the tuples are sent between instances of those spouts and bolts. What do we mean by this? Let's take a step back and look at our commit count topology. We have two streams in our GitHub commit count topology. Each of these streams will have their own stream grouping defined, telling Storm how to send individual tuples between instances of the spout and bolts (figure 2.13).

Storm comes with several stream groupings out of the box. We'll cover most of these throughout this book, starting with the two most common groupings in this chapter: the shuffle grouping and fields grouping.

SHUFFLE GROUPING

The stream between our spout and first bolt uses a shuffle grouping. A *shuffle grouping* is a type of stream grouping where tuples are emitted to instances of bolts at random, as shown in figure 2.14.

In this example, we don't care how tuples are passed to the instances of our bolts, so we choose the shuffle grouping to distribute tuples at random. Using a shuffle grouping will guarantee that each bolt instance should receive a relatively equal number of tuples, thus spreading the load across all bolt instances. Shuffle grouping assignment is done randomly rather than round robin so exact equality of distribution isn't guaranteed.

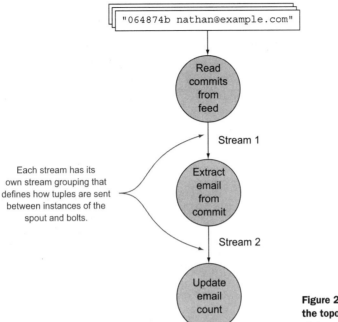

Each stream has its own stream grouping that defines how tuples are sent between instances of the spout and bolts.

Figure 2.13   Each stream in the topology will have its own stream grouping.

This grouping is useful in many basic cases where you don't have special requirements about how your data is passed to bolts. But sometimes you have scenarios where sending tuples to random bolt instances won't work based on your requirements—as in the case of our scenario for sending tuples between the bolt that extracts the email and the bolt that updates the email. We'll need a different type of stream grouping for this.

FIELDS GROUPING
The stream between the bolt that extracts the email and the bolt that updates the email will need to use a fields grouping. A *fields grouping* ensures that tuples with the same value for a particular field name are always emitted to the same instance of a bolt. To understand why a fields grouping is necessary for our second stream, let's look at the consequences of using an in-memory map to track the number of commits per email.

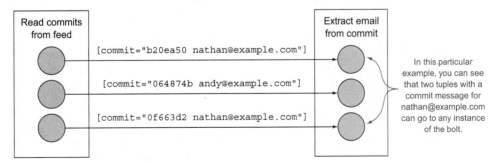

Figure 2.14   Using a shuffle grouping between our spout and first bolt

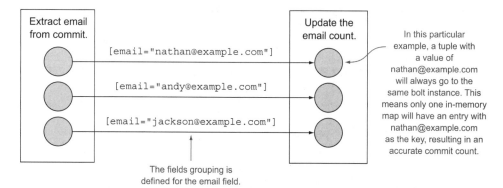

Figure 2.15   Use a fields grouping for the bolt that will have a separate in-memory map for each bolt instance.

Each bolt instance will have its own map for the email/commit count pairs, so it's necessary that the same email go to the same bolt instance in order for the count for each email to be accurate across all bolt instances. A fields grouping provides exactly this (figure 2.15).

In this example, the decision to use an in-memory map for the email count implementation resulted in the need for a fields grouping. We could've used a resource that was shared across bolt instances and eliminated that need. We'll explore design and implementation considerations like this one in chapter 3 and beyond, but for now let's shift our focus to the code that we'll need to get our topology up and running.

2.3   *Implementing a GitHub commit count dashboard in Storm*

Now that we've covered all the important concepts in Storm, it's time to get into writing the code for our topology. This section will start with the code for the individual spout and bolts and introduce the relevant Storm interfaces and classes. Some of these interfaces and classes you'll use directly and some you won't; regardless, understanding the overall Storm API hierarchy will give you a fuller understanding of your topology and associated code.

After we've introduced the code for the spout and bolts, we'll go over the code required for putting it all together. If you remember from our earlier discussion, our topology contains streams and stream groupings. The code for the spout and bolts is only part of the picture—you still need to define where and how tuples are emitted between components in the topology. In our discussion of the code needed for building the topology, you'll encounter some of Storm's configuration options, most of which will be covered in greater detail later in the book.

Finally, after we've wired everything up by defining the streams and stream groupings in the topology, we'll show you how to run your topology locally, allowing you to test whether everything works as expected. But before we dive into all this code, let's set you up with a basic Storm project.

2.3.1 Setting up a Storm project

The easiest way to get the Storm JARs on your classpath for development is to use Apache Maven.

> **NOTE** You can find other ways to set up Storm at http://storm.apache.org/documentation/Creating-a-new-Storm-project.html, but Maven is by far the simplest. Check out http://maven.apache.org/ for information on Maven.

Add the code shown in the next listing to your project's pom.xml file.

Listing 2.2   pom.xml

```
<project>
..
  <dependencies>
  ..
    <dependency>
      <groupId>org.apache.storm</groupId>
      <artifactId>storm-core</artifactId>
      <version>0.9.3/version>
      <!-- <scope>provided</scope> -->
    </dependency>
  ..
  </dependencies>
</project>
```

This is the most recent version of Storm as of this writing.

For topologies that will be deployed to a real cluster, scope should be set to provided. But we're leaving it commented out as we're still in learning mode.

Once you've made these additions to your pom.xml file, you should have all the necessary dependencies for writing code and running Storm topologies locally on your development machine.

2.3.2 Implementing the spout

Because the spout is where data enters a topology, this is where we'll begin our coding. Before diving into the details, let's examine the general interface and class structure within Storm for the spout. Figure 2.16 explains this class hierarchy.

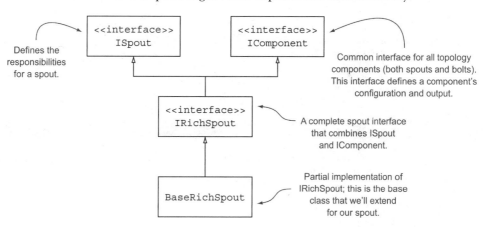

Figure 2.16   Storm's class hierarchy for the spout

In this design, the spout listens to a live feed of commits being made to a particular GitHub project using the GitHub API and emits tuples, each containing an entire commit message, as shown in figure 2.17.

Setting up a spout to listen to a live feed requires a bit of work that we feel is a distraction from understanding the basic code. Because of this, we're going to cheat and simulate a live feed by having our spout continuously read from a file of commit messages, emitting a tuple for each line in the file. Don't worry; in later chapters we'll wire up spouts to live feeds, but for now our focus is on the basics. The file changelog.txt will live next to the class for our spout and contain a list of commit messages in the expected format (shown in the following listing).

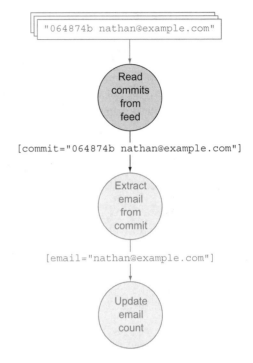

Figure 2.17   The spout listens to the feed of commit messages and emits a tuple for each commit message.

Listing 2.3   An excerpt from our simple data source: changelog.txt

```
b20ea50 nathan@example.com
064874b andy@example.com
28e4f8e andy@example.com
9a3e07f andy@example.com
cbb9cd1 nathan@example.com
0f663d2 jackson@example.com
0a4b984 nathan@example.com
1915ca4 derek@example.com
```

Once we've defined the source of our data, we can move to the spout implementation, as shown in the next listing.

Listing 2.4   CommitFeedListener.java

```
public class CommitFeedListener extends BaseRichSpout {
    private SpoutOutputCollector outputCollector;
    private List<String> commits;
```

Base class providing basic functionality, requiring us to override three methods

Emits tuples

List of strings for the commit messages read from changelog.txt

```
                   @Override
                   public void declareOutputFields(OutputFieldsDeclarer declarer) {
                     declarer.declare(new Fields("commit"));
                   }

                   @Override
                   public void open(Map configMap,
                                    TopologyContext context,
                                    SpoutOutputCollector outputCollector) {
                     this.outputCollector = outputCollector;

                     try {
                       commits = IOUtils.readLines(
                         ClassLoader.getSystemResourceAsStream("changelog.txt"),
                         Charset.defaultCharset().name()
                       );
                     } catch (IOException e) {
                       throw new RuntimeException(e);
                     }
                   }

                   @Override
                   public void nextTuple() {
                     for (String commit : commits) {
                       outputCollector.emit(new Values(commit));
                     }
                   }
                 }
```

Where we define the field names for all tuples emitted by the spout

Gets called when Storm prepares the spout to be run

Indicates that the spout emits a tuple with a field named commit

Reads the contents of changelog.txt into our list of strings

Called by Storm when it's ready to read the next tuple for the spout

Emits a tuple for each commit message

Quite a bit is going on with our spout. We start by extending BaseRichSpout, which gives us three methods that need to be overridden. The first of these methods is declareOutputFields. Remember earlier in the chapter when we said we'd discuss how Storm assigns names to tuples? Well, here we are. The declareOutputFields method is where we define the names for the values in tuples being emitted by this spout. Defining names for emitted tuple values is done with the Fields class, whose constructor accepts multiple strings; each string is the name of a value in an emitted tuple. The order of the names in the Fields constructor must match the order of the values emitted in the tuple via the Values class. Because the tuple emitted by our spout contains a single value, we have a single argument, commit, passed into Fields.

The next method we need to override is open; this is where we read the contents of changelog.txt into our list of strings. If we're writing code for a spout that deals with a live data source, such as a message queue, this is where we'd put the code for connecting to that data source. You'll see more on this beginning in chapter 3.

The final method we need to override is nextTuple. This is the method Storm calls when it's ready for the spout to read and emit a new tuple and is usually invoked periodically as determined by Storm. In our example we're emitting a new tuple for each value in our list every time nextTuple is called, but for something that reads from a live data source, such as a message queue, a new tuple will only be emitted if a new piece of data is available.

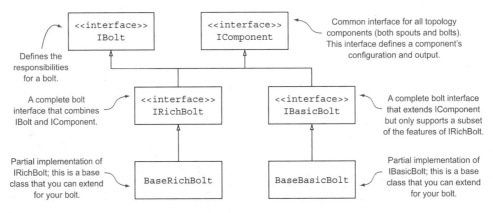

Figure 2.18   Storm's class hierarchy for the bolt

You'll also notice a class called SpoutOutputCollector. Output collectors are something you'll see quite a bit for both spouts and bolts. They're responsible for emitting and failing tuples.

Now that we know how our spout obtains commit messages from our data source and emits new tuples for each commit message, we need to implement the code that transforms these commit messages into a map of emails to commit counts.

2.3.3   *Implementing the bolts*

We've implemented the spout that serves as the source of a stream, so now it's time to move on to the bolts. Figure 2.18 explains the general interface and class structure within Storm for bolts.

You'll notice in figure 2.18 that the class hierarchy for a bolt is a little more complex than that of a spout. The reason is that Storm has additional classes for bolts that have incredibly simple implementations (IBasicBolt/BaseBasicBolt). These take over the responsibilities usually accessible to a developer with IRichBolt, so it makes simpler bolt implementations more concise. The simplicity of IBasic-Bolt does come at the cost of taking away some of the fluency of the rich feature set

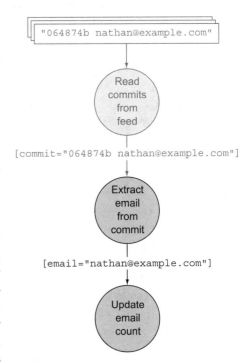

Figure 2.19   The two bolts in our topology: the first bolt extracts the email from the commit message and the second bolt maintains an in-memory map of emails to commit counts.

made accessible through IRichBolt. We'll cover the differences between BaseRich-Bolt and BaseBasicBolt and explain when to use either in more detail in chapter 4. In this chapter, we'll use BaseBasicBolt because the bolt implementations are quite straightforward.

To revisit our design, remember that we have two bolts in our topology (see figure 2.19). One bolt accepts a tuple containing the full commit message, extracts the email from the commit message, and emits a tuple containing the email. The second bolt maintains an in-memory map of emails to commit counts.

Let's take a look at the code for these bolts, starting with EmailExtractor.java in the next listing.

Listing 2.5   EmailExtractor.java

```
public class EmailExtractor extends BaseBasicBolt {
  @Override
  public void declareOutputFields(OutputFieldsDeclarer declarer) {
    declarer.declare(new Fields("email"));
  }

  @Override
  public void execute(Tuple tuple,
                      BasicOutputCollector outputCollector) {
    String commit = tuple.getStringByField("commit");
    String[] parts = commit.split(" ");
    outputCollector.emit(new Values(parts[1]));
  }
}
```

Where we define the field names for all tuples emitted by the bolt

Extending BaseBasicBolt since we have a simple implementation.

Indicates the bolt emits a tuple with a field named email

Gets called when a tuple has been emitted to this bolt

Emits a new tuple containing the email

Extracts the value for the field named commit

The implementation for EmailExtractor.java is quite small, which is the main reason we decided to extend BaseBasicBolt. If you look a little deeper into the code, you'll notice some similarities to our spout code, namely the manner in which we declare the names for the values in tuples emitted by this bolt. Here we've defined a single field with a name of email.

As far as the bolt's execute method is concerned, all we're doing is splitting the string on the whitespace in order to obtain the email and emitting a new tuple with that email. Remember the output collector we mentioned in the previous spout implementation? We have something similar here with BasicOutputCollector, which emits this tuple, sending it to the next bolt in the topology, the email counter.

The code in the email counter is similar in structure to EmailExtractor.java but with a little more setup and implementation, as shown in the next listing.

Listing 2.6   EmailCounter.java

In-memory map for mapping emails to commit counts

```java
public class EmailCounter extends BaseBasicBolt {
  private Map<String, Integer> counts;

  @Override
  public void declareOutputFields(OutputFieldsDeclarer declarer) {
    // This bolt does not emit anything and therefore does
    // not declare any output fields.
  }

  @Override
  public void prepare(Map config,
                      TopologyContext context) {
    counts = new HashMap<String, Integer>();
  }

  @Override
  public void execute(Tuple tuple,
                      BasicOutputCollector outputCollector) {
    String email = tuple.getStringByField("email");
    counts.put(email, countFor(email) + 1);
    printCounts();
  }

  private Integer countFor(String email) {
    Integer count = counts.get(email);
    return count == null ? 0 : count;
  }

  private void printCounts() {
    for (String email : counts.keySet()) {
      System.out.println(
        String.format("%s has count of %s", email, counts.get(email)));
    }
  }
}
```

Extending BaseBasicBolt since we have a simple implementation.

Gets called when Storm prepares this bolt to be run

Extracts the value for the field named email

Again, we've decided to extend `BaseBasicBolt`. Even though EmailCounter.java is more complex than EmailExtractor.java, we can still get away with the functionality accessible by `BaseBasicBolt`. One difference you'll notice is that we've overridden the `prepare` method. This method gets called as Storm prepares the bolt before execution and is the method where we'd perform any setup for our bolt. In our case, this means instantiating the in-memory map.

Speaking of the in-memory map, you'll notice this is a private member variable that's specific to a single instance of this bolt. This should ring a bell, as it's something we mentioned in section 2.2.6, and it's why we were forced to use a fields grouping for the stream between our two bolts.

So here we are; we have code for our spout and two bolts. What's next? We need to somehow tell Storm where the streams are and identify the stream groupings for each of those streams. And we imagine you're eager to run this topology and see it in action. Here's where wiring everything together comes into play.

2.3.4 *Wiring everything together to form the topology*

Our spout and bolt implementations aren't useful on their own. We need to build up the topology, defining the streams and stream groupings between the spout and bolts. After that, we'd like to be able to run a test to make sure it all works as expected. Storm provides all the classes you need to do this. These classes include the following:

- `TopologyBuilder`—This class is used to piece together spouts and bolts, defining the streams and stream groupings between them.
- `Config`—This class is used for defining topology-level configuration.
- `StormTopology`—This class is what `TopologyBuilder` builds and is what's submitted to the cluster to be run.
- `LocalCluster`—This class simulates a Storm cluster in-process on our local machine, allowing us to easily run our topologies for testing purposes.

With a basic understanding of these classes, we'll build our topology and submit it to a local cluster, as seen in the next listing.

Listing 2.7 LocalTopologyRunner.java

Used for wiring together the spout and bolts

Adds the commit feed listener to the topology with an ID of commit-feed-listener

Adds the email counter to the topology with an ID of email-counter

Class for defining topology-level configuration; we're keeping it simple with debug output turned on.

Main method that will get called to run our topology locally in-process

Adds the email extractor to the topology with an ID of email-extractor

Defines the stream between the commit feed listener and email extractor

Defines the stream between the email extractor and email counter

Creates the topology

Defines a local cluster that can be run in-memory

Submits the topology and configuration to the local cluster

Kills the topology

Shuts down the local cluster

```java
public class LocalTopologyRunner {
  private static final int TEN_MINUTES = 600000;

  public static void main(String[] args) {
    TopologyBuilder builder = new TopologyBuilder();

    builder.setSpout("commit-feed-listener", new CommitFeedListener());

    builder
      .setBolt("email-extractor", new EmailExtractor())
      .shuffleGrouping("commit-feed-listener");

    builder
      .setBolt("email-counter", new EmailCounter())
      .fieldsGrouping("email-extractor", new Fields("email"));

    Config config = new Config();
    config.setDebug(true);

    StormTopology topology = builder.createTopology();

    LocalCluster cluster = new LocalCluster();
    cluster.submitTopology("github-commit-count-topology",
      config,
      topology);

    Utils.sleep(TEN_MINUTES);
    cluster.killTopology("github-commit-count-topology");
    cluster.shutdown();
  }
}
```

You can think of the main method as being split into three sections. The first is where we build the topology and tell Storm where the streams are and identify the stream groupings for each of these streams. The next part is creating the configuration. In our example, we've turned on debug logging. Many more configuration options are available that we'll cover later in this book. The final part is where we submit both the configuration and built topology to the local cluster to be run. Here we run the local cluster for 10 minutes, continuously emitting tuples for each commit message in our changelog.txt file. This should provide plenty of activity within our topology.

If we were to run the main method of LocalTopologyRunner.java via `java -jar`, we would see debug log messages flying by in the console showing tuples being emitted by our spout and processed by our bolts. And there you have it; you've built your first topology! With the basics covered, we still need to address some of the topics we alluded to in this chapter. We'll start with addressing some good topology design practices to follow in chapter 3.

2.4   *Summary*

In this chapter, you learned that

- A topology is a graph where the nodes represent a single process or computation and the edges represent the result of one computation being passed as the input to another computation.
- A tuple is an ordered list of values where each value in the list is assigned a name. A tuple represents the data passed between two components.
- The flow of tuples between two components is called a stream.
- Spouts act as the source of a stream; their sole purpose is to read data from a source and emit tuples to its output stream.
- Bolts are where the core logic in a topology exists, performing operations such as filters, aggregations, joins, and talking to databases.
- Both spouts and bolts (called components) execute as one or more individual instances, emitting tuples to other instances of bolts.
- The manner in which tuples flow between individual instances of components is defined with a stream grouping.
- Implementing the code for your spouts and bolts is only part of the picture; you still need to wire them together and define the streams and stream groupings.
- Running a topology in local mode is the quickest way to test that your topology is working.

Topology design 3

This chapter covers

- Decomposing a problem to fit Storm constructs
- Working with unreliable data sources
- Integrating with external services and data stores
- Understanding parallelism within a Storm topology
- Following best practices for topology design

In the previous chapter, we got our feet wet by building a simple topology that counts commits made to a GitHub project. We broke it down into Storm's two primary components—spouts and bolts—but we didn't concern ourselves with details as to why. This chapter expands on those basic Storm concepts by showing you how to think about modeling and designing solutions with Storm. You'll learn strategies for problem analysis that can help you end up with a good design: a model for representing the workflow of the problem at hand.

In addition, it's important that you learn how scalability (or parallelization of units of work) is built into Storm because that affects the approach that you'll take with topology design. We'll also explore strategies for gaining the most out of your topology in terms of speed.

After reading this chapter, not only will you be able to easily take apart a problem and see how it fits within Storm, but you'll also be able to determine whether Storm is the right solution for tackling that problem. This chapter will give you a solid understanding of topology design so that you can envision solutions to big data problems.

Let's get started by exploring how you can approach topology design and then get into breaking down a real-world scenario using the steps we've outlined.

3.1   Approaching topology design

The approach to topology design can be broken down into the following five steps:

1   *Defining the problem/forming a conceptual solution*—This step serves to provide a clear understanding of the problem being tackled. It also serves as a place to document the requirements to be placed on any potential solution (including requirements with regard to speed, which is a common criterion in big data problems). This step involves modeling a solution (not an implementation) that addresses the core need(s) of the problem.

2   *Mapping the solution to Storm*—In this step, you follow a set of tenets for breaking down the proposed solution in a manner that allows you to envision how it will map to Storm primitives (aka Storm concepts). At this stage, you'll come up with a design for your topology. This design will be tuned and adjusted as needed in the following steps.

3   *Implementing the initial solution*—Each of the components will be implemented at this point.

4   *Scaling the topology*—In this step, you'll turn the knobs that Storm provides for you to run this topology at scale.

5   *Tuning based on observations*—Finally, you'll adjust the topology based on observed behavior once it's running. This step may involve additional tuning for achieving scale as well as design changes that may be warranted for efficiency.

Let's apply these steps to a real-world problem to show how you'd go about completing each of the steps. We'll do this with a social heat map, which encapsulates several challenging topics related to topology design.

3.2   Problem definition: a social heat map

Imagine this scenario: it's Saturday night and you're out drinking at a bar, enjoying the good life with your friends. You're finishing your third drink and you're starting to feel like you need a change of scene. Maybe switch it up and go to a different bar? So many choices—how do you even choose? Being a socialite, of course you'd want to end up in the bar that's most popular. You don't want to go somewhere that was voted best in your neighborhood glossy magazine. That was so last week. You want to be where the action is right now, not last week, not even last hour. You are the trendsetter. You have a responsibility to show your friends a good time.

Okay, maybe that's not you. But does that represent the average social network user? Now what can we do to help this person? If we can represent the answer this person is looking for in a graphical form factor, it'd be ideal—a map that identifies the neighborhoods with highest density of activity in bars as hot zones can convey everything quickly. A heat map can identify the general neighborhood in a big city like New York or San Francisco, and generally when a picking a popular bar, it's better to have a few choices within close proximity to one another, just in case.

Other case studies for heat maps

What kind of problems benefit from visualization using a heat map? A good candidate would allow you to use the heat map's intensity to model the relative importance of a set of data points as compared to others within an area (geographical or otherwise):

- The spread of a wildfire in California, an approaching hurricane on the East Coast, or the outbreak of a disease can be modeled and represented as a heat map to warn residents.
- On an election day, you might want to know
  - Which political districts had the most voters turn out? You can depict this on a heat map by modeling the turnout numbers to reflect the intensity.
  - You can depict which political party/candidate/issue received the most votes by modeling the party, candidate, or issue as a different color, with the intensity of the color reflecting the number of votes.

We've provided a general problem definition. Before moving any further, let's form a conceptual solution.

3.2.1 Formation of a conceptual solution

Where should we begin? Multiple social networks incorporate the concept of check-ins. Let's say we have access to a data fire hose that collects check-ins for bars from all of these networks. This fire hose will emit a bar's address for every check-in. This gives us a starting point, but it's also good to have an end goal in mind. Let's say that our end goal is a geographical map with a heat map overlay identifying neighborhoods with the most popular bars. Figure 3.1 illustrates our proposed solution where we'll transform multiple check-ins from different venues to be shown in a heat map.

The solution that we need to model within Storm becomes the method of transforming (or aggregating) check-ins into a data set that can be depicted on a heat map.

3.3 Precepts for mapping the solution to Storm

The best way to start is to contemplate the nature of data flowing through this system. When we better understand the peculiarities contained within the data stream, we can become more attuned to requirements that can be placed on this system realistically.

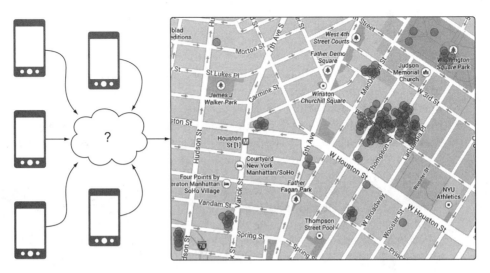

Figure 3.1   Using check-ins to build a heat map of bars

3.3.1   *Consider the requirements imposed by the data stream*

We have a fire hose emitting addresses of bars for each check-in. But this stream of check-ins doesn't reliably represent every single user who went to a bar. A check-in isn't equivalent to a physical presence at a location. It's better to think of it as a sampling of real life because not every single user checks in. But that leads us to question whether check-in data is even useful for solving this problem. For this example, we can safely assume that check-ins at bars are proportional to people at those locations.

So we know the following:

- Check-ins are a sampling of real-life scenarios, but they're not complete.
- They're proportionately representative.

NOTE   Let's make the assumption here that the data volume is large enough to compensate for data loss and that any data loss is intermittent and not sustained long enough to cause a noticeable disruption in service. These assumptions help us portray a case of working with an unreliable data source.

We have our first insight about our data stream: a proportionately representative but possibly incomplete stream of check-ins. What's next? We know our users want to be notified about the latest trends in activity as soon as possible. In other words, we have a strict speed requirement: get the results to the user as quickly as possible because the value of data diminishes with time.

What emerges from consideration of the data stream is that we don't need to worry too much about data loss. We can come to this conclusion because we know that our incoming data set is incomplete, so accuracy down to some arbitrary, minute degree of precision isn't necessary. But it's proportionately representative and that's good enough for determining popularity. Combine this with the requirement of speed and we know that as long as we get recent data quickly to our users, they'll be happy. Even if data loss occurs, the past results will be replaced soon.

This scenario maps directly to the idea of working with an unreliable data source in Storm. With an unreliable data source, you don't have the ability to retry a failed operation; the data source may not have the ability to replay a data point. In our case, we're sampling real life by way of check-ins and that mimics the availability of an incomplete data set.

In contrast, there may be cases where you work with a reliable data source—one that has the ability to replay data points that fail. But perhaps accuracy is less important than speed and you may not want to take advantage of the replayability of a reliable data source. Then approximations can be just as acceptable, and you're treating the reliable data source as if it was unreliable by choosing to ignore any reliability measures it provides.

NOTE We'll cover reliable data sources along with fault tolerance in chapter 4.

Having defined the source of the data, the next step is to identify how the individual data points will flow through our proposed solution. We'll explore this topic next.

3.3.2 *Represent data points as tuples*

Our next step is to identify the individual data points that flow through this stream. It's easy to accomplish this by considering the beginning and end. We begin with a series of data points composed of street addresses of bars with activity. We'll also need to know the time the check-in occurred. So our input data point can be represented as follows:

```
[time="9:00:07 PM", address="287 Hudson St New York NY 10013"]
```

That's the time and an address where the check-in happened. This would be our input tuple that's emitted by the spout. As you'll recall from chapter 2, a *tuple* is a Storm primitive for representing a data point and a *spout* is a source of a stream of tuples.

We have the end goal of building a heat map with the latest activity at bars. So we need to end up with data points representing timely coordinates on a map. We can attach a time interval (say 9:00:00 PM to 9:00:15 PM, if we want 15-second increments) to a set of coordinates that occurred within that interval. Then at the point of display within the heat map, we can pick the latest available time interval. Coordinates on a map can be expressed by way of latitude and longitude (say, 40.7142° N, 74.0064° W for New York, NY). It's standard form to represent 40.7142° N, 74.0064° W as (40.7142, -74.0064). But there might be multiple coordinates representing multiple check-ins within a time window. So we need a list of coordinates for a time interval. Then our end data point starts to look like this:

```
[time-interval="9:00:00 PM to 9:00:15 PM",
 hotzones=List((40.719908,-73.987277),(40.72612,-74.001396))]
```

That's an end data point containing a time interval and two corresponding check-ins at two different bars.

What if there's two or more check-ins at the same bar within that time interval? Then that coordinate will be duplicated. How would we handle that? One option is to keep counts of occurrences within that time window for that coordinate. This involves determining sameness of coordinates based on some arbitrary but useful degree of precision. To avoid all that, let's keep duplicates of any coordinate within a time interval with multiple check-ins. By adding multiples of the same coordinates to a heat map, we can let the map generator make use of multiple occurrences as a level of hotness (rather than using occurrence count for that purpose).

Our end data point will look like this:

```
[time-interval="9:00:00 PM to 9:00:15 PM",
 hotzones=List((40.719908,-73.987277),
               (40.72612,-74.001396),
               (40.719908,-73.987277))]
```

Note that the first coordinate is duplicated. This is our end tuple that will be served up in the form of a heat map. Having a list of coordinates grouped by a time interval has these advantages:

- Allows us to easily build a heat map by using the Google Maps API. We can do this by adding a heat map overlay on top of a regular Google Map.
- Let us go back in time to any particular time interval and see the heat map for that point in time.

Having the input data points and final data points is only part of the picture; we still need to identify how we get from point A to point B.

3.3.3   *Steps for determining the topology composition*

Our approach for designing a Storm topology can be broken down into three steps:

1   Determine the input data points and how they can be represented as tuples.
2   Determine the final data points needed to solve the problem and how they can be represented as tuples.
3   Bridge the gap between the input tuples and the final tuples by creating a series of operations that transform them.

We already know our input and desired output:

Input tuples:

```
[time="9:00:07 PM", address="287 Hudson St New York NY 10013"]
```

End tuples:

```
[time-interval="9:00:00 PM to 9:00:15 PM",
 hotzones=List((40.719908,-73.987277),
               (40.72612,-74.001396),
               (40.719908,-73.987277))]
```

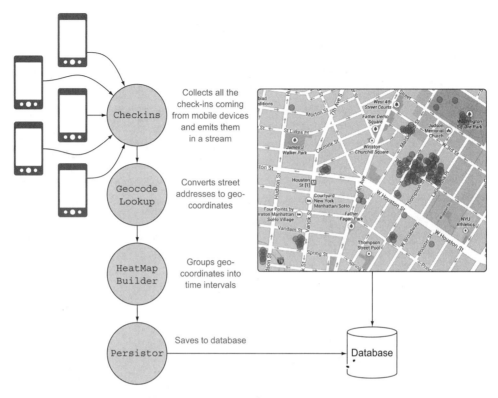

Figure 3.2   Transforming input tuples to end tuples via a series of operations

Somewhere along the way, we need to transform the addresses of bars into these end tuples. Figure 3.2 shows how we can break down the problem into these series of operations.

Let's take these steps and see how they map onto Storm primitives (we're using the terms *Storm primitives* and *Storm concepts* interchangeably).

OPERATIONS AS SPOUTS AND BOLTS

We've created a series of operations to transform input tuples to end tuples. Let's see how these four operations map to Storm primitives:

- Checkins—This will be the source of input tuples into the topology, so in terms of Storm concepts this will be our spout. In this case, because we're using an unreliable data source, we'll build a spout that has no capability of retrying failures. We'll get into retrying failures in chapter 4.

- GeocodeLookup—This will take our input tuple and convert the street address to a geocoordinate by querying the Google Maps Geocoding API. This is the first bolt in the topology.

- HeatMapBuilder—This is the second bolt in the topology, and it'll keep a data structure in memory to map each incoming tuple to a time interval, thereby

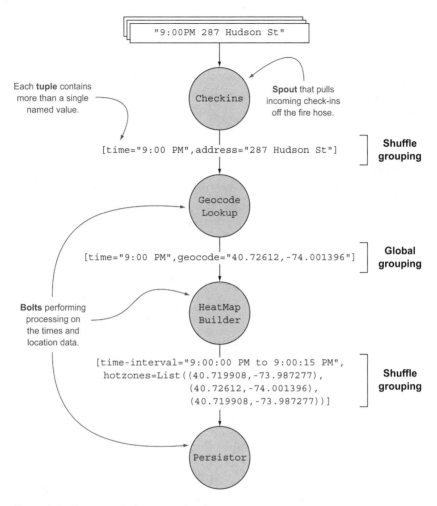

Each **tuple** contains more than a single named value.

"9:00PM 287 Hudson St"

Checkins

Spout that pulls incoming check-ins off the fire hose.

[time="9:00 PM",address="287 Hudson St"]

} **Shuffle grouping**

Geocode Lookup

[time="9:00 PM",geocode="40.72612,-74.001396"]

} **Global grouping**

Bolts performing processing on the times and location data.

HeatMap Builder

[time-interval="9:00:00 PM to 9:00:15 PM",
  hotzones=List((40.719908,-73.987277),
               (40.72612,-74.001396),
               (40.719908,-73.987277))]

} **Shuffle grouping**

Persistor

Figure 3.3 Heat map design mapped to Storm concepts

grouping check-ins by time interval. When each time interval is completely passed, it'll emit the list of coordinates associated with that time interval.

- `Persistor`—We'll use this third and final bolt in our topology to save our end tuples to a database.

Figure 3.3 provides an illustration of the design mapped to Storm concepts.

So far we've discussed the tuples, spout, and bolts. One thing in figure 3.3 that we haven't talked about is the stream grouping for each stream. We'll get into each grouping in more detail when we cover the code for the topology in the next section.

3.4 *Initial implementation of the design*

With the design complete, we're ready to tackle the implementation for each of the components. Much as we did in chapter 2, we'll start with the code for the spout and bolts, and finish with the code that wires it all together. Later we'll adjust each of these implementations for efficiency or to address some of their shortcomings.

3.4.1 *Spout: read data from a source*

In our design, the spout listens to a fire hose of social check-ins and emits a tuple for each individual check-in. Figure 3.4 provides a reminder of where we are in our topology design.

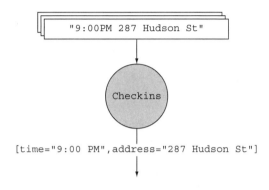

"9:00PM 287 Hudson St"

Checkins

[time="9:00 PM",address="287 Hudson St"]

Figure 3.4   The spout listens to the fire hose of social check-ins and emits a tuple for each check-in.

For the purpose of this chapter, we'll use a text file as our source of data for check-ins. To feed this data set into our Storm topology, we need to write a spout that reads from this file and emits a tuple for each line. The file, checkins.txt, will live next to the class for our spout and contain a list of check-ins in the expected format (see the following listing).

Listing 3.1   An excerpt from our simple data source, checkins.txt

```
1382904793783, 287 Hudson St New York NY 10013
1382904793784, 155 Varick St New York NY 10013
1382904793785, 222 W Houston St New York NY 10013
1382904793786, 5 Spring St New York NY 10013
1382904793787, 148 West 4th St New York NY 10013
```

The next listing shows the spout implementation that reads from this file of check-ins. Because our input tuple is a time and address, we'll represent the time as a `Long` (millisecond-level Unix timestamp) and the address as a `String`, with the two separated by a comma in our text file.

Listing 3.2   `Checkins.java`

```
public class Checkins extends BaseRichSpout {
    private List<String> checkins;
    private int nextEmitIndex;
    private SpoutOutputCollector outputCollector;

    @Override
    public void declareOutputFields(OutputFieldsDeclarer declarer) {
```

Store the static check-ins from a file in List.

⟵ **Checkins spout extends BaseRichSpout.**

⟵ **nextEmitIndex will keep track of our current position in the list as we'll recycle the static list of check-ins.**

```
    declarer.declare(new Fields("time", "address"));
}

@Override
public void open(Map config,
                 TopologyContext topologyContext,
                 SpoutOutputCollector spoutOutputCollector) {
  this.outputCollector = spoutOutputCollector;
  this.nextEmitIndex = 0;

  try {
    checkins =
    IOUtils.readLines(ClassLoader.getSystemResourceAsStream("checkins.txt"),
                      Charset.defaultCharset().name());
  } catch (IOException e) {
    throw new RuntimeException(e);
  }
}

@Override
public void nextTuple() {
  String checkin = checkins.get(nextEmitIndex);
  String[] parts = checkin.split(",");
  Long time = Long.valueOf(parts[0]);
  String address = parts[1];
  outputCollector.emit(new Values(time, address));

  nextEmitIndex = (nextEmitIndex + 1) % checkins.size();
}
}
```

Let Storm know that this spout will emit a tuple containing two fields named time and address.

When Storm requests the next tuple from the spout, look up the next check-in from our in-memory List and parse it into time and address components.

Use the SpoutOutput-Collector provided in the spout open method to emit the relevant fields.

Because we're treating this as an unreliable data source, the spout remains simple; it doesn't need to keep track of which tuples failed and which ones succeeded in order to provide fault tolerance. Not only does that simplify the spout implementation, it also removes quite a bit of bookkeeping that Storm needs to do internally and speeds things up. When fault tolerance isn't necessary and we can define a service-level agreement (SLA) that allows us to discard data at will, an unreliable data source can be beneficial. It's easier to maintain and provides fewer points of failure.

3.4.2 Bolt: connect to an external service

The first bolt in the topology will take the address data point from the tuple emitted by the Checkins spout and translate that address into a coordinate by querying the Google Maps Geocoding Service. Figure 3.5 highlights the bolt we're currently implementing.

The code for this bolt can be seen in listing 3.3. We're using the Google Geocoder Java API from https://code.google.com/p/geocoder-java/ to retrieve the coordinates.

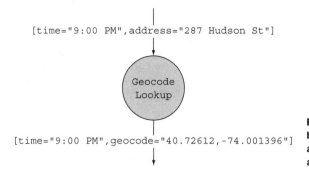

[time="9:00 PM",address="287 Hudson St"]

[time="9:00 PM",geocode="40.72612,-74.001396"]

Figure 3.5 The geocode lookup bolt accepts a social check-in and retrieves the coordinates associated with that check-in.

Listing 3.3 GeocodeLookup.java

```java
public class GeocodeLookup extends BaseBasicBolt {
  private Geocoder geocoder;

  @Override
  public void declareOutputFields(OutputFieldsDeclarer fieldsDeclarer) {
    fieldsDeclarer.declare(new Fields("time", "geocode"));
  }

  @Override
  public void prepare(Map config,
                      TopologyContext context) {
    geocoder = new Geocoder();
  }

  @Override
  public void execute(Tuple tuple,
                      BasicOutputCollector outputCollector) {
    String address = tuple.getStringByField("address");
    Long time = tuple.getLongByField("time");

    GeocoderRequest request = new GeocoderRequestBuilder()
      .setAddress(address)
      .setLanguage("en")
      .getGeocoderRequest();
    GeocodeResponse response = geocoder.geocode(request);
    GeocoderStatus status = response.getStatus();
    if (GeocoderStatus.OK.equals(status)) {
      GeocoderResult firstResult = response.getResults().get(0);
      LatLng latLng = firstResult.getGeometry().getLocation();
      outputCollector.emit(new Values(time, latLng));
    }
  }
}
```

- **GeocodeLookup bolt extends BaseBasicBolt.**
- **Inform Storm that this bolt will emit two fields, time and geocode.**
- **Initialize the Google Geocoder.**
- **Extract the time and address fields from the tuple sent by the Checkins spout.**
- **Query Google Maps Geocoding API with the address value from the tuple.**
- **Use the first result from the Google Geocoding API for the geocoordinate and emit it along with the time.**

We've intentionally kept our interaction with Google Geocoding API simple. In a real implementation we should be handling for error cases when addresses may not be valid. Additionally, the Google Geocoding API imposes a quota when used in this way that's quite small and not practical for big data applications. For a big data application like this, you'd need to obtain an access level with a higher quota from Google if you wanted to use them as a provider for Geocoding. Other approaches to consider include locally caching geocoding results within your data center to avoid making unnecessary invocations to Google's API.

We now have the time and geocoordinate of every check-in. We took our input tuple

```
[time="9:00:07 PM", address="287 Hudson St New York NY 10013"]
```

and transformed it into this:

```
[time="9:00 PM", geocode="40.72612,-74.001396"]
```

This new tuple will then be sent to the bolt that maintains groups of check-ins by time interval, which we'll look at now.

3.4.3   *Bolt: collect data in-memory*

Next, we'll build the data structure that represents the heat map. Figure 3.6 illustrates our location in the design.

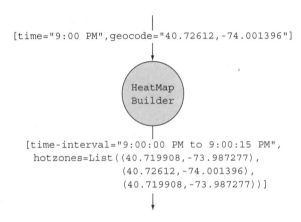

Figure 3.6   **The heat map builder bolt accepts a tuple with time and geocode and emits a tuple containing a time interval and a list of geocodes.**

What kind of data structure is suitable here? We have tuples coming into this bolt from the previous `GeocodeLookup` bolt in the form of [time="9:00 PM", geocode= "40.72612,-74.001396"]. We need to group these by time intervals—let's say 15-second intervals because we want to display a new heat map every 15 seconds. Our end tuples need to be in the form of [time-interval="9:00:00 PM to 9:00:15 PM", hotzones= List((40.719908,-73.987277),(40.72612,-74.001396),(40.719908,-73.987277))].

To group geocoordinates by time interval, let's maintain a data structure in memory and collect incoming tuples into that data structure isolated by time interval. We can model this as a map:

```
Map<Long, List<LatLng>> heatmaps;
```

This map is keyed by the time that starts our interval. We can omit the end of the time interval because each interval is of the same length. The value will be the list of coordinates that fall into that time interval (including duplicates—duplicates or coordinates in closer proximity would indicate a hot zone or intensity on the heat map).

Let's start building the heat map in three steps:

1 Collect incoming tuples into an in-memory map.
2 Configure this bolt to receive a signal at a given frequency.
3 Emit the aggregated heat map for elapsed time intervals to the `Persistor` bolt for saving to a database.

Let's look at each step individually, and then we can put everything together, starting with the next listing.

Listing 3.4 `HeatMapBuilder.java`: step 1, collecting incoming tuples into an in-memory map

```
private Map<Long, List<LatLng>> heatmaps;

@Override
public void prepare(Map config,
                    TopologyContext context) {
  heatmaps = new HashMap<Long, List<LatLng>>();     ◁── Initialize the in-memory map.
}

@Override
public void execute(Tuple tuple,
                    BasicOutputCollector outputCollector) {
  Long time = tuple.getLongByField("time");
  LatLng geocode = (LatLng) tuple.getValueByField("geocode");   ◁── Select the time interval that the tuple falls into.

  Long timeInterval = selectTimeInterval(time);
  List<LatLng> checkins = getCheckinsForInterval(timeInterval);
  checkins.add(geocode);     ◁── Add the geocoordinate to the list of check-ins associated with that time interval.
}

private Long selectTimeInterval(Long time) {
  return time / (15 * 1000);
}

private List<LatLng> getCheckinsForInterval(Long timeInterval) {
  List<LatLng> hotzones = heatmaps.get(timeInterval);
  if (hotzones == null) {
    hotzones = new ArrayList<LatLng>();
    heatmaps.put(timeInterval, hotzones);
  }
  return hotzones;
}
```

The absolute time interval the incoming tuple falls into is selected by taking the check-in time and dividing it by the length of the interval—in this case, 15 seconds. For example, if check-in time is 9:00:07.535 PM, then it should fall into the time interval 9:00:00.000–9:00:15.000 PM. What we're extracting here is the beginning of that time interval, which is 9:00:00.000 PM.

Now that we're collecting all the tuples into a heat map, we need to periodically inspect it and emit the coordinates from completed time intervals so that they can be persisted into a data store by the next bolt.

TICK TUPLES

Sometimes you need to trigger an action periodically, such as aggregating a batch of data or flushing some writes to a database. Storm has a feature called *tick tuples* to handle this eventuality. Tick tuples can be configured to be received at a user-defined frequency and when configured, the execute method on the bolt will receive the tick tuple at the given frequency. You need to inspect the tuple to determine whether it's one of these system-emitted tick tuples or whether it's a normal tuple. Normal tuples within a topology will flow through the default stream, whereas tick tuples are flowing through a system tick stream, making them easily identifiable. The following listing shows the code for configuring and handling tick tuples in the HeatMapBuilder bolt.

Listing 3.5   `HeatMapBuilder.java`: step 2, configuring to receive a signal at a given frequency

```
@Override
public Map<String, Object> getComponentConfiguration() {       ◁──┐  Overriding this
  Config conf = new Config();                                        method allows us
  conf.put(Config.TOPOLOGY_TICK_TUPLE_FREQ_SECS, 60);                to configure various
  return conf;                                                       aspects of how our
}                                                                    component runs—in
                                                                     this case, setting the
@Override                                                            tick tuple frequency.
public void execute(Tuple tuple,
                    BasicOutputCollector outputCollector) {
  if (isTickTuple(tuple)) {                                    ◁──┐  When we get
    // . . . take periodic action                                   a tick tuple,
  } else {                                                          do something
    Long time = tuple.getLongByField("time");                      different. For a
    LatLng geocode = (LatLng) tuple.getValueByField("geocode");    regular tuple,
                                                                   we take the
    Long timeInterval = selectTimeInterval(time);                  same action
    List<LatLng> checkins = getCheckinsForInterval(timeInterval);  as before.
    checkins.add(geocode);
  }
}

private boolean isTickTuple(Tuple tuple) {
  String sourceComponent = tuple.getSourceComponent();
  String sourceStreamId = tuple.getSourceStreamId();
  return sourceComponent.equals(Constants.SYSTEM_COMPONENT_ID)   ◁──┐
      && sourceStreamId.equals(Constants.SYSTEM_TICK_STREAM_ID);
}
```

Tick tuples are easily identifiable because they're emitted on the system tick stream by system components rather than being emitted by one of our own components on the default stream for our topology.

Looking at the code in listing 3.5, you'll notice that tick tuples are configured at the bolt level, as demonstrated by the getComponentConfiguration implementation. The tick tuple in question will only be sent to instances of this bolt.

> ### Emit frequencies of tick tuples
>
> We configured our tick tuples to be emitted at a frequency of every 60 seconds. This doesn't mean they'll be emitted exactly every 60 seconds; it's done on a best-effort basis. Tick tuples that are sent to a bolt are queued behind the other tuples currently waiting to be consumed by the `execute()` method on that bolt. A bolt may not necessarily process the tick tuples at the frequency that they're emitted if the bolt is lagging behind due to high latency in processing its regular stream of tuples.

Now let's use that tick tuple as a signal to select time periods that have passed for which we no longer expect any incoming coordinates, and emit them from this bolt so that the next bolt down the line can take them on (see the next listing).

Listing 3.6 `HeatMapBuilder.java`: step 3, emitting the aggregated HeatMap for elapsed time intervals

```
@Override
public void execute(Tuple tuple,
                    BasicOutputCollector outputCollector) {
  if (isTickTuple(tuple)) {
    emitHeatmap(outputCollector);            ⟵   If we got a
  } else {                                         tick tuple,
    Long time = tuple.getLongByField("time");      interpret that
    LatLng geocode = (LatLng) tuple.getValueByField("geocode");   as a signal to
                                                   see whether
    Long timeInterval = selectTimeInterval(time);  there are any
    List<LatLng> checkins = getCheckinsForInterval(timeInterval);  heat maps
    checkins.add(geocode);                         that can be
  }                                                emitted.
}

private void emitHeatmap(BasicOutputCollector outputCollector) {
  Long now = System.currentTimeMillis();
  Long emitUpToTimeInterval = selectTimeInterval(now);      ⟵
  Set<Long> timeIntervalsAvailable = heatmaps.keySet();
  for (Long timeInterval : timeIntervalsAvailable) {
    if (timeInterval <= emitUpToTimeInterval) {
      List<LatLng> hotzones = heatmaps.remove(timeInterval);
      outputCollector.emit(new Values(timeInterval, hotzones));
    }
  }
}

private Long selectTimeInterval(Long time) {
  return time / (15 * 1000);
}
```

For all time intervals we're currently keeping track of: if they've elapsed, remove them from the in-memory data structure and emit them.

Heat maps that can be emitted are considered to have check-ins that occurred before the beginning of the current time-interval. That's why we're passing the current time into selectTimeInterval(), which will give us the beginning of the current time interval.

Steps 1, 2, and 3 provide a complete `HeatMapBuilder` implementation, showing how you can maintain state with an in-memory map and also how you can use Storm's built-in tick tuple to emit a tuple at particular time intervals. With this implementation complete, let's move on to persisting the results of the tuples emitted by `Heat-MapBuilder`.

Thread safety

We're collecting coordinates into an in-memory map, but we created it as an instance of a regular `HashMap`. Storm is highly scalable, and there are multiple tuples coming in that are added to this map, and we're also periodically removing entries from that map. Is modifying an in-memory data structure like this thread-safe?

Yes, it's thread-safe because `execute()` is processing only one tuple at a time. Whether it's our regular stream of tuples or a tick tuple, only one JVM thread of execution will be going through and processing code within an instance of this bolt. So within a given bolt instance, there will never be multiple threads running through it.

Does that mean you never need to worry about thread safety within the confines of your bolt? No, in certain cases you might.

One such case has to do with how values within a tuple are serialized on a different thread when being sent between bolts. For example, when you emit your in-memory data structure without copying it and it's serialized on a different thread, if that data structure is changed during the serialization process, you'll get a `Concurrent-ModificationException`. Theoretically, everything emitted to an `OutputCollector` should guard against such scenarios. One way to do this is make any emitted values immutable.

Another case is where you may create threads of your own with the bolt's `execute()` method. For example, if instead of using tick tuples, you spawned a background thread that periodically emits heat maps, then you'll need to concern yourself with thread safety, because you'll have your own thread and Storm's thread of execution both running through your bolt.

3.4.4 *Bolt: persisting to a data store*

We have the end tuples that represent a heat map. At this point, we're ready to persist that data to some data store. Our JavaScript-based web application can read the heat map values from this data store and interact with the Google Maps API to build a geographical visualization from these calculated values. Figure 3.7 illustrates the final bolt in our design.

Because we're storing and accessing heat maps based on time interval,

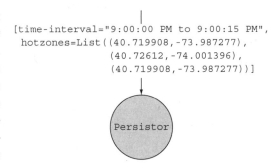

```
[time-interval="9:00:00 PM to 9:00:15 PM",
    hotzones=List((40.719908,-73.987277),
                  (40.72612,-74.001396),
                  (40.719908,-73.987277))]
```

Figure 3.7 The `Persistor` bolt accepts a tuple with a time interval and a list of geocodes and persists that data to a data store.

it makes sense to use a key-value data model for storage. For this case study, we'll use Redis, but any data store that supports the key-value model will suffice (such as Membase, Memcached, or Riak). We'll store the heat maps keyed by time interval with the heat map itself as a JSON representation of the list of coordinates. We'll use Jedis as a Java client for Redis and the Jackson JSON library for converting the heat map to JSON.

NoSQL and other data stores with Storm

Examining the various NoSQL and data storage solutions available for working with large data sets is outside the scope of this book, but make sure you start off on the right foot when making your selections with regard to data storage solutions.

It's common for people to consider the various options available to them and ask themselves, "Which one of these NoSQL solutions should I pick?" This is the wrong approach. Instead, ask yourself questions about the functionality you're implementing and the requirements they impose on any data storage solution.

You should be asking whether your use case requires a data store that supports the following:

- Random reads or random writes
- Sequential reads or sequential writes
- High read throughput or high write throughput
- Whether the data changes or remains immutable once written
- Storage model suitable for your data access patterns
  - Column/column-family oriented
  - Key-value
  - Document oriented
  - Schema/schemaless
- Whether consistency or availability is most desirable

Once you've determined your mix of requirements, it's easy to figure out which of the available NoSQL, NewSQL, or other solutions are suitable for you. There's no right NoSQL solution for all problems. There's also no perfect data store for use with Storm—it depends on the use case.

So let's take a look at the code for writing to this NoSQL data store (see the following listing).

Listing 3.7 `Persistor.java`

```
public class Persistor extends BaseBasicBolt {
  private final Logger logger = LoggerFactory.getLogger(Persistor.class);

  private Jedis jedis;
  private ObjectMapper objectMapper;
```

Convert the list of LatLng to a list of Strings where each String is of the form (latitude, longitude).

Write the heat map JSON to Redis keyed by the time interval.

Instantiate Jedis and have it connect to a Redis instance running on localhost.

Instantiate the Jackson JSON ObjectMapper for serializing our heat map.

Serialize the list of geocoordinates (currently in String form) to JSON.

We aren't retrying any database failures because this is an unreliable stream.

Close the connection to Redis when the Storm topology is stopped.

This is the last bolt, so no tuples are emitted from it. This means no fields need to be declared.

```
@Override
public void prepare(Map stormConf,
                    TopologyContext context) {
    jedis = new Jedis("localhost");
    objectMapper = new ObjectMapper();
}

@Override
public void execute(Tuple tuple,
                    BasicOutputCollector outputCollector) {
    Long timeInterval = tuple.getLongByField("time-interval");
    List<LatLng> hz = (List<LatLng>) tuple.getValueByField("hotzones");
    List<String> hotzones = asListOfStrings(hz);

    try {
        String key = "checkins-" + timeInterval;
        String value = objectMapper.writeValueAsString(hotzones);
        jedis.set(key, value);
    } catch (Exception e) {
        logger.error("Error persisting for time: " + timeInterval, e);
    }
}

private List<String> asListOfStrings(List<LatLng> hotzones) {
    List<String> hotzonesStandard = new ArrayList<String>(hotzones.size());
    for (LatLng geoCoordinate : hotzones) {
        hotzonesStandard.add(geoCoordinate.toUrlValue());
    }
    return hotzonesStandard;
}

@Override
public void cleanup() {
    if (jedis.isConnected()) {
        jedis.quit();
    }
}

@Override
public void declareOutputFields(OutputFieldsDeclarer declarer) {
    // No output fields to be declared
}
}
```

Working with Redis is simple, and it serves as a good store for our use case. But for larger-scale applications and data sets, a different data store may be necessary. One thing to note is that because we're working with an unreliable data stream, we're simply logging any errors that may occur while saving to the database. Some errors may be able to be retried (say, a timeout), and when working with a reliable data stream, we'd consider how to retry them, as you'll see in chapter 4.

3.4.5 *Defining stream groupings between the components*

In chapter 2, you learned two ways of connecting components within a topology to one another—shuffle grouping and fields grouping. To recap:

- You use shuffle grouping to distribute outgoing tuples from one component to the next in a manner that's random but evenly spread out.
- You use fields grouping when you want to ensure tuples with the same values for a selected set of fields always go to the same instance of the next bolt.

A shuffle grouping should suffice for the streams between `Checkins/GeocodeLookup` and `HeatMapBuilder/Persistor`.

But we need to send the entire stream of outgoing tuples from the `GeocodeLookup` bolt to the `HeatMapBuilder` bolt. If different tuples from `GeocodeLookup` end up going to different instances of `HeatMapBuilder`, then we won't be able to group them into time intervals because they'll be spread out among different instances of `HeatMap-Builder`. This is where global grouping comes in. *Global grouping* will ensure that the entire stream of tuples will go to one specific instance of `HeatMapBuilder`. Specifically, the entire stream will go to the instance of `HeatMapBuilder` with the lowest task ID (an ID assigned internally by Storm). Now we have every tuple in one place and we can easily determine which time interval any tuple falls into and group them into their corresponding time intervals.

> **NOTE** Instead of using a global grouping you could have a single instance of the `HeatMapBuilder` bolt with a shuffle grouping. This will also guarantee that everything goes to the same `HeatMapBuilder` instance, as there is only one. But we favor being explicit in our code, and using a global grouping clearly conveys the desired behavior here. A global grouping is also slightly cheaper, as it doesn't have to pick a random instance to emit to as in a shuffle grouping.

Let's take a look at how we'd define these stream groupings in the code for building and running our topology.

3.4.6 *Building a topology for running in local cluster mode*

We're almost done. We just need to wire everything together and run the topology in local cluster mode, just like we did in chapter 2. But in this chapter, we're going to deviate from having all the code in a single `LocalTopologyRunner` class and split the code into two classes: one class for building the topology and another for running it. This is a common practice and while you might not see the benefits immediately in this chapter, hopefully in chapters 4 and 5 you'll see why we've decided to do this.

The following listing shows you the code for building the topology.

Listing 3.8 `HeatmapTopologyBuilder.java`

We use
global
grouping
to connect
HeatMap-
Builder to
Checkins.

Wire in the topology and connect all
the bolts and spout together in order.
In this particular topology, these
components are connected to one
another in order, in serial fashion.

```java
public class HeatmapTopologyBuilder {
  public StormTopology build() {
    TopologyBuilder builder = new TopologyBuilder();

    builder.setSpout("checkins", new Checkins());
    builder.setBolt("geocode-lookup", new GeocodeLookup())
        .shuffleGrouping("checkins");
    builder.setBolt("heatmap-builder", new HeatMapBuilder())
        .globalGrouping("geocode-lookup");
    builder.setBolt("persistor", new Persistor())
        .shuffleGrouping("heatmap-builder");

    return builder.createTopology();
  }
}
```

These two bolts are
connected to their
corresponding
previous components
using shuffle grouping,
so these bolts receive
their incoming tuples
in a random but evenly
distributed manner.

With the code for building the topology defined, the next listing shows how to implement LocalTopologyRunner.

Listing 3.9 `LocalTopologyRunner.java`

A basic Storm
config with
no changes
to the default
configuration

```java
public class LocalTopologyRunner {
  public static void main(String[] args) {
    Config config = new Config();

    StormTopology topology = HeatmapTopologyBuilder.build();

    LocalCluster localCluster = new LocalCluster();
    localCluster.submitTopology("local-heatmap", config, topology);
  }
}
```

A simple Java class with a
main() method is usually
used to start the topology.

Create a local
cluster.

Submit the topology and start
running it in local cluster mode.

Now we have a working topology. We read check-in data from our spout, and in the end, we persist the coordinates grouped by time intervals into Redis and complete the heat map topology implementation. All we have left to do is read the data from Redis using a JavaScript application and use the heat map overlay feature of the Google Maps API to build the visualization.

This simple implementation will run, but will it scale? Will it be fast enough? Let's do some digging and find out.

3.5   *Scaling the topology*

Let's review where we are so far. We have a working topology for our service that looks similar to the one shown in figure 3.8.

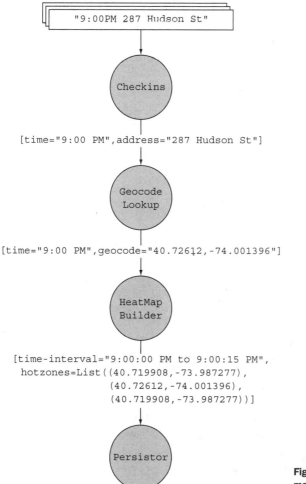

```
"9:00PM 287 Hudson St"


                    Checkins


[time="9:00 PM",address="287 Hudson St"]


                    Geocode
                    Lookup


[time="9:00 PM",geocode="40.72612,-74.001396"]


                    HeatMap
                    Builder


[time-interval="9:00:00 PM to 9:00:15 PM",
 hotzones=List((40.719908,-73.987277),
               (40.72612,-74.001396),
               (40.719908,-73.987277))]


                    Persistor
```

Figure 3.8 Heat map topology

There are problems with it. As it stands right now, this topology operates in a serial fashion, processing one check-in at a time. That isn't web-scale—that's Apple IIe scale. If we were to put this live, everything would back up and we would end up with unhappy customers, an unhappy ops team, and probably unhappy investors.

What is web-scale?

A system is web-scale when it can grow simply without downtime to cater to the demand brought about by the network effect that is the web. When each happy user tells 10 of their friends about your heat map, service and demand increase exponentially. This increase in demand is known as web-scale.

We need to process multiple check-ins at a time, so we'll introduce parallelism into our topology. One property that makes Storm so alluring is how easy it is to parallelize workflows such as our heat map. Let's take a look at the parts of the topology again and discuss how they can be parallelized. We'll begin with check-ins.

3.5.1   *Understanding parallelism in Storm*

Storm has additional primitives that serve as knobs for tuning how it can scale. If you don't touch them, the topology can still work, but all components will run in a more or less linear fashion. This may be fine for topologies that only have a small stream of data flowing through them. For something like the heat map topology that'll receive data from a large fire hose, we would want to address the bottlenecks in it. In this section, we'll look at two of the primitives that deal with scaling. There are additional primitives for scaling that we'll consider later in the next chapter.

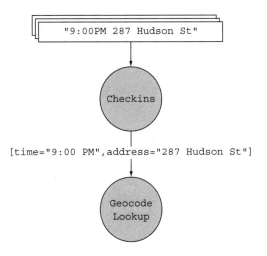

Figure 3.9   **Focusing our parallelization changes on the** Checkins **spout**

PARALLELISM HINTS

We know we're going to need to process many check-ins rapidly, so we want to parallelize the spout that handles check-ins. Figure 3.9 gives you an idea of what part of the topology we're working on here.

Storm allows you to provide a parallelism hint when you define any spouts or bolts. In code, this would involve transforming

```
builder.setSpout("checkins", new Checkins());
```

to

```
builder.setSpout("checkins", new Checkins(), 4);
```

The additional parameter we provide to setSpout is the parallelism hint. That's a bit of a mouthful: *parallelism hint*. So what is a parallelism hint? For right now, let's say that the parallelism hint tells Storm how many check-in spouts to create. In our example, this results in four spout instances being created. There's more to it than that, but we'll get to that in a bit.

Now when we run our topology, we should be able to process check-ins four times as fast—except simply introducing more spouts and bolts into our topology isn't enough. Parallelism in a topology is about both input and output. The Checkins spout can now

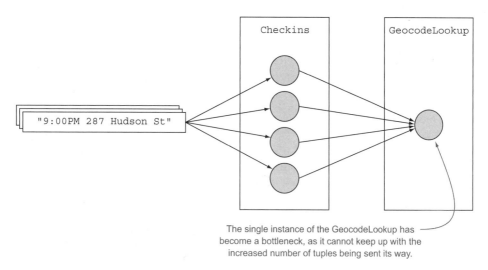

The single instance of the GeocodeLookup has
become a bottleneck, as it cannot keep up with the
increased number of tuples being sent its way.

Figure 3.10 Four Checkins instances emitting tuples to one GeocodeLookup instance results in the GeocodeLookup instance being a bottleneck.

process more check-ins at a time, but the GeocodeLookup bolt is still being handled serially. Simultaneously passing four check-ins to a single GeocodeLookup instance isn't going to work out well. Figure 3.10 illustrates the problem we've created.

Right now, what we have is akin to a circus clown car routine where many clowns all try to simultaneously pile into a car through the same door. This bottleneck needs to be resolved; let's try parallelizing the geocode lookup bolt as well. We could just parallelize the geocode bolt in the same way we did check-ins. Going from this

```
builder.setBolt("geocode-lookup", new GeocodeLookup());
```

to this

```
builder.setBolt("geocode-lookup", new GeocodeLookup(), 4);
```

will certainly help. Now we have one GeocodeLookup instance for each Checkins instance. But GeocodeLookup is going to take a lot longer than receiving a check-in and handing it off to our bolt. So perhaps we can do something more like this:

```
builder.setBolt("geocode-lookup", new GeocodeLookup(), 8);
```

Now if GeocodeLookup takes two times as long as check-in handling, tuples should continue to flow through our system smoothly, resulting in figure 3.11.

We're making progress here, but there's something else to think about: what happens as our service becomes more popular? We're going to need to be able to continue to scale to keep pace with our ever expanding traffic without taking our application offline, or at least not taking it offline very often. Luckily Storm provides a way to do

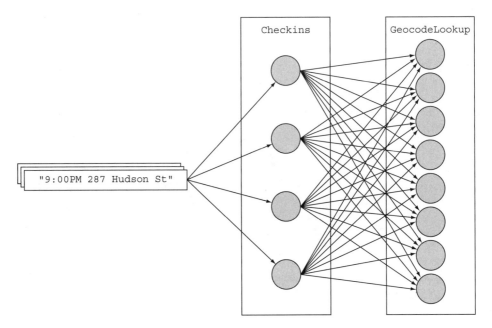

Figure 3.11 **Four** Checkins **instances emitting tuples to eight** GeocodeLookup **instances**

that. We loosely defined the parallelism hint earlier but said there was a little more to it. Well, here we are. That parallelism hint maps into two Storm concepts we haven't covered yet: executors and tasks.

EXECUTORS AND TASKS

So what are executors and tasks? Truly understanding the answer to this question requires deeper knowledge of a Storm cluster and its various parts. Although we won't learn any details about a Storm cluster until chapter 5, we can provide you with a sneak peek into certain parts of a Storm cluster that'll help you understand what executors and tasks are for the purpose of scaling our topology.

So far, we know that our spouts and bolts are each running as one or more instances. Each of these instances is running somewhere, right? There has to be some machine (physical or virtual) that's actually executing our components. We'll call this machine a worker node, and though a worker node isn't the only type of node running on a Storm cluster, it is the node that executes the logic in our spouts and bolts. And because Storm runs on the JVM, each of these worker nodes is executing our spouts and bolts on a JVM. Figure 3.12 shows what we have so far.

There's a little more to a worker node, but what's important for now is that you understand that it runs the JVM that executes our spout and bolt instances. So we pose the question again: what are executors and tasks? Executors are a thread of execution

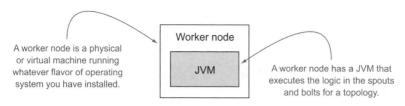

Figure 3.12 A worker node is a physical or virtual machine that's running a JVM, which executes the logic in the spouts and bolts.

on the JVM, and tasks are the instances of our spouts and bolts running within a thread of execution. Figure 3.13 illustrates this relationship.

It's really that simple. An executor is a thread of execution within a JVM. A task is an instance of a spout or bolt running within that thread of execution. When discussing scalability in this chapter, we're referring to changing the number of executors and tasks. Storm provides additional ways to scale by changing the number of worker nodes and JVMs, but we're saving those for chapters 6 and 7.

Let's go back to our code and revisit what this means in terms of parallelism hints. Setting the parallelism hint to 8, as we did with GeocodeLookup, is telling Storm to create eight executors (threads) and run eight tasks (instances) of GeocodeLookup. This is seen with the following code:

```
builder.setBolt("geocode-lookup", new GeocodeLookup(), 8)
```

By default, the parallelism hint is setting both the number of executors and tasks to the same value. We can override the number of tasks with the setNumTasks() method as follows:

```
builder.setBolt("geocode-lookup", new GeocodeLookup(), 8).setNumTasks(8)
```

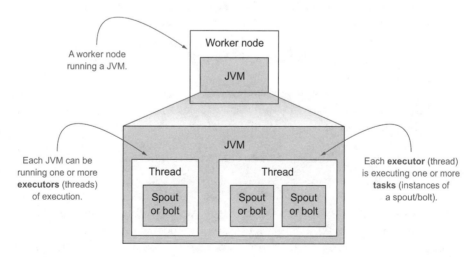

Figure 3.13 Executors (threads) and tasks (instances of spouts/bolts) run on a JVM.

Why provide the ability to set the number of tasks to something different than the number of executors? Before we answer this question, let's take a step back and revisit how we got here. We were talking about how we'll want to scale our heat map in the future without taking it offline. What's the easiest way to do this? The answer: increase the parallelism. Fortunately, Storm provides a useful feature that allows us to increase the parallelism of a running topology by dynamically increasing the number of executors (threads). You'll learn more on how this is done in chapter 6.

What does this mean for our `GeocodeLookup` bolt with eight instances being run across eight threads? Well, each of those instances will spend most of its time waiting on network I/O. We suspect that this means `GeocodeLookup` is going to be a source of contention in the future and will need to be scaled up. We can allow for this possibility with

```
builder.setBolt("geocode-lookup", new GeocodeLookup(), 8).setNumTasks(64)
```

Now we have 64 tasks (instances) of `GeocodeLookup` running across eight executors (threads). As we need to increase the parallelism of `GeocodeLookup`, we can keep increasing the number of executors up to a maximum of 64 without stopping our topology. We repeat: *without stopping the topology.* As we mentioned earlier, we'll get into the details of how to do this in a later chapter, but the key point to understand here is that the number of executors (threads) can be dynamically changed in a running topology.

Storm breaks parallelism down into two distinct concepts of executors and tasks to deal with situations like we have with our `GeocodeLookup` bolt. To illustrate why, let's go back to the definition of a fields grouping:

> A fields grouping is a type of stream grouping where tuples with the same value for a particular field name are always emitted to the same instance of a bolt.

Within that definition lurks our answer. Fields groupings work by consistently hashing tuples across a set number of bolts. To keep keys with the same value going to the same bolt, the number of bolts can't change. If it did, tuples would start going to different bolts. That would defeat the purpose of what we were trying to accomplish with a fields grouping.

It was easy to configure the executors and tasks on the `Checkins` spout and `GeocodeLookup` bolt in order to scale them at a later point in time. Sometimes, though, parts of our design won't work well for scaling. Let's look at that next.

3.5.2 *Adjusting the topology to address bottlenecks inherent within design*

`HeatMapBuilder` is up next. Earlier we hit a bottleneck on `GeocodeLookup` when we increased the parallelism hint on the `Checkins` spout. But we were able to address this easily by increasing the parallelism on the `GeocodeLookup` bolt accordingly. We can't do that here. It doesn't make sense to increase the parallelism on `HeatMapBuilder` as it's connected to the previous bolt using global grouping. Because global grouping dictates that every tuple goes to one specific instance of `HeatMapBuilder`, increasing parallelism on it doesn't have any effect; only one instance will be actively working on the stream. There's a bottleneck that's inherent in the design of our topology.

This is the downside of using global grouping. With global grouping, we're trading our ability to scale and introducing an intentional bottleneck with being able to see the entire stream of tuples in one specific bolt instance.

So what can we do? Is there no way we can parallelize this step in our topology? If we can't parallelize this bolt, it makes little sense to parallelize the bolts that follow. This is the choke point. It can't be parallelized with the current design. When we come across a problem like this, the best approach is to take a step back and see what we can change about the topology design to achieve our goal.

The reason why we can't parallelize `HeatMapBuilder` is because all tuples need to go in to the same instance. All tuples have to go to the same instance because we need to ensure that every tuple that falls into any given time interval can be grouped together. So if we can ensure that every tuple that falls into given time interval goes into the same instance, we can have multiple instances of `HeatMapBuilder`.

Right now, we use the `HeatMapBuilder` bolt to do two things:

- Determine which time interval a given tuple falls into
- Group tuples by time interval

If we can move these two actions into separate bolts, we can get closer to our goal. Let's look at the part of the `HeatMapBuilder` bolt that determines which time interval a tuple falls into in the next listing.

> **Listing 3.10   Determining time interval for a tuple in `HeatMapBuilder.java`**

```
public void execute(Tuple tuple,
                      BasicOutputCollector outputCollector) {
  if (isTickTuple(tuple)) {
    emitHeatmap(outputCollector);
  } else {
    Long time = tuple.getLongByField("time");
    LatLng geocode = (LatLng) tuple.getValueByField("geocode");

    Long timeInterval = selectTimeInterval(time);
    List<LatLng> checkins = getCheckinsForInterval(timeInterval);
    checkins.add(geocode);
  }
}

private Long selectTimeInterval(Long time) {
  return time / (15 * 1000);
}
```

`HeatMapBuilder` receives a check-in time and a geocoordinate from `GeocodeLookup`. Let's move this simple task of extracting the time interval out of tuple emitted by `GeocodeLookup` into another bolt. This bolt—let's call it `TimeIntervalExtractor`— can emit a time interval and a coordinate that can be picked up by `HeatMapBuilder` instead, as shown in the following listing.

Listing 3.11 `TimeIntervalExtractor.java`

```java
public class TimeIntervalExtractor extends BaseBasicBolt {
  @Override
  public void declareOutputFields(OutputFieldsDeclarer declarer) {
    declarer.declare(new Fields("time-interval", "geocode"));
  }

  @Override
  public void execute(Tuple tuple,
                      BasicOutputCollector outputCollector) {
    Long time = tuple.getLongByField("time");
    LatLng geocode = (LatLng) tuple.getValueByField("geocode");

    Long timeInterval = time / (15 * 1000);
    outputCollector.emit(new Values(timeInterval, geocode));
  }
}
```

Calculates the time interval and emits that time interval and geocoordinate (instead of time and geocoordinate) to be picked up by HeatMapBuilder

Introducing `TimeIntervalExtractor` requires a change in `HeatMapBuilder`. Instead of retrieving the time from the input tuple, we need to update that bolt's `execute()` method to accept a time interval, as you can see in the next listing.

Listing 3.12 Updating `execute()` in `HeatMapBuilder.java` to use the precalculated time interval

```java
@Override
public void execute(Tuple tuple,
                    BasicOutputCollector outputCollector) {
  if (isTickTuple(tuple)) {
    emitHeatmap(outputCollector);
  } else {
    Long timeInterval = tuple.getLongByField("time-interval");
    LatLng geocode = (LatLng) tuple.getValueByField("geocode");

    List<LatLng> checkins = getCheckinsForInterval(timeInterval);
    checkins.add(geocode);
  }.
}
```

The components in our topology now include the following:

- `Checkins` spout, which emits the time and address
- `GeocodeLookup` bolt, which emits the time and geocoordinate
- `TimeIntervalExtractor` bolt, which emits the time interval and geocoordinate
- `HeatMapBuilder` bolt, which emits the time interval as well as a list of grouped geocoordinates
- `Persistor` bolt, which emits nothing because it's the last bolt in our topology

Figure 3.14 shows an updated topology design that reflects these changes.

Now when we wire `HeatMapBuilder` to `TimeIntervalExtractor` we don't need to use global grouping.

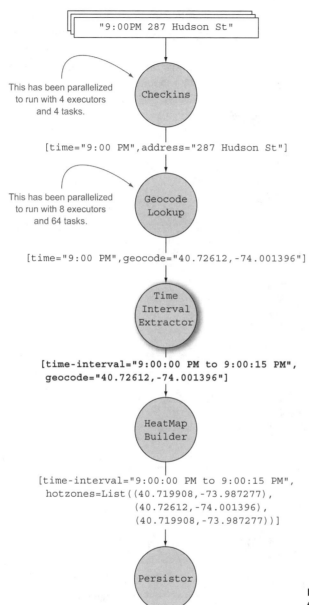

"9:00PM 287 Hudson St"

Checkins

This has been parallelized
to run with 4 executors
and 4 tasks.

[time="9:00 PM",address="287 Hudson St"]

Geocode
Lookup

This has been parallelized
to run with 8 executors
and 64 tasks.

[time="9:00 PM",geocode="40.72612,-74.001396"]

Time
Interval
Extractor

**[time-interval="9:00:00 PM to 9:00:15 PM",
geocode="40.72612,-74.001396"]**

HeatMap
Builder

[time-interval="9:00:00 PM to 9:00:15 PM",
hotzones=List((40.719908,-73.987277),
(40.72612,-74.001396),
(40.719908,-73.987277))]

Persistor

**Figure 3.14 Updated topology with
the `TimeIntervalExtractor` bolt**

We have the time interval precalculated, so now we need to ensure the same `HeatMap-`
`Builder` bolt instance receives all values for the given time interval. It doesn't matter
whether different time intervals go to different instances. We can use *fields grouping* for
this. Fields grouping lets us group values by a specified field and send all tuples that
arrive with that given value to a specific bolt instance. What we've done is segment the
tuples into time intervals and send each segment into different `HeatMapBuilder`

instances, thereby allowing us to achieve parallelism by running the segments in parallel. Figure 3.15 shows the updated stream groupings between our spout and bolts.

Let's take a look at the code we would need to add to `HeatmapTopologyBuilder` in order to incorporate our new `TimeIntervalExtractor` bolt along with changing to the appropriate stream groupings, as listing 3.13 shows.

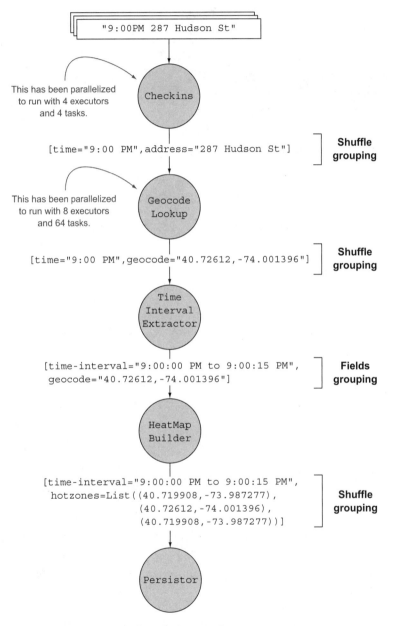

Figure 3.15   Updated topology stream groupings

Listing 3.13   New bolt added to `HeatmapTopologyBuilder.java`

The new bolt is inserted between Geocode-Lookup and HeatMap-Builder. It will bind to Geocode-Lookup with shuffle grouping because random assignment of tuples is okay.

```
public class HeatmapTopologyBuilder {
  public StormTopology build() {
    TopologyBuilder builder = new TopologyBuilder();

    builder.setSpout("checkins", new Checkins(), 4);
    builder.setBolt("geocode-lookup", new GeocodeLookup(), 8)
           .setNumTasks(64)
           .shuffleGrouping("checkins");
    builder.setBolt("time-interval-extractor", new TimeIntervalExtractor())
           .shuffleGrouping("geocode-lookup");
    builder.setBolt("heatmap-builder", new HeatMapBuilder())
           .fieldsGrouping("time-interval-extractor",
                           new Fields("time-interval"));
    builder.setBolt("persistor", new Persistor())
           .shuffleGrouping("heatmap-builder");

    return builder.createTopology();
  }
}
```

HeatMapBuilder can now receive tuples from the new bolt. We can change it to use fields grouping so that it can be parallelized.

As the listing shows, we've completely removed the global grouping and we're now using a series of shuffle groupings with a single fields grouping for the time intervals.

Global grouping

We scaled this bolt by replacing global grouping with fields grouping after some minor design changes. So does global grouping fit well with any real-world scenarios where we actually need scale? Don't discount global grouping; it does serve a useful purpose when deployed at the right junction.

In this case study, we used global grouping at the point of aggregation (grouping coordinates by time interval). When used at the point of aggregation, it doesn't indeed scale because we're forcing it to crunch a larger data set. But if we were to use global grouping postaggregation, it'd be dealing with a smaller stream of tuples and we wouldn't have as great a need for scale as we would preaggregation.

If you need to see the entire stream of tuples, global grouping is highly useful. What you'd need to do first is aggregate them in some manner (shuffle grouping for randomly aggregating sets of tuples or fields grouping for aggregating selected sets of tuples) and then use global grouping on the aggregation to get the complete picture:

```
builder.setBolt("aggregation-bolt", new AggregationBolt(), 10)
       .shuffleGrouping("previous-bolt");
builder.setBolt("world-view-bolt", new WorldViewBolt())
       .globalGrouping("aggregation-bolt");
```

`AggregationBolt` in this case can be scaled, and it'll trim down the stream into a smaller set. Then `WorldViewBolt` can look at the complete stream by using global grouping on already aggregated tuples coming from `AggregationBolt`. We don't have to scale `WorldViewBolt` because it's looking at a smaller data set.

Parallelizing `TimeIntervalExtractor` is simple. To start, we can give it the same level of parallelism as the `Checkins` spout—there's no waiting on an external service as with the `GeocodeLookup` bolt:

```
builder.setBolt("time-interval-extractor", new TimeIntervalExtractor(), 4)
    .shuffleGrouping("geocode-lookup");
```

Next up, we can clear our troublesome choke point in the topology:

```
builder.setBolt("heatmap-builder", new HeatMapBuilder(), 4)
        .fieldsGrouping("time-interval-extractor", new Fields("time-interval"));
```

Finally we address the `Persistor`. This is similar to `GeocodeLookup` in the sense that we expect we'll need to scale it later on. So we'll need more tasks than executors for the reasons we covered under our `GeocodeLookup` discussion earlier:

```
builder.setBolt("persistor", new Persistor(), 1)
    .setNumTasks(4)
    .shuffleGrouping("heatmap-builder");
```

Figure 3.16 illustrates the parallelism changes that were just applied.

It looks like we're done with scaling this topology…or are we? We've configured every component (that is, every spout and bolt) for parallelism within the topology. Each bolt or spout may be configured for parallelism, but that doesn't necessarily mean it will run at scale. Let's see why.

3.5.3   *Adjusting the topology to address bottlenecks inherent within a data stream*

We've parallelized every component within the topology, and this is in line with the technical definition of how every grouping (shuffle grouping, fields grouping, and global grouping) we use affects the flow of tuples within our topology. Unfortunately, it's still not effectively parallel.

Although we were able to parallelize `HeatMapBuilder` with the changes from the previous section, what we forgot to consider is how the nature of our data stream affects parallelism. We're grouping the tuples that flow through the stream into segments of 15 seconds, and that's the source of our problem. For a given 15-second window, all tuples that fall into that window will go through one instance of the `Heat-MapBuilder` bolt. It's true that with the design changes we made `HeatMapBuilder` became technically parallelizable, but it's effectively not parallel yet. The shape of the data stream that flows through your topology can hide problems with scaling that may be hard to spot. It's wise to always question the impact of how data flows through your topology.

How can we parallelize this? We were right to group by time interval because that's the basis for our heat map generation. What we need is an additional level of grouping under the time interval; we can refine our higher-level solution so that we're

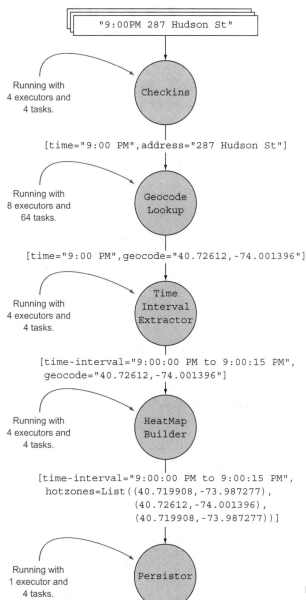

Figure 3.16 Parallelizing all the components in our topology

delivering heat maps by time interval by city. When we add an additional level of grouping by city, we'll have multiple data flows for a given time interval and they may flow through different instances of the HeatmapBuilder. In order to add this additional level of grouping, we first need to add city as a field in the output tuple of GeocodeLookup, as shown in the next listing.

Listing 3.14   Adding city as a field in the output tuple of `GeocodeLookup.java`

```java
public class GeocodeLookup extends BaseBasicBolt {
  private Geocoder geocoder;

  @Override
  public void declareOutputFields(OutputFieldsDeclarer fieldsDeclarer) {
    fieldsDeclarer.declare(new Fields("time", "geocode", "city"));    ◄─────┐
  }                                                                          │
                                                               Add city as an
  @Override                                                    additional field
  public void prepare(Map config,                              that will be
                      TopologyContext context) {               emitted from
    geocoder = new Geocoder();                                 this bolt
  }

  @Override
  public void execute(Tuple tuple,
                      BasicOutputCollector outputCollector) {
    String address = tuple.getStringByField("address");
    Long time = tuple.getLongByField("time");

    GeocoderRequest request = new GeocoderRequestBuilder()
      .setAddress(address)
      .setLanguage("en")
      .getGeocoderRequest();
    GeocodeResponse response = geocoder.geocode(request);           Extract city
    GeocoderStatus status = response.getStatus();                   name from
    if (GeocoderStatus.OK.equals(status)) {                         the already
      GeocoderResult firstResult = response.getResults().get(0);    available
      LatLng latLng = firstResult.getGeometry().getLocation();      geocoded
      String city = extractCity(firstResult);          ◄──────┘     result
      outputCollector.emit(new Values(time, latLng, city));
    }
  }

  private String extractCity(GeocoderResult result) {
    for (GeocoderAddressComponent component : result.getAddressComponents())
    {
      if (component.getTypes().contains("locality"))
        return component.getLongName();
    }
    return "";
  }
}
```

GeocodeLookup now includes city as a field in its output tuple. We'll need to update `TimeIntervalExtractor` to read and emit this value, as shown in the following listing.

Listing 3.15   Pass city field along in `TimeIntervalExtractor.java`

```java
public class TimeIntervalExtractor extends BaseBasicBolt {
  @Override
  public void declareOutputFields(OutputFieldsDeclarer declarer) {
    declarer.declare(new Fields("time-interval", "geocode", "city"));
  }
```

```
@Override
public void execute(Tuple tuple,
                    BasicOutputCollector outputCollector) {
  Long time = tuple.getLongByField("time");
  LatLng geocode = (LatLng) tuple.getValueByField("geocode");
  String city = tuple.getStringByField("city");

  Long timeInterval = time / (15 * 1000);
  outputCollector.emit(new Values(timeInterval, geocode, city));
  }
}
```

Finally, we need to update our `HeatmapTopologyBuilder` so the fields grouping between `TimeIntervalExtractor` and `HeatMapBuilder` is based on both the time-interval and city fields, as shown in the next listing.

Listing 3.16 Added second-level grouping to `HeatmapTopologyBuilder.java`

```
public class HeatmapTopologyBuilder {
  public StormTopology build() {
    TopologyBuilder builder = new TopologyBuilder();

    builder.setSpout("checkins", new Checkins(), 4);
    builder.setBolt("geocode-lookup", new GeocodeLookup(), 8)
           .setNumTasks(64)
           .shuffleGrouping("checkins");
    builder.setBolt("time-interval-extractor", new TimeIntervalExtractor(), 4)
           .shuffleGrouping("geocode-lookup");
    builder.setBolt("heatmap-builder", new HeatMapBuilder(), 4)
           .fieldsGrouping("time-interval-extractor",
                       new Fields("time-interval", "city"));   ◁─┐ Secondary
    builder.setBolt("persistor", new Persistor(), 1)              │ grouping
           .setNumTasks(4)                                        │ allows effective
           .shuffleGrouping("heatmap-builder");                   │ parallelization
                                                                  │ of HeatMap-
    return builder.createTopology();                              │ Builder
  }
}
```

Now we have a topology that isn't only technically parallelized but is also effectively running in parallel fashion. We've made a few changes here, so let's take an updated look at our topology and the transformation of the tuples in figure 3.17.

We've covered the basics of parallelizing a Storm topology. The approach we followed here is based on making educated guesses driven by our understanding of how each topology component works. There's more work that can be done on parallelizing this topology, including additional parallelism primitives and approaches to achieving optimal tuning based on observed metrics. We'll visit them at appropriate points throughout the book. In this chapter, we built up the understanding of parallelism needed to properly design a Storm topology. The ability to scale a topology depends heavily on the makeup of a topology's underlying component breakdown and design.

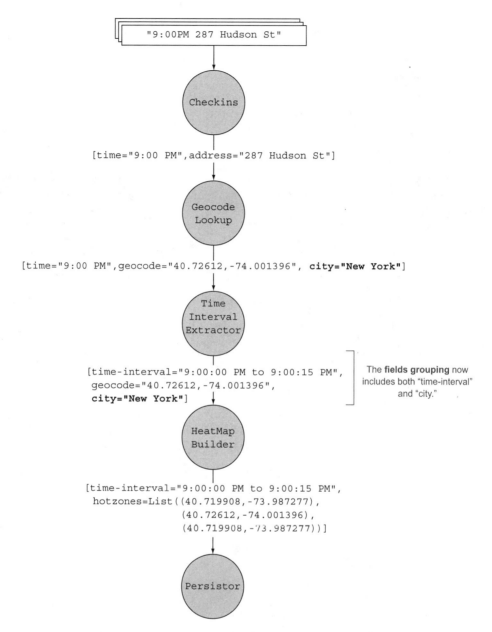

Figure 3.17   Adding city to the tuple being emitted by `GeocodeLookup` **and having**
`TimeIntervalExtractor` **pass the city along in its emitted tuple**

3.6   *Topology design paradigms*

Let's recap how we designed the heat map topology:

1   We examined our data stream, and determined that our input tuples are based on what we start with. Then we determined the resulting tuples we need to end up with in order to achieve our goal (the end tuples).

2   We created a series of operations (as bolts) that transform the input tuples into end tuples.

3   We carefully examined each operation to understand its behavior and scaled it by making educated guesses based on our understanding of its behavior (by adjusting its executors/tasks).

4   At points of contention where we could no longer scale, we rethought our design and refactored the topology into scalable components.

This is a good approach to topology design. It's quite common for most people to fall into the trap of not having scalability in mind when creating their topologies. If we don't do this early on and leave scalability concerns for later on, the amount of work you have to do to refactor or redesign your topology will increase by an order of magnitude.

> Premature optimization is the root of all evil.
>
> —Donald Knuth

As engineers we're fond of using this quote from Donald Knuth whenever we talk about performance considerations early on. This is indeed true in most cases, but let's look at the complete quote to give us more context to what Dr. Knuth was trying to say (rather than the sound bite we engineers normally use to make our point):

> You should forget about small efficiencies, say about 97% of the time;
> premature optimization is the root of all evil.

You're not trying to achieve small efficiencies—you're working with big data. Every efficiency enhancement you make counts. One minor performance block can be the difference in not achieving the performance SLA you need when working with large data sets. If you're building a racecar, you need to keep performance in mind starting on day one. You can't refactor your engine to improve it later if it wasn't built for performance from the ground up. So steps 3 and 4 are critical pieces in designing a topology.

The only caveat here is a lack of knowledge about the problem domain. If your knowledge about the problem domain is limited, that might work against you if you try to scale it too early. When we say *knowledge about the problem domain*, what we're referring to is both the nature of the data that's flowing through your system as well as the inherent choke points within your operations. It's always okay to defer scaling concerns until you have a good understanding of it. Similar to building an expert system, when you have a true understanding of the problem domain, you might have to scrap your initial solution and start over.

3.6.1 *Design by breakdown into functional components*

Let's observe how we broke down the series of operations within our topology (figure 3.18).

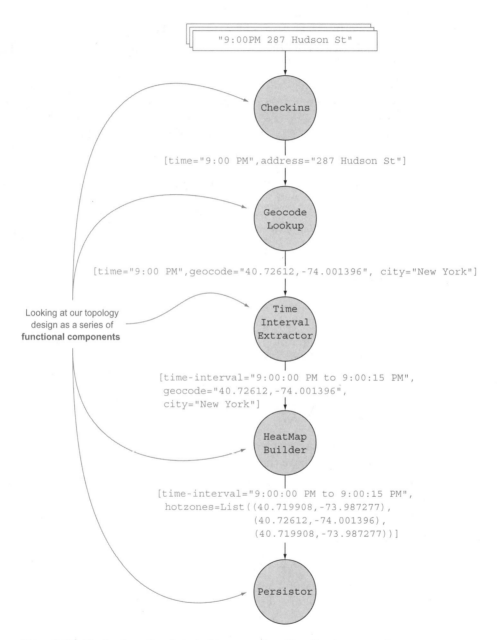

Figure 3.18 **The heat map topology design as a series of functional components**

We decomposed the topology makeup into separate bolts by giving each bolt a specific responsibility. This is in line with the *principle of single responsibility*. We encapsulated a specific responsibility within each bolt and everything within each bolt is narrowly aligned with its responsibility and nothing else. In other words, each bolt represents a functional whole.

There's a lot of value in this approach to design. Giving each bolt a single responsibility makes it easy to work with a given bolt in isolation. It also makes it easy to scale a single bolt without interference from the rest of the topology because parallelism is tuned at the bolt level. Whether it's scaling or troubleshooting a problem, when you can zoom in and focus your attention on a single component, the productivity gains to be had from that will allow you to reap the benefits of the effort spent on designing your components in this manner.

3.6.2 *Design by breakdown into components at points of repartition*

There's a slightly different approach to breaking down a problem into its constituent parts. It provides a marked improvement in terms of performance over the approach of breaking down into functional components discussed earlier. With this pattern, instead of decomposing the problem into its simplest possible functional components, we think in terms of separation points (or join points) between the different components. In other words, we think of the points of connection between the different bolts. In Storm, the different stream groupings are markers between different bolts (as the groupings define how the outgoing tuples from one bolt are distributed to the next).

At these points, the stream of tuples flowing through the topology gets repartitioned. During a stream repartition, the way tuples are distributed changes. That is in fact the functionality of a stream grouping. Figure 3.19 illustrates our design by points of repartition.

With this pattern of topology design, we strive to minimize the number of repartitions within a topology. Every time there's a repartitioning, tuples will be sent from one bolt to another across the network. This is an expensive operation due to a number of reasons:

- The topology operates within a distributed cluster. When tuples are emitted, they may travel across the cluster and this may incur network overhead.
- With every emit, a tuple will need to be serialized and deserialized at the receiving point.
- The higher the number of partitions, the higher the number of resources needed. Each bolt will require a number of executors and tasks and a queue in front for all the incoming tuples.

NOTE We'll discuss the makeup of a Storm cluster and the internals that support a bolt in later chapters.

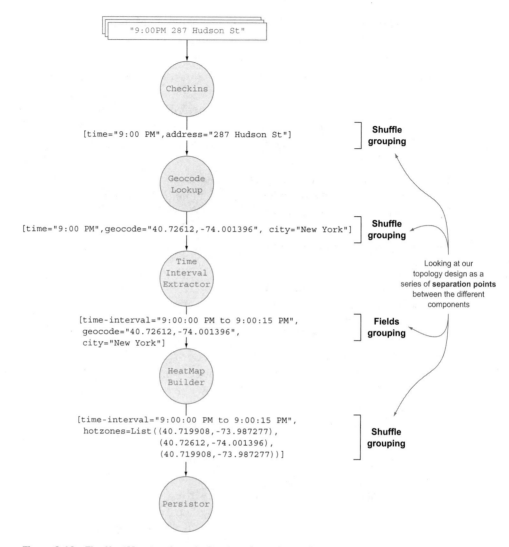

Figure 3.19   The HeatMap topology design as points of repartition

For our topology, what can we do to minimize the number of partitions? We'll have to collapse a few bolts together. To do so, we must figure out what's different about each functional component that makes it need its own bolt (and the resources that come with a bolt):

- `Checkins` (spout)—4 executors (reads a file)
- `GeocodeLookup`—8 executors, 64 tasks (hits an external service)
- `TimeIntervalExtractor`—4 executors (internal computation; transforms data)
- `HeatMapBuilder`—4 executors (internal computation; aggregates tuples)
- `Persistor`—1 executor, 4 tasks (writes to a data store)

And now for the analysis:

- `GeocodeLookup` and `Persistor` interact with an external entity and the time spent waiting on interactions with that external entity will dictate the way executors and tasks are allocated to these two bolts. It's unlikely that we'll be able to coerce the behavior of these bolts to fit within another. Maybe something else might be able to fit within the resources necessary for one of these two.

- `HeatMapBuilder` does the aggregation of geocoordinates by time interval and city. It's somewhat unique compared to others because it buffers data in memory and you can't proceed to the next step until the time interval has elapsed. It's peculiar enough that collapsing it with another will require careful consideration.

- `Checkins` is a spout and normally you wouldn't modify a spout to contain operations that involve computation. Also, because the spout is responsible for keeping track of the data that has been emitted, rarely would we perform any computation within one. But certain things related to adapting the initial tuples (such as parsing, extracting, and converting) do fit within the responsibilities of a spout.

- That leaves `TimeIntervalExtractor`. This is simple—all it does is transform a "time" entry into a "time interval." We extracted it out of `HeatMapBuilder` because we needed to know the time interval prior to `HeatMapBuilder` so that we could group by the time interval. This allowed us to scale the `HeatMapBuilder` bolt. Work done by `TimeIntervalExtractor` can technically happen at any point before the `HeatMapBuilder`:
  - If we merge `TimeIntervalExtractor` with `GeocodeLookup`, it'll need to fit within resources allocated to `GeocodeLookup`. Although they have different resource configurations, the simplicity of `TimeIntervalExtractor` will allow it to fit within resources allocated to `GeocodeLookup`. On a purely idealistic sense, they also fit—both operations are data transformations (going from time to time interval and address to geocoordinate). One of them is incredibly simple and the other requires the network overhead of using an external service.
  - Can we merge `TimeIntervalExtractor` with the `Checkins` spout? They have the exact same resource configurations. Also, transforming a "time" to a "time interval" is one of the few types of operations from a bolt that can make sense within a spout. The answer is a resounding yes. This begs the question of whether `GeocodeLookup` can also be merged with the `Checkins` spout. Although `GeocodeLookup` is also a data transformer, it's a much more heavyweight computation because it depends on an external service, meaning it doesn't fit within the type of actions that should happen in a spout.

Should we merge `TimeIntervalExtractor` with `GeocodeLookup` or the `Checkins` spout? From an efficiency perspective, either will do, and that's the right answer. We would merge it with the spout because we have a preference for keeping external service interactions untangled with much simpler tasks like `TimeIntervalExtractor`. We'll let you make the needed changes in your topology to make this happen.

You might wonder why in this example we chose not to merge `HeatMapBuilder` with `Persistor`. `HeatMapBuilder` emits the aggregated geocoordinates periodically (whenever it receives a tick tuple) and at the point of emitting, it can be modified to write the value to the data store instead (the responsibility of `Persistor`). Although this makes sense conceptually, it changes the observable behavior of the combined bolt. The combined `HeatMapBuilder/Persistor` behaves very differently on the two types of tuples it receives. The regular tuple from the stream will perform with low latency whereas the tick tuple for writing to the data store will have comparably higher latency. If we were to monitor and gather data about the performance of this combined bolt, it'd be difficult to isolate the observed metrics and make intelligent decisions on how to tune it further. This unbalanced nature of latency makes it very inelegant.

Designing a topology by considering the points of repartitioning of the stream and trying to minimize them will give you the most efficient use of resources with a topology makeup that has a higher likelihood of performing with low latency.

3.6.3   *Simplest functional components vs. lowest number of repartitions*

We've discussed two approaches to topology design. Which one is better? Having the lowest number of repartitions will provide the best performance as long as careful consideration is given to what kind of operations can be grouped into one bolt.

Usually it isn't one or the other. As a Storm beginner, you should always start by designing the simplest functional components; doing so allows you to reason about different operations easily. Also, if you start with more complex components tasked with multiple responsibilities, it's much harder to break down into simpler components if your design is wrong.

You can always start with the simplest functional components and then advance toward combining different operations together to reduce the number of partitions. It's much harder to go the other way around. As you gain more experience with working with Storm and develop intuition for topology design, you'll be able start with the lowest number of repartitions from the beginning.

3.7   *Summary*

In this chapter, you learned

- How to take a problem and break it down into constructs that fit within a Storm topology
- How to take a topology that runs in a serial fashion and introduce parallelism

- How to spot problems in your design and refine and refactor
- The importance of paying attention to the effects of the data stream on the limitations it imposes on the topology
- Two different approaches to topology design and the delicate balance between the two

These design guidelines serve as best practices for building Storm topologies. Later on in the book, you'll see why these design decisions aid greatly in tuning Storm for optimal performance.

Creating robust topologies

This chapter covers

- Guaranteed message processing
- Fault tolerance
- Replay semantics

So far, we've defined many of Storm's core concepts. Along the way, we've implemented two separate topologies, each of which runs in a local cluster. This chapter is no different in that we'll be designing and implementing another topology for a new scenario. But the problem we're solving has stricter requirements for guaranteeing tuples are processed and fault tolerance is maintained. To help us meet these requirements, we'll introduce some new concepts related to reliability and failure. You'll learn about the tools Storm gives us to handle failure, and we'll also dive into the various types of guarantees we can make about processing data. Armed with this knowledge, we'll be ready to venture out into the world and create production-quality topologies.

4.1 Requirements for reliability

In the previous chapter, our heat map application needed to quickly process a large amount of time-sensitive data. Further, merely sampling a portion of that data could provide us with what we needed: an approximation of the popularity of establishments within a given geographic area *right now*. If we failed to process a given tuple within a short time window, it lost its value. The heat map was all about right now. We didn't need to guarantee that each message was processed—*most* was good enough.

But there are domains where this is strictly unacceptable; each tuple is sacred. In these scenarios, we need to guarantee that each and every one is processed. Reliability is more important than timeliness here. If we have to keep retrying a tuple for 30 seconds or 10 minutes or an hour (or up to some threshold that makes sense), it has just as much value in our system as it did when we first tried. There's a need for reliability.

Storm provides the ability to guarantee that each tuple is processed. This serves as a reliability measure we can count on to ensure accurate implementation of functionality. On a high level, Storm provides reliability by keeping track of which tuples are successfully processed and which ones aren't and then replaying the ones that have failed until they succeed.

4.1.1 *Pieces of the puzzle for supporting reliability*

Storm has many moving parts that need to come together in order to deliver reliability:

- A reliable data source with a correspondingly reliable spout
- An anchored tuple stream
- A topology that acknowledges each tuple as it's processed or notifies you of the failure
- A fault-tolerant Storm cluster infrastructure

In this chapter, we'll look at how the first three of these components fall into place to enable reliability. Then chapter 5 introduces you to the Storm cluster and talks about how it provides fault tolerance.

4.2 *Problem definition: a credit card authorization system*

When you think about using Storm to solve a problem within your domain, take time to think about what guarantees you need to have around processing; it's an important part of "thinking in Storm." Let's dive into a problem that has a reliability requirement.

Imagine that we run a large e-commerce site that deals with shipping physical goods to people. We know that the vast majority of orders placed on our site are authorized for payment successfully and only a small percentage are declined. Traditionally in e-commerce, the more steps our user needs to take to place an order, the higher the risk of losing the sale. When we're billing at the time an order is placed, we're losing business. Handling billing as a separate, "offline" operation improves conversions and directly affects our bottom line. We also need this offline billing process to scale well to support peak seasons such as the holidays (think Amazon) or even flash sales (think Gilt).

This is a scenario that requires reliability. Each order has to be authorized before it's shipped. If we encounter a problem during our attempts to authorize, we should retry. In short, we need guaranteed message processing. Let's take a look at what such a system may look like, keeping in mind how we can incorporate retry characteristics.

4.2.1   *A conceptual solution with retry characteristics*

This system deals solely with authorizing credit cards related to orders that have already been placed. Our system doesn't deal with customers placing orders; that happens earlier in the pipeline.

ASSUMPTIONS ON UPSTREAM AND DOWNSTREAM SYSTEMS

Distributed systems are defined by the interactions amongst different systems. For our use case we can assume the following:

- The same order will never be sent to our system more than once. This is guaranteed by an upstream system that handles the placing of customer orders.
- The upstream system that places orders will put the order on a queue and our system will pull the order off the queue so it can be authorized.
- A separate downstream system will handle a processed order, either fulfilling the order if the credit card was authorized or notifying the customer of a denied credit card.

With these assumptions in hand, we can move forward with a design that's limited in scope but maps well to the Storm concepts we want to cover.

FORMATION OF A CONCEPTUAL SOLUTION

Let's begin with how orders flow through our system. The following steps are taken when the credit card for an order must be authorized:

1 Pull the order off the message queue.
2 Attempt to authorize the credit card by calling an external credit card authorization service.
3 If the service call succeeds, update the order status in the database.
4 If it fails, we can try again later.
5 Notify a separate downstream system that the order has been processed.

These steps are illustrated in figure 4.1.

We have our basic flow. The next step in defining our problem is to look at the data points being worked with in our topology; with this knowledge, we can determine what's being passed along in our tuples.

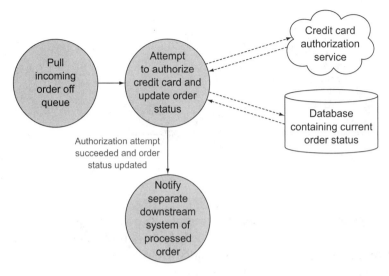

Figure 4.1   Conceptual solution of the e-commerce credit card authorization flow

4.2.2   *Defining the data points*

With the flow of transactions defined, we can take a look at the data involved. The flow of data starts with incoming orders being pulled off a queue as JSON (see the following listing).

Listing 4.1   Order JSON

```json
{
  "id":1234,
  "customerId":5678,
  "creditCardNumber":1111222233334444,
  "creditCardExpiration":"012014",
  "creditCardCode":123,
  "chargeAmount":42.23
}
```

This JSON will be converted into Java objects and our system will deal internally with these serialized Java objects. The next listing defines the class for this.

Listing 4.2   `Order.java`

```java
public class Order implements Serializable {
    private long id;
    private long customerId;
    private long creditCardNumber;
    private String creditCardExpiration;
    private int creditCardCode;
    private double chargeAmount;
```

```
public Order(long id,
             long customerId,
             long creditCardNumber,
             String creditCardExpiration,
             int creditCardCode,
             double chargeAmount) {
    this.id = id;
    this.customerId = customerId;
    this.creditCardNumber = creditCardNumber;
    this.creditCardExpiration = creditCardExpiration;
    this.creditCardCode = creditCardCode;
    this.chargeAmount = chargeAmount;
}
...
}
```

This approach of defining a problem in terms of data points and components that act on them should be familiar to you; it's exactly how we broke down the problems in chapters 2 and 3 when creating our topologies. We now need to map this solution to components Storm can use to build our topology.

4.2.3 *Mapping the solution to Storm with retry characteristics*

Now that we have a basic design and have identified the data that will flow through our system, we can map both our data and our components to Storm concepts. Our topology will have three main components, one spout, and two bolts:

- RabbitMQSpout—Our spout will consume messages from the queue, where each message is JSON representing an order, and emit a tuple containing a serialized Order object. We'll use RabbitMQ for our queue implementation—hence the name. We'll delve into the details of this spout when we discuss guaranteed message processing later in this chapter.
- AuthorizeCreditCard—If the credit card was authorized, this bolt will update the status of the order to "ready-to-ship." If the credit card was denied, this bolt will update the status of the order to "denied." Regardless of the status, this bolt will emit a tuple containing the Order to the next bolt in the stream.
- ProcessedOrderNotification—A bolt that notifies a separate system that an order has been processed.

In addition to the spout, bolts, and tuples, we must define stream groupings for how tuples are emitted between each of the components. The following stream groupings will be used:

- Shuffle grouping between the RabbitMQSpout and AuthorizeCreditCard bolt
- Shuffle grouping between AuthorizeCreditCard bolt and the ProcessedOrder-Notification bolt

In chapter 2 we used a fields grouping to ensure the same GitHub committer email was routed to the same bolt instance. In chapter 3 we used a fields grouping to ensure the same grouping of geocoordinates by time interval was routed to the same bolt

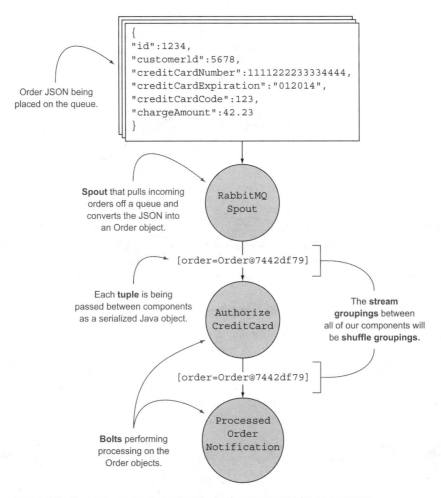

Figure 4.2   E-commerce credit card authorization mapped to Storm concepts

instance. We don't need the same assurances; any given bolt instance can process any given tuple, so a shuffle grouping will suffice.

All of the Storm concepts we just discussed are shown in figure 4.2.

With an idea of what our topology looks like, we'll next cover the code for our two bolts before getting into guaranteed message processing and what's required to achieve it. We'll discuss the code for the spout a bit later.

4.3   Basic implementation of the bolts

This section will cover the code for our two bolts: AuthorizeCreditCard and ProcessedOrderNotification. Understanding what's happening within each of the bolts will provide some context when we discuss guaranteed message processing in section 4.4.

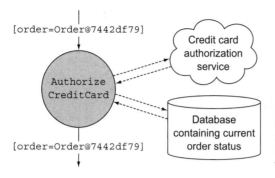

Figure 4.3 The `AuthorizeCreditCard` bolt accepts an incoming tuple from the `RabbitMQSpout` and emits a tuple regardless of whether or not the credit card was authorized.

We're leaving the implementation of the `RabbitMQSpout` for the end of the guaranteed message processing section because much of the code in the spout is geared toward retrying failed tuples. A complete understanding of guaranteed message processing will help you focus on the relevant parts of the spout code.

Let's begin with a look at the first bolt in our topology: `AuthorizeCreditCard`.

4.3.1   *The AuthorizeCreditCard implementation*

The `AuthorizeCreditCard` bolt accepts an `Order` object from the `RabbitMQSpout`. This bolt then attempts to authorize the credit card by talking to an external service. The status of the order will be updated in our database based on the results of the authorization attempt. After that, this bolt will emit a tuple containing the `Order` object it received. Figure 4.3 illustrates where we are in the topology.

The code for this bolt is presented in the next listing.

Listing 4.3   `AuthorizeCreditCard.java`

```
public class AuthorizeCreditCard extends BaseBasicBolt {
  private AuthorizationService authorizationService;
  private OrderDao orderDao;

  @Override
  public void declareOutputFields(OutputFieldsDeclarer declarer) {
    declarer.declare(new Fields("order"));
  }

  @Override
  public void prepare(Map config,
                      TopologyContext context) {
    orderDao = new OrderDao();
    authorizationService = new AuthorizationService();
  }

  @Override
  public void execute(Tuple tuple,
                      BasicOutputCollector outputCollector) {
    Order order = (Order) tuple.getValueByField("order");
    boolean isAuthorized = authorizationService.authorize(order);
```

Service for authorizing the credit card → `private AuthorizationService authorizationService;`

DAO for updating the status of the order in the database ← `private OrderDao orderDao;`

Indicates the bolt emits a tuple with a field named order ← `declarer.declare(new Fields("order"));`

Attempt to authorize the credit card by calling out to the authorization service. → `boolean isAuthorized = authorizationService.authorize(order);`

Obtain the order from the input tuple. ← `Order order = (Order) tuple.getValueByField("order");`

The status of the order is updated to "ready-to-ship" in the database.

```
    if (isAuthorized) {
        orderDao.updateStatusToReadyToShip(order);
    } else {
        orderDao.updateStatusToDenied(order);
    }
    outputCollector.emit(new Values(order));
    }
}
```

The status of the order is updated to "denied" in the database.

Emit a tuple containing the order down the stream.

Once the billing has been approved or denied, we're ready to notify the downstream system of the processed order; the code for this is seen next in `ProcessedOrder-Notification`.

4.3.2 The ProcessedOrderNotification implementation

The second and final bolt in our stream, `ProcessedOrderNotification`, accepts an `Order` from the `AuthorizeCreditCard` bolt and notifies an external system the order has been processed. This bolt doesn't emit any tuples. Figure 4.4 shows this final bolt in the topology.

The following listing shows the code for this bolt.

Listing 4.4 `ProcessedOrderNotification.java`

```java
public class ProcessedOrderNotification extends BaseBasicBolt {
    private NotificationService notificationService;

    @Override
    public void declareOutputFields(OutputFieldsDeclarer declarer) {
        // This bolt does not emit anything. No output fields will be declared.
    }

    @Override
    public void prepare(Map config,
                        TopologyContext context) {
        notificationService = new NotificationService();
    }

    @Override
    public void execute(Tuple tuple,
                        BasicOutputCollector outputCollector) {
        Order order = (Order) tuple.getValueByField("order");
        notificationService.notifyOrderHasBeenProcessed(order);
    }
}
```

Notification service that notifies some downstream system the order has been processed

Extract the order from the input tuple.

The notification service notifies the downstream system the order has been processed.

`[order=Order@7442df79]`

Processed Order Notification

Figure 4.4 The `ProcessedOrderNotification` bolt accepts an incoming tuple from the `AuthorizeCreditCard` bolt and notifies an external system without emitting a tuple.

After the downstream system has been notified of the processed order, there's nothing left for our topology to do, so this is where the implementation of our bolts comes to an end. We have a well-defined solution at this point (minus the spout, which we'll discuss next). The steps we took to come up with a design/implementation in this chapter match the same steps we took in chapters 2 and 3.

Where this implementation will differ from those chapters is the requirement to ensure all tuples are processed by all the bolts in the topology. Dealing with financial transactions is much different than GitHub commit counts or heat maps for social media check-ins. Remember the pieces of the puzzle needed for supporting reliability mentioned earlier in section 4.1.1?

- A reliable data source with a corresponding reliable spout
- An anchored tuple stream
- A topology that acknowledges each tuple as it's processed or notifies us of the failure
- A fault-tolerant Storm cluster infrastructure

We are at a point where we can start addressing the first three pieces. So how will our implementation change in order to provide these pieces? Surprisingly, it won't! The code for our bolts is already set up to support guaranteed message processing in Storm. Let's examine in detail how Storm is doing this as well as take a look at our reliable `RabbitMQSpout` next.

4.4   *Guaranteed message processing*

What's a message and how does Storm guarantee it gets processed? A message is synonymous with a tuple, and Storm has the ability to ensure a tuple being emitted from a spout gets fully processed by the topology. So if a tuple fails at some point in the stream, Storm knows a failure occurred and can replay the tuple, thus making sure it gets processed. The Storm documentation commonly uses the phrase *guaranteed message processing*, as will we throughout the book.

Understanding guaranteed message processing is essential if you want to develop reliable topologies. The first step in gaining this understanding is to know what it means for a tuple to be either fully processed or failed.

4.4.1   *Tuple states: fully processed vs. failed*

A tuple that's emitted from a spout can result in many additional tuples being emitted by the downstream bolts. This creates a *tuple tree*, with the tuple emitted by the spout acting as the root. Storm creates and tracks a tuple tree for every tuple emitted by the spout. Storm will consider a tuple emitted by a spout to be fully processed when all the leaves in the tree for that tuple have been marked as processed. Here are two things you need to do with the Storm API to make sure Storm can create and track the tuple tree:

- Make sure you anchor to input tuples when emitting new tuples from a bolt. It's a bolt's way of saying, "Okay, I'm emitting a new tuple and here's the initial input tuple as well so you can make a connection between the two."
- Make sure your bolts tell Storm when they've finished processing an input tuple. This is called *acking* and it's a bolt's way of saying, "Hey Storm, I'm done processing this tuple so feel free to mark it as processed in the tuple tree."

Storm will then have all it needs to create and track a tuple tree.

Directed acyclic graph and tuple trees

Though we call it a tuple tree, it's actually a directed acyclic graph (DAG). A directed graph is a set of nodes connected by edges, where the edges have a direction to them. A DAG is a directed graph such that you can't start at one node and follow a sequence of edges to eventually get back to that same node. Early versions of Storm only worked with trees; even though Storm now supports DAGs, the term "tuple tree" has stuck.

In an ideal world, you could stop here and tuples emitted by the spout would always be fully processed without any problems. Unfortunately, the world of software isn't always ideal; you should expect failures. Our tuples are no different and will be considered failed in one of two scenarios:

- All of the leaves in a tuple tree aren't marked as processed (acked) within a certain time frame. This time frame is configurable at the topology level via the `TOPOLOGY_MESSAGE_TIMEOUT_SECS` setting, which defaults to 30 seconds. Here's how you'd override this default when building your topology:

```
Config config = new Config();
config.setMessageTimeoutSecs(60);.
```

- A tuple is manually failed in a bolt, which triggers an immediate failure of the tuple tree.

We keep mentioning the phrase *tuple tree*, so let's walk through the life of a tuple tree in our topology to show you how this works.

Going down the rabbit hole with Alice...or a tuple

Figure 4.5 starts things off by showing the initial state of the tuple tree after our spout emits a tuple. We have a tree with a single root node.

The first bolt in the stream is the `Authorize-CreditCard` bolt. This bolt will perform the authorization and then emit a new tuple. Figure 4.6 shows the tuple tree after emitting.

We'll need to ack the input tuple in the `AuthorizeCreditCard` bolt so Storm can mark that tuple as processed. Figure 4.7 shows the tuple tree after this ack has been performed.

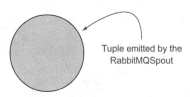

Figure 4.5 Initial state of the tuple tree

Once a tuple has been emitted by the `Authorize-CreditCard` bolt, it makes its way to the `Processed-OrderNotification` bolt. This bolt doesn't emit a tuple, so no tuples will be added to the tuple tree. But we do need to ack the input tuple and thus tell Storm this bolt has completed processing. Figure 4.8 shows the tuple tree after this ack has been performed. At this point the tuple is considered fully processed.

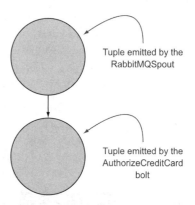

Figure 4.6   Tuple tree after the `AuthorizeCreditCard` bolt emits a tuple

With a clear definition of a tuple tree in mind, let's move on to the code that's needed in our bolts for anchoring and acking. We'll also discuss failing tuples and the various types of errors we need to watch out for.

4.4.2   *Anchoring, acking, and failing tuples in our bolts*

There are two ways to implement anchoring, acking, and failing of tuples in our bolts: *implicit* and *explicit*. We mentioned earlier that our bolt implementations are already set up for guaranteed message processing. This is done via implicit anchoring, acking, and failing, which we'll discuss next.

IMPLICIT ANCHORING, ACKING, AND FAILING

In our implementation, all of our bolts extended the `BaseBasicBolt` abstract class. The beauty of using `BaseBasicBolt` as our base class is that it automatically provides anchoring and acking for us. The following list examines how Storm does this:

- *Anchoring*—Within the `execute()` method of the `BaseBasicBolt` implementation, we'll be emitting a tuple to be passed on to the next bolt. At this point of emitting, the provided `BasicOutputCollector` will take on the responsibility of anchoring the output tuple to the input tuple. In the `AuthorizeCreditCard`

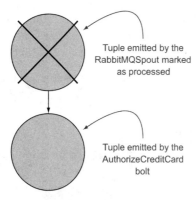

Figure 4.7   Tuple tree after the `AuthorizeCreditCard` bolt acks its input tuple

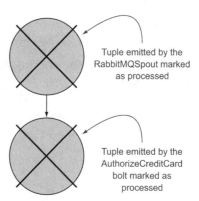

Figure 4.8   Tuple tree after the `ProcessedOrderNotification` bolt acks its input tuple

bolt, we emit the order. This outgoing order tuple will be automatically anchored to the incoming order tuple:

```
outputCollector.emit(new Values(order));
```

- *Acking*—When the execute() method of the BaseBasicBolt implementation completes, the tuple that was sent to it will be automatically acked.
- *Failing*—If there's a failure within the execute() method, the way to handle that is to notify BaseBasicBolt by throwing a FailedException or ReportedFailedException. Then BaseBasicBolt will take care of marking that tuple as failed.

Using BaseBasicBolt to keep track of tuple states through implicit anchoring, acking, and failing is easy. But BaseBasicBolt isn't suitable for every use case. It's generally helpful only in use cases where a single tuple enters the bolt and a single corresponding tuple is emitted from that bolt immediately. That is the case with our credit card authorization topology, so it works here. But for more complex examples, it's not sufficient. This is where explicit anchoring, acking, and failing come into play.

EXPLICIT ANCHORING, ACKING, AND FAILING
When we have bolts that perform more complex tasks such as these

- Aggregating on multiple input tuples (collapsing)
- Joining multiple incoming streams (we won't cover multiple streams in this chapter, but we did have two streams going through a bolt in the heat map chapter, chapter 3, when we had a tick tuple stream in addition to the default stream)

then we'll have to move beyond the functionality provided by BaseBasicBolt. BaseBasicBolt is suitable when behavior is predictable. When you need to programmatically decide when a tuple batch is complete (when aggregating, for example) or at runtime decide when two or more streams should be joined, then you need to programmatically decide when to anchor, ack, or fail. In these cases, you need to use BaseRichBolt as a base class instead of BaseBasicBolt. The following list shows what needs to be done inside an implementation of a bolt extending BaseRichBolt:

- *Anchoring*—To explicitly anchor, we need to pass the input tuple into the emit() method on the outputCollector within the bolt's execute method: outputCollector.emit(new Values(order)) becomes outputCollector.emit(tuple, new Values(order)).
- *Acking*—To explicitly ack, we need to call the ack method on the outputCollector within the bolt's execute method: outputCollector.ack(tuple).
- *Failing*—This is achieved by calling the fail method on the outputCollector within the bolt's execute method: throw new FailedException() becomes outputCollector.fail(tuple);

Although we can't use BaseBasicBolt for all use cases, we can use BaseRichBolt for everything that the former can do and more because it provides more fine-grained control over when and how you anchor, ack, or fail. Our credit card authorization topology can be expressed in terms of BaseBasicBolt with desired reliability, but it can be written with BaseRichBolt just as easily. The following listing rewrites one of the bolts from our credit card authorization topology using BaseRichBolt.

Listing 4.5   Explicit anchoring and acking in `AuthorizeCreditCard.java`

```
public class AuthorizeCreditCard extends BaseRichBolt {        ◁──┐ Switch to extending
  private AuthorizationService authorizationService;                BaseRichBolt from
  private OrderDao orderDao;                                         BaseBasicBolt.
  private OutputCollector outputCollector;

  @Override
  public void declareOutputFields(OutputFieldsDeclarer declarer) {
    declarer.declare(new Fields("order"));
  }

  @Override
  public void prepare(Map config,
                      TopologyContext context,
                      OutputCollector collector) {
    orderDao = new OrderDao();                               Store the
    authorizationService = new AuthorizationService();       OutputCollector in
    outputCollector = collector;                      ◁──┘   an instance variable.
  }

  @Override
  public void execute(Tuple tuple,
                      BasicOutputCollector outputCollector) {
    Order order = (Order) tuple.getValueByField("order");
    boolean isAuthorized = authorizationService.authorize(order);
    if (isAuthorized) {
      orderDao.updateStatusToReadyToShip(order);
    } else {
      orderDao.updateStatusToDenied(order);
    }                                                              Anchor to the
    outputCollector.emit(tuple, new Values(order));     ◁──┘       input tuple.
    outputCollector.ack(tuple);                   ◁──┐ Ack the
  }                                                    input tuple.
}
```

One thing to note is that with BaseBasicBolt, we were given a BasicOutputCollector with each call of the execute() method. But with BaseRichBolt, we are responsible for maintaining tuple state by using an OutputCollector that will be provided via the prepare() method at the time of bolt initialization. BasicOutputCollector is a stripped-down version of OutputCollector; it encapsulates an OutputCollector but hides the more fine-grained functionality with a simpler interface.

Another thing to be mindful of is that when using BaseRichBolt, if we don't anchor our outgoing tuple(s) to the incoming tuple, we'll no longer have any reliability downstream from that point on. BaseBasicBolt did the anchoring on your behalf:

- *Anchored*—outputCollector.emit(tuple, new Values(order));
- *Unanchored*—outputCollector.emit(new Values(order));

Having covered anchoring and acking, let's move on to something that isn't as straight-forward: handling errors. The act of failing a tuple itself is easy; it's knowing when an error can be retried that requires some thought.

HANDLING FAILURES AND KNOWING WHEN TO RETRY

We've covered a lot of concepts related to guaranteed message processing. We have anchoring and acking down pat. But we have yet to address how we want to handle failures. We know that we can fail a tuple by either throwing a `FailedException`/ `ReportedFailedException` (when using `BaseBasicBolt`) or calling `fail` on the `Output-Collector` (when using `BaseRichBolt`). Let's look at this in the context of our `AuthorizeCreditCard` bolt, shown in the next listing. We're showing only the changes to the `execute()` method that incorporate explicit failing.

Listing 4.6 Anchoring, acking, and failing in `AuthorizeCreditCard.execute()`

```
public void execute(Tuple tuple) {
  Order order = (Order) tuple.getValueByField("order");
  try {
    boolean isAuthorized = authorizationService.authorize(order);
    if (isAuthorized) {
      orderDao.updateStatusToReadyToShip(order);      Anchor to the
    } else {                                          input tuple.
      orderDao.updateStatusToDenied(order);
    }                                                   Ack the
    outputCollector.emit(tuple, new Values(order));   input tuple.
    outputCollector.ack(tuple);
  } catch (ServiceException e) {          Fail the input tuple
    outputCollector.fail(tuple);         in the case of a
  }                                       service exception.
}
```

Failing a tuple in this way will cause the entire tuple tree to be replayed starting at the spout. This is the key to guaranteed message processing, because this is the main trigger for the retry mechanism. It's important to know when a tuple should be failed. This seems obvious, but tuples should be failed when they're *retriable* (can be retried). The question then becomes what can/should be retried. The following list discusses the various types of errors:

- *Known errors*—These can be broken down into two groups:
  - *Retriable*—For known specific, retriable errors (say, a socket timeout exception while connecting to a service), we'll want to fail the tuple so it gets replayed and retried.
  - *Nonretriable*—For known errors that can't be safely retried (like a POST to REST API) or when it doesn't make sense for something to be retried (like a `ParseException` while handling JSON or XML), you shouldn't fail the tuple. When you have one of these nonretriable errors, instead of failing the tuple you'll need to ack the tuple (without emitting a new one), because you don't want to engage the replay mechanism for it. We recommend some sort of logging or reporting here so you'll know there was an error in your topology.

- *Unknown errors*—Generally, unknown or unexpected errors will be a small percentage of errors observed, so it's customary to fail them and retry them. After you've seen them once, they become a known error (assuming logging is in place), and you can take action on them as either a retriable or nonretriable known error.

NOTE Having data on errors within a Storm topology can be useful, as you'll see in chapter 6 when we discuss metrics.

This brings our discussion of anchoring, acking, and failing in our bolts to a close. Now it's time to shift gears and move to the spout. We mentioned that when the replay mechanism gets engaged, the replaying starts at the spout and works its way down. Let's see how that works.

4.4.3 A spout's role in guaranteed message processing

So far our focus has been centered on what we need to do in our bolts to achieve guaranteed message processing. This section will complete the sequence and discuss the role a spout plays in guaranteeing a tuple it emits gets fully processed or replayed on failure. The next listing shows the spout interface from chapter 2.

Listing 4.7   ISpout.java interface

```
public interface ISpout extends Serializable {
    void open(Map config,
              TopologyContext context,
              SpoutOutputCollector outputCollector);

    void close();

    void nextTuple();                          ← ❶

    void ack(Object messageId);                ← ❷

    void fail(Object messageId);               ← ❸
}
```

How does a spout tie into guaranteeing messages are processed? Here's a hint: The ack ❷ and fail ❸ methods have something to do with it. The following steps give a more complete picture in terms of what happens before a spout emits a tuple and after that tuple is either fully processed or failed:

1 Storm requests a tuple by calling nextTuple ❶ on the spout.

2 The spout uses the SpoutOutputCollector to emit a tuple to one of its streams.

3 When emitting the tuple, the spout provides a messageId that's used to identify that particular tuple. This may look something like this:

```
spoutOutputCollector.emit(tuple, messageId);.
```

4 The tuple gets sent to the bolts downstream and Storm tracks the tuple tree of messages that are created. Remember, this is done via anchoring and acking within the bolts so Storm can build up the tree and mark leaves as processed.

5 If Storm detects that a tuple is fully processed, it will call the `ack` ❷ method on the originating spout task with the message ID the spout provided to Storm.

6 If the tuple timed out or one of the consuming bolts explicitly failed the tuple (such as in our `AuthorizeCreditCard` bolt), Storm will call the `fail` ❸ method on the originating spout task with the message ID the spout provided to Storm.

Steps 3, 5, and 6 are the keys to guaranteed message processing from a spout's perspective. Everything starts with providing a `messageId` when emitting a tuple. Not doing this means Storm can't track the tuple tree. You should add code to the `ack` method to perform any required cleanup for a fully processed tuple, if necessary. You should also add code to the `fail` method to replay the tuple.

Storm acker tasks

Storm uses special "acker" tasks to keep track of tuple trees in order to determine whether a spout tuple has been fully processed. If an acker task sees a tuple tree is complete, it'll send a message to the spout that originally emitted the tuple, resulting in that spout's `ack` method being called.

It looks like we need to write an implementation of a spout that supports all these criteria. In the previous chapter, we introduced the concept of an unreliable data source. An unreliable data source won't be able to support acking or failing. Once that data source hands your spout a message, it assumes you've taken responsibility for that message. A reliable data source, on the other hand, will pass messages to the spout but won't assume you've taken responsibility for them until you've provided an acknowledgment of some sort. In addition, a reliable data source will allow you to fail any given tuple with the guarantee that it will later be able to replay it. In short, a reliable data source will support steps 3, 5, and 6.

The best way to demonstrate how a reliable data source's capabilities tie into a spout API is to implement a solution with a commonly used data source. Kafka, RabbitMQ, and Kestrel are all commonly used with Storm. Kafka is a valuable tool in your arsenal of infrastructure that works great with Storm, which we'll cover in detail in chapter 9. For now we're going with RabbitMQ, which is an excellent match for our use case.

A RELIABLE SPOUT IMPLEMENTATION

Let's go over a RabbitMQ-based spout implementation that'll provide all the reliability we need for this use case.[1] Keep in mind our main point of interest isn't RabbitMQ, but rather how a well-implemented spout together with a reliable data source provide guaranteed message processing. If you don't follow the underpinnings of the RabbitMQ client API, don't worry; we've emphasized the important parts that you need to follow in the next listing.

---

[1] You can find a more robust, configurable, and performant implementation of the spout implementation for RabbitMQ on GitHub at https://github.com/ppat/storm-rabbitmq.

Listing 4.8   RabbitMQSpout.java

```
public class RabbitMQSpout extends BaseRichSpout {
  private Connection connection;
  private Channel channel;
  private QueueingConsumer consumer;
  private SpoutOutputCollector outputCollector;

  @Override
  public void declareOutputFields(OutputFieldsDeclarer declarer) {
    declarer.declare(new Fields("order"));
  }

  @Override
  public void open(Map config,
                   TopologyContext topologyContext,
                   SpoutOutputCollector spoutOutputCollector) {
    outputCollector = spoutOutputCollector;
    connection = new ConnectionFactory().newConnection();
    channel = connection.createChannel();
    channel.basicQos(25);
    consumer = new QueueingConsumer(channel);
    channel.basicConsume("orders", false /*auto-ack=false*/, consumer);
  }


  @Override
  public void nextTuple() {
    QueueingConsumer.Delivery delivery = consumer.nextDelivery(1L);
    if (delivery == null) return; /* no messages yet */
    Long msgId = delivery.getEnvelope().getDeliveryTag();
    byte[] msgAsbytes = delivery.getBody();
    String msgAsString = new String(msgAsbytes, Charset.forName("UTF-8"));
    Order order = new Gson().fromJson(msgAsString, Order.class);
    outputCollector.emit(new Values(order), msgId);
  }
```

Extend the BaseRichSpout abstract class, which implements ISpout.

Connect to a RabbitMQ node running on localhost with default credentials and settings.

Consume and locally buffer 25 messages at a time from RabbitMQ.

When we take messages off a RabbitMQ queue, we'll buffer them locally inside this consumer.

Emit the order tuple but anchor it with message-id provided by RabbitMQ.

Storm will call next tuple when it's ready to send the next message to downstream bolt.

Deserialize the message into the Order object by using Google GSON JSON parsing library.

Set up subscription that consumes off a RabbitMQ queue. The messages consumed will be kept in a local buffer in a consumer object and we won't ack them until downstream bolts send their acks back.

Identify this message by the message ID assigned to it by RabbitMQ (common vernacular between RabbitMQ and Storm to refer to this message).

Pick the next message off the local buffer of the RabbitMQ queue. A timeout of 1 ms is imposed as nextTuple shouldn't be allowed to block for thread safety issues within Storm.

Storm will call ack on the spout when all downstream bolts have fully processed this message. This will be called with same message ID that the spout anchored to when it emitted that message.

All downstream bolts have fully processed this message, so we can tell RabbitMQ we're done with it and have it removed from the queue.

```
@Override
public void ack(Object msgId) {
    channel.basicAck((Long) msgId, false /* only acking this msgId */);
}

@Override
public void fail(Object msgId) {
    channel.basicReject((Long) msgId, true /* requeue enabled */);
}

@Override
public void close() {
    channel.close();
    connection.close();
}
}
```

Storm will call fail when anything downstream fails this message.

We tell RabbitMQ to re-queue this message to be retried.

Storm gives you the tools to guarantee the tuples being emitted by your spout are fully processed while they're in transit within the Storm infrastructure. But for guaranteed message processing to take effect, you must use a reliable data source that has the capability of replaying a tuple. Additionally, the spout implementation has to make use of the replay mechanism provided by its data source. Understanding this is essential if you want to be successful with guaranteed message processing in your topologies.

Emitting anchored vs. unanchored tuples from a spout

The topologies we created in earlier chapters didn't take advantage of guaranteed message processing or fault tolerance. We may have used `BaseBasicBolt` in those chapters and that may have bought us implicit anchoring and acking, but our tuples in those chapters didn't originate from a reliable spout. Because of the unreliable nature of those data sources, when we emitted tuples at the spout, they were sent "unanchored" via `outputCollector.emit(new Values(order))`. When you don't anchor to the input tuple starting from the spout, it can't guarantee that they'll be fully processed. This is because replaying always starts at the spout. So the decision to emit tuples unanchored should always be a conscious one, as we made in the heat map example.

We're now ready to write a robust topology and introduce it to the world. We've covered three pieces of the puzzle needed for supporting reliability:

- A data source with a corresponding reliable spout
- An anchored tuple stream
- A topology that acknowledges each tuple as it gets processed or notifies of failure

But before moving on to chapter 5 to discuss the last piece of the puzzle—the Storm cluster—let's talk about replay semantics and whether our current topology implementation is good enough for what we want.

4.5 *Replay semantics*

Each of the four pieces of the puzzle to reliability plays a key role and is necessary if we want to build a robust topology. But when you consider the replay characteristics of streams as they flow through your topology, you'll begin to recognize that Storm provides varying guarantees of reliability when it comes to event processing. We can assign different semantics to reliability when we become aware of different requirements being met by our streams. Let's take a look at these varying degrees of reliability.

4.5.1 *Degrees of reliability in Storm*

Much like we saw different kinds of scaling problems when we carefully examined data streams in chapter 3, we see varying degrees of reliability when we carefully examine our topology design. We identify three degrees of reliability here:

- At-most-once processing
- At-least-once processing
- Exactly once processing

Let's elaborate a little further what we mean by each of these.

AT-MOST-ONCE PROCESSING

You'd use *at-most-once processing* when you want to guarantee that no single tuple ever gets processed more than once. In this case, no replaying will ever happen. If it succeeds, great, but if it fails the tuple will be discarded. Regardless, this semantic provides no reliability that all operations will be processed, and it's the simplest semantic you can choose. We used at-most-once processing in the preceding chapters, because those use cases didn't dictate a need for reliability. We may have used `BaseBasicBolt` (with its automated anchoring and acking) in previous chapters, but we didn't anchor the tuples when we first emitted them from the spout.

You don't need to do anything special to achieve this type of reliability in Storm, which isn't true for our next degree of reliability.

AT-LEAST-ONCE PROCESSING

At-least-once processing can be used when you want to guarantee that every single tuple must be processed successfully at least once. If a single tuple is replayed several times, and for some reason it succeeds more than once, that's okay under this replay semantic. Your primary concern is that it must succeed, even if that means doing redundant work.

To achieve at-least-once processing in Storm, you need a reliable spout with a reliable data source and an anchored stream with acked or failed tuples. This leads us to the strictest degree of reliability.

EXACTLY ONCE PROCESSING

Exactly once processing is similar to at-least-once processing in that it can guarantee that every tuple is processed successfully. But exactly once processing takes care to ensure that once a tuple is processed, it can't be processed ever again.

As with at-least-once processing, you need a reliable spout with a reliable data source and an anchored stream with acked or failed tuples. But what sets this degree apart from at-least-once processing is that you also need logic in your bolt(s) to guarantee tuples are processed only once.

To understand what each type of processing requires of your system, it's important to understand the subtleties and problems that arise from our most stringent of options: exactly once.

4.5.2 Examining exactly once processing in a Storm topology

There's a lot of complexity hiding behind that simple phrase *exactly once*. This means that you have to be able to know whether you've already done a unit of work, which in turn means that you have to do the following:

1 Do the unit of work.
2 Record that you've done the unit of work.

Further, these two steps must be performed as an atomic operation—you can't do the work and then fail to record the result. You need to be able to do the work and record that it was done in one step. If you can do the work but have a failure before recording that the work was done, then you don't actually have *exactly once*—you have *usually once*. The vast majority of the time, the work will be done one time, but from time to time, it'll be done more often. That's an exceedingly rigorous qualification to meet.

At-least-once processing shares the same two steps, except that these operations aren't required to occur atomically. If for some reason a failure occurs during or immediately after performing your unit of work, it is okay to redo the work and reattempt to record the result. If it isn't okay to redo the work, then you need to add an important requirement: the end result of your unit of work must be idempotent. An action is *idempotent* when performed more than once, it has no additional effect on its subject after the first time it's performed. For example:

- "Set x to 2" is an idempotent operation.
- "Add 2 to variable x" isn't an idempotent operation.

Operations with external side effects such as sending an email are decidedly non-idempotent. Repeating that unit of work would send more than one email and is assuredly not what you want to do.

If your unit of work is non-idempotent, then you must fall back to at-most-once processing. You want to do the unit of work, but it's more important that the result of this work not be duplicated than doing the actual work.

4.5.3 Examining the reliability guarantees in our topology

How can we provide a stricter degree of reliability in our topology? Do we even need to, or are we already in a good enough state? To answer these questions, it makes sense to identify what level of reliability our topology is currently at.

IDENTIFYING THE CURRENT LEVEL OF RELIABILITY

Which type of processing do we have with our topology? We have guaranteed message processing so that if we have a failure, we'll retry the tuple. This rules out at-most-once as our semantics. That's good. We certainly want to charge people for the goods we're shipping them.

Do we have exactly once semantics or at-least-once semantics? Let's break this down. Our "unit of work" is charging a customer's credit card along with updating the status of the order. This is seen in the following listing.

Listing 4.9 Examining the `execute()` method of `AuthorizeCreditCard.java`

```
public void execute(Tuple tuple) {
  Order order = (Order) tuple.getValueByField("order");
  try {
    boolean isAuthorized = authorizationService.authorize(order);     ◁—❶
    if (isAuthorized) {
      orderDao.updateStatusToReadyToShip(order);                       ◁—❷
    } else {
      orderDao.updateStatusToDenied(order);                            ◁—┐
    }                                                                     ❸
    outputCollector.emit(tuple, new Values(order));
    outputCollector.ack(tuple);
  } catch (ServiceException e) {
    outputCollector.fail(tuple);
  }
}
```

The question is this: are the two steps a single atomic operation? The answer is no. It's possible for us to charge a user's credit card and then not update the order status. Between charging the credit card ❶ and changing the order status (❷, ❸), a couple of things could happen:

- Our process could crash.
- The database might be unavailable to record the result.

This means we don't have exactly once semantics; we have at-least-once. Looking at our topology as it currently stands, that's problematic. Retrying a tuple can result in multiple charges to a customer's card. What can we do to lessen this danger? We know that exactly once is impossible for us, but we should be able to make at-least-once safer.

PROVIDING BETTER AT-LEAST-ONCE PROCESSING WHEN AUTHORIZING AN ORDER

The first question we want to ask ourselves in making our at-least-once processing safer is whether our operation can be made idempotent. The answer is probably not. We'd need the external credit card service's assistance with that. If we could provide the order ID as a unique transaction identifier and the service would throw an error such as `DuplicateTransactionException`, then we could update our records to indicate the order is ready to ship and continue processing. Handling such an error is seen in the following listing.

Listing 4.10 Updating `AuthorizeCreditCard.java` to handle a `DuplicateTransactionException`

```
public void execute(Tuple tuple) {
  Order order = (Order) tuple.getValueByField("order");
  try {
    boolean isAuthorized = authorizationService.authorize(order);
    if (isAuthorized) {
      orderDao.updateStatusToReadyToShip(order);
    } else {
      orderDao.updateStatusToDenied(order);
    }
    outputCollector.emit(tuple, new Values(order));
    outputCollector.ack(tuple);
  }
  catch (DuplicateTransactionException e) {
    orderDao.updateStatusToReadyToShip(order);
    outputCollector.ack(tuple);
  }
  catch (ServiceException e) {
    outputCollector.fail(tuple);
  }
}
```

If the order has already been processed and is a duplicate, ensure that the status is updated and ack the tuple.

Without that external cooperation, what's the best we can do? If our process crashes between charging a customer and recording that we charged, there isn't anything we can do but accept that it'll happen from time to time and be prepared to address it in a nontechnical fashion (such as customer service responding to a refund request). Realistically, if our system is stable, this should be a relatively rare occurrence.

For the "system of record being unavailable" scenario, we can add a partially preventive measure. We can verify the database for storing the updated order status is available before attempting to charge the credit card. This approach reduces the chance of a situation arising where we charge the credit card and then fail to update the order status because the database is down.

In general, this is good practice. If you're computing a non-idempotent result within a topology and will then store "doneness," verify at the time you begin your unit of work that you'll be able record it. This check can be seen in the next listing.

Listing 4.11 Updating `AuthorizeCreditCard.java` to check for database availability before processing

```
public void execute(Tuple tuple) {
  Order order = (Order) tuple.getValueByField("order");
  try {
    if (orderDao.systemIsAvailable()) {
      boolean isAuthorized = authorizationService.authorize(order);
      if (isAuthorized) {
        orderDao.updateStatusToReadyToShip(order);
      } else {
        orderDao.updateStatusToDenied(order);
      }
```

Check to see if the database is available.

```
        outputCollector.emit(tuple, new Values(order));
        outputCollector.ack(tuple);
    } else {
        outputCollector.fail(tuple);           Fail the tuple if
    }                                          the database
} catch (ServiceException e) {                 isn't available.
    outputCollector.fail(tuple);
    }
}
}
```

So we've improved our reliability, but we have a feeling we can do better. Looking back at our steps, we have the following:

1 Authorize the credit card.
2 Update the order status.
3 Notify an external system of the change.

Looks like there's more work to do to address step 3.

PROVIDING BETTER AT-LEAST-ONCE PROCESSING ACROSS ALL STEPS

What happens if we manage to do the first two steps but we experience a failure while doing the third? Perhaps our process crashes; perhaps our tuple times out before notifying the external system. However it happens, it has happened, and Storm is going to replay the tuple. So what can we do to address this scenario?

Before processing the credit card, we should assure that the system of record is available (as we did previously) and verify that the order status isn't already "ready to ship." If the order isn't ready to ship, then we proceed as normal. It's probably the first time we're trying this order and the database is up and running. If the order is ready to ship, then we probably had a failure between our "update order status" and "notify external system" steps. In that case, we would want to skip charging the card again and move directly to notifying the external system of the change.

If we control this external system, then we can make a request to ship the same order more than once an idempotent operation where subsequent attempts are dropped. If not, the caveats we encountered earlier around lack of idempotence of credit card processing applies as well.

The steps in our conceptual framework have changed somewhat; step 2 is new:

1 Pull the order off the message queue.
2 Determine whether the order has been marked as "ready to ship" and do one of two things:
   a. If the order has been marked as "ready to ship," skip to step 6.
   b. If the order hasn't been marked as "ready to ship," continue to step 3.
3 Attempt to authorize the credit card by calling an external credit card authorization service.
4 If the service call succeeded, update the order status.
5 If it fails, we can try again later.
6 Notify a separate downstream system that the order has been processed.

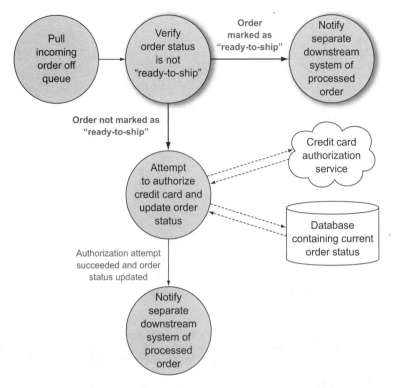

Figure 4.9 Conceptual solution of the e-commerce credit card authorization flow with an extra step for providing better at-least-once processing

These updated steps are illustrated in figure 4.9, with the new steps highlighted.

We could map this conceptual solution onto our topology in a couple ways:

- Add a new bolt that performs the status verification step. We could call this something like `VerifyOrderStatus`.
- Perform the status verification step in the `AuthorizeCreditCard` bolt.

We'll choose option number two and update the `AuthorizeCreditCard` bolt to perform the verification step. We'll leave adding a new `VerifyOrderStatus` bolt as an exercise for you. The following listing shows the updated code for `Authorize-CreditCard`.

Listing 4.12 Updating `AuthorizeCreditCard.java` to check the order status before processing

```
public void execute(Tuple tuple) {
  Order order = (Order) tuple.getValueByField("order");
  try {
    if(orderDao.systemIsAvailable()) {
      if (!orderDao.orderIsReadyToShip(order)) {
```

Not only are we checking the order status, but we're also verifying that our system of record is available as we previously discussed.

```
        boolean isAuthorized = authorizationService.authorize(order);
        if (isAuthorized) {
          orderDao.updateStatusToReadyToShip(order);
        } else {
          orderDao.updateStatusToDenied(order);
        }
        outputCollector.emit(tuple, new Values(order));
      }
      outputCollector.ack(tuple);           ◁───┐  Always ack the
    } else {                                     │  input tuple if there
      outputCollector.fail(tuple);               │  wasn't an error.
    }
  } catch (ServiceException e) {
    outputCollector.fail(tuple);
  }
}
```

And just like that, we're done. Or are we? We missed something here. We still need to always notify the external system when we are done processing the order even if "done" just means that we checked that the order was ready to ship and did nothing. The updated code for this can be seen in the next code listing; we just need to emit a tuple with the order whenever we "process" it.

Listing 4.13   Updating `AuthorizeCreditCard.java` to emit a tuple whenever an order is "processed"

```
public void execute(Tuple tuple) {
  Order order = (Order) tuple.getValueByField("order");
  try {
    if (orderDao.systemIsAvailable()) {
      if (!orderDao.orderIsReadyToShip(order)) {
        boolean isAuthorized = authorizationService.authorize(order);
        if (isAuthorized) {
          orderDao.updateStatusToReadyToShip(order);
        } else {
          orderDao.updateStatusToDenied(order);
        }                                              Always emit a tuple
      }                                                with the order,
      outputCollector.emit(tuple, new Values(order));  ◁──  making sure our
      outputCollector.ack(tuple);                           external system
    } else {                                                knows to do
      outputCollector.fail(tuple);                          something.
    }
  } catch (ServiceException e) {
    outputCollector.fail(tuple);
  }
}
```

This brings us to a solution we feel comfortable with. And although we haven't been able to achieve exactly once processing, we have been able to achieve a better at-least-once processing by including some additional logic in our `AuthorizeCreditCard` bolt. Follow this process whenever you're designing a topology with reliability requirements.

You need to map out your basic conceptual problem and then figure out what your semantics are, at least once or at most once. If it's at least once, start looking at all the ways it can fail and make sure you address them.

4.6 *Summary*

In this chapter, you learned that

- The varying degrees of reliability you can achieve in Storm are
  - At-most-once processing
  - At-least-once processing
  - Exactly once processing
- Different problems require varying levels of reliability, and it's your job as a developer to understand the reliability requirements of your problem domain.
- Storm supports reliability with four main parts:
  - A reliable data source with a corresponding reliable spout
  - An anchored tuple stream
  - A topology that acknowledges each tuple as it gets processed or notifies of failure
  - A fault-tolerant Storm cluster infrastructure (to be addressed next)
- Storm is able to tell if a tuple emitted by a spout is fully processed by tracking a tuple tree for that tuple.
- In order for Storm to be able to track a tuple tree, you must anchor input tuples to output tuples and ack any input tuples.
- Failing a tuple either via a timeout or manually will trigger the retry mechanism in Storm.
- Tuples should be failed for known/retriable errors and unknown errors. Tuples should not be failed for known/non-retriable errors.
- A spout must be implemented to explicitly handle and retry failures while being hooked up to a reliable data source in order to truly achieve guaranteed message processing.

Moving from local to remote topologies

5

This chapter covers

- The Storm cluster
- Fault tolerance within a Storm cluster
- Storm cluster installation
- Deploying and running topologies on a Storm cluster
- The Storm UI and the role it plays

Imagine the following scenario. You're tasked with implementing a Storm topology for performing real-time analysis on events logged within your company's system. As a conscientious developer, you've decided to use this book as a guideline for developing the topology. You've built it using the core Storm components covered in chapter 2. You've applied the topology design patterns you learned about in chapter 3 while determining what logic should go into each bolt, and you've followed the steps in chapter 4 to provide at-least-once processing for all tuples coming into your topology. You're ready to hook the topology up to a queue receiving logging events and have it hum along. What do you do next?

You can run your topology locally as in chapters 2, 3, and 4, but doing so won't scale to the data volume and velocity that you're expecting. You need to be able to deploy your topology to an environment that's built for handling production-level data. This is where the "remote" (also known as "production") Storm cluster comes into play—an environment built to handle the demands of production-level data.

> **NOTE** As you learned in chapter 1, *volume* refers to the amount of data entering your system and *velocity* refers to the pace at which that data flows through your system.

Running our topologies locally and simulating a Storm cluster within a single process has served our needs so far and is useful for development and testing purposes. But local mode doesn't support the scaling discussed in chapter 3 nor the first-class guaranteed processing we learned about in chapter 4. An actual Storm cluster is needed for both of these.

This chapter will begin by explaining the parts of a Storm cluster and the roles they play, followed by a Q&A session on how Storm provides fault tolerance. We'll then move on to installing a Storm cluster and deploying and running your topologies against the installed cluster. We'll also cover an important tool you can use to make sure your topology is healthy: the Storm UI. Along the way, we'll provide a preview into the tuning and troubleshooting topics that will be covered in chapters 6 and 7.

It all starts with the Storm cluster, so let's expand on our worker nodes discussion from chapter 3.

5.1 The Storm cluster

Chapter 3 scratched the surface of a worker node and how it runs a JVM, which in turn runs executors and tasks. In this section, we're going to go much deeper, starting with the Storm cluster as a whole. A Storm cluster consists of two types of nodes: the master node and the worker nodes. A *master* node runs a daemon called Nimbus, and the *worker* nodes each run a daemon called a Supervisor. Figure 5.1 shows a Storm cluster with one master node and four worker nodes. Storm supports only a single master node, whereas it's likely your cluster will have a different number of worker nodes based on your needs (we'll cover how to determine this number in chapters 6 and 7).

The master node can be thought of as the control center. In addition to the responsibilities listed in figure 5.1, this is where you'd run any of the commands—such as activate, deactivate, rebalance, or kill—available in a Storm cluster (more on these commands later in the chapter). The worker nodes are where the logic in the spouts and bolts is executed.

Another big part of a Storm cluster is *Zookeeper*. Storm relies on Apache Zookeeper[1] for coordinating communication between Nimbus and the Supervisors. Any state needed to coordinate between Nimbus and the Supervisors is kept in Zookeeper. As a result, if Nimbus or a Supervisor goes down, once it comes back up it can recover state from Zookeeper, keeping the Storm cluster running as if nothing happened.

---

[1] http://zookeeper.apache.org/

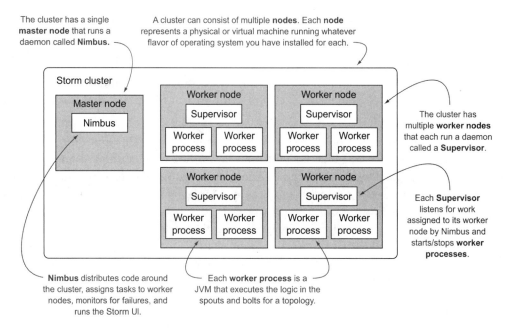

The cluster has a single **master node** that runs a daemon called **Nimbus.**

A cluster can consist of multiple **nodes**. Each **node** represents a physical or virtual machine running whatever flavor of operating system you have installed for each.

The cluster has multiple **worker nodes** that each run a daemon called a **Supervisor**.

Each **Supervisor** listens for work assigned to its worker node by Nimbus and starts/stops **worker processes**.

Nimbus distributes code around the cluster, assigns tasks to worker nodes, monitors for failures, and runs the Storm UI.

Each **worker process** is a JVM that executes the logic in the spouts and bolts for a topology.

Figure 5.1   Nimbus and Supervisors and their responsibilities inside a Storm cluster

Figure 5.2 shows a cluster of Zookeeper nodes integrated into the Storm cluster. We've removed the worker processes from this figure so you can focus on where Zookeeper fits as it coordinates communication between Nimbus and Supervisors.

Throughout the remainder of the book, any time we mention "Storm cluster," we're referring to the master, worker, and Zookeeper nodes.

Although the master node and Zookeeper are important parts of a Storm cluster, we're going to shift our focus to worker nodes for now. Worker nodes are where the spout and bolt processing occurs, making them the central place for much of our tuning and troubleshooting efforts in chapters 6 and 7.

> **NOTE** Chapters 6 and 7 will explain when you might want to increase the number of worker processes running on a worker node and when and how you might reach a point of diminishing returns. These chapters will also discuss tuning within a worker process, so it makes sense to explain the various parts of a worker process.

5.1.1 The anatomy of a worker node

As mentioned earlier, each worker node has a Supervisor daemon that's tasked with administering the worker processes and keeping them in a running state. If a Supervisor notices that one of the worker processes is down, it will immediately restart it. What's a worker process exactly? We mentioned that it was a JVM, but as you know from chapter 3, there's more to it.

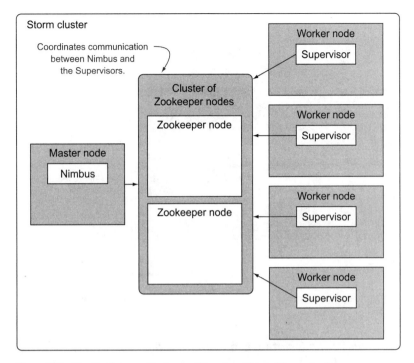

Figure 5.2 The Zookeeper Cluster and its role within a Storm cluster

Each worker process executes a subset of a topology. This means that each worker process belongs to a specific topology and that each topology will be run across one or more worker processes. Normally, these worker processes are run across many machines within the Storm cluster.

In chapter 3, you learned about executors (threads) and tasks (instances of spouts/bolts). We discussed how a worker process (JVM) runs one or more executors (threads), with each thread executing one or more instances of spouts/bolts (tasks). Figure 5.3 illustrates this concept.

Here are the key takeaways:

- A worker process is a JVM.
- An executor is a thread of execution within a JVM.
- A task is an instance of a spout or bolt being run within a thread of execution on the JVM.

Understanding these mappings is extremely important for the purposes of tuning and troubleshooting. For example, chapter 6 answers questions such as why you might want many tasks per executor, so understanding the relationship between an executor and its tasks is essential.

To bring the discussion of a worker node, worker processes, executors, and tasks full circle, let's present them within the context of the credit card authorization topology from chapter 4.

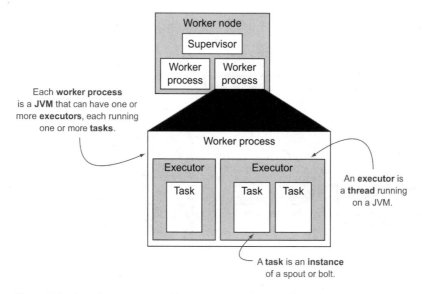

Each **worker process** is a **JVM** that can have one or more **executors**, each running one or more **tasks**.

An **executor** is a **thread** running on a JVM.

A **task** is an **instance** of a spout or bolt.

Figure 5.3   A worker process consists of one or more executors, with each executor consisting of one or more tasks.

5.1.2   *Presenting a worker node within the context of the credit card authorization topology*

In this section we'll present a hypothetical configuration for the credit card authorization topology in order to help you make the connection between the number of worker processes, executors, and tasks in the figures and the code for doing so. This hypothetical configuration can be seen in figure 5.4.

The setup in figure 5.4 would be achieved via the code in the following listing.

Listing 5.1   Configuration for our hypothetical Storm cluster

Set the number of worker processes (JVMs) to 2.

```
Config config = new Config();
config.setNumWorkers(2);
config.setMessageTimeoutSecs(60);
```

Configure how long each tuple tree has to complete before it gets failed automatically.

Parallelism hint that sets the number of executors (threads) to 1 for this spout, with the default number of tasks (instances) also set to 1

```
TopologyBuilder builder = new TopologyBuilder();
```

Set the number of executors (threads) to 1.

```
builder.setSpout("rabbitmq-spout", new RabbitMQSpout(), 1);

builder.setBolt("check-status", new VerifyOrderStatus(), 1)
        .shuffleGrouping("rabbitmq-spout")
        .setNumTasks(2);
```

Set the number of tasks (instances) to 2.

Set the number of executors (threads) to 1.

```
builder.setBolt("authorize-card", new AuthorizeCreditCard(), 1)
        .shuffleGrouping("check-status")
        .setNumTasks(2);
```

Set the number of tasks (instances) to 2.

```
builder.setBolt("notification", new ProcessedOrderNotification(), 1)
    .shuffleGrouping("authorize-card")
    .setNumTasks(1);
```

**Set the number
of executors
(threads) to 1.**

**Set the number
of tasks to 1.**

When we set the numWorkers in the Config, we're configuring the worker processes desired for running this topology. We don't actually force both worker processes to end up on the same worker node as depicted in figure 5.4. Storm will pick where they end up based on which worker nodes in the cluster have vacant slots for running worker processes.

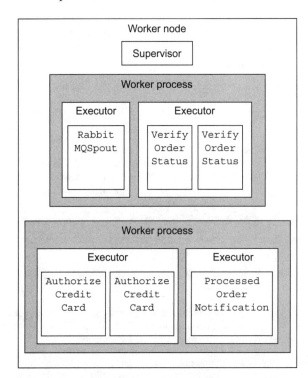

Figure 5.4   A hypothetical breakdown of a worker node with multiple worker processes, executors, and tasks for the credit card authorization topology

Parallelism vs. concurrency: what's the difference?

Parallelism is when two threads are executing simultaneously. *Concurrency* is when at least two threads are making progress on some sort of computation. Concurrency doesn't necessarily mean the two threads are executing simultaneously—something like time slicing may be used to simulate parallelism.

Having revisited the breakdown of a worker node, let's see how Storm provides fault tolerance across the cluster's various parts.

5.2   *Fail-fast philosophy for fault tolerance within a Storm cluster*

Remember the four pieces to the reliability puzzle discussed in chapter 4?

- A reliable data source with a corresponding reliable spout
- An anchored tuple stream
- A topology that acknowledges each tuple as it gets processed or notifies you of failure
- A fault-tolerant Storm cluster infrastructure

We're finally at a point to discuss the last piece, a fault-tolerant Storm cluster infrastructure. The components of a Storm cluster have been designed with fault tolerance in mind. The easiest way to explain how Storm handles fault tolerance is to answer questions in the form of "What does Storm do when *x* happens?" The most important questions on fault tolerance are addressed in table 5.1.

Table 5.1   Fault tolerance questions and answers

Question	Answer
What if a worker node dies?	Supervisor will restart it and new tasks will be assigned to it. All tuples that weren't fully acked at time of death will be fully replayed by the spout. This is why the spout needs to support replaying (reliable spout) *and* the data source behind the spout also needs to be reliable (supporting replay).
What if a worker node continuously fails to start up?	Nimbus will reassign tasks to another worker.
What if an actual machine that runs worker nodes dies?	Nimbus will reassign the tasks on that machine to healthy machines.
What if Nimbus dies?	Because Nimbus is being run under supervision (using a tool like daemontools or monit), it should get restarted and continue processing like nothing happened.
What if a Supervisor dies?	Because Supervisors are being run under supervision (using a tool like daemontools or monit), they should get restarted like nothing happened.
Is Nimbus a single point of failure?	Not necessarily. Supervisors and worker nodes will continue to process, but you lose the ability to reassign workers to other machines or deploy new topologies.

You can see that Storm maintains a fail-fast philosophy in the sense that every piece within this infrastructure can be restarted and will recalibrate itself and move on. If tuples were in mid-process during a failure, they'll be failed automatically.

It doesn't matter whether the unit of infrastructure that failed is an instance (task) or a thread (executor) or a JVM (worker process) or a VM (worker node). At each level, safeguards are in place to ensure that everything gets restarted automatically (because everything runs under supervision).

We've talked about the benefits a Storm cluster provides in terms of parallelism and fault tolerance. How do you go about getting such a cluster up and running?

5.3   *Installing a Storm cluster*

The Storm wiki does an excellent job describing how to set up a Storm cluster. The steps found on the wiki include these:

1   Find information on setting up Zookeeper along with some helpful tips on maintaining the Zookeeper cluster.
2   Install the required Storm dependencies on the master and worker machines.
3   Download and extract a Storm release to the master and worker machines.
4   Configure the master and worker nodes via the storm.yaml file.
5   Launch the Nimbus and Supervisor daemons under supervision using the Storm script.

We'll cover each of these steps in more detail next.

> **NOTE**   What does it mean to run a process under supervision? It means that some supervisory process manages the actual process being run. Therefore, if the process being "supervised" fails, the supervisory process can automatically restart the failed process. This is a key element in providing fault tolerance in Storm.

5.3.1   *Setting up a Zookeeper cluster*

The steps for setting up a Zookeeper cluster are outside the scope of this book. You can find a thorough explanation of how to install Zookeeper on the Apache Zookeeper project page at http://zookeeper.apache.org. Follow those steps to get your cluster up and running.

Keep the following in mind when running Zookeeper:

- Zookeeper is designed to "fail fast," meaning it will shut down if an error occurs that it can't recover from. This isn't desirable within a Storm cluster because Zookeeper coordinates communication between Nimbus and the Supervisors. Because of this, we must have a supervisory process manage the Zookeeper instances so that if a Zookeeper instance does go down, the cluster as a whole can continue handling requests. The supervisory process will handle restarting any failed individual Zookeeper server, allowing the Zookeeper cluster to be self-healing.
- Because Zookeeper is a long-running process, its transaction logs can get quite large. This will eventually result in Zookeeper running out of disk space. Therefore, it's critical to set up some sort of process to compact (and even archive) the data produced in these logs.

5.3.2 Installing the required Storm dependencies to master and worker nodes

The next step is to install the required Storm dependencies to the machines you've dedicated to running Nimbus and the Supervisors. Table 5.2 lists these dependencies.

Table 5.2 External dependencies for Storm master and worker nodes

Dependency	Why it's needed	Link to download
Java 6+	Storm runs on the JVM and the latest version of Storm runs on Java 6.	www.oracle.com/us/technologies/java/overview/index.html
Python 2.6.6	The standard command-line tool for Storm is Python wrapped around Java.	https://www.python.org/downloads/

Once the required external dependencies have been installed to each of the machines hosting Nimbus and the Supervisors, you can install Storm to those machines.

5.3.3 Installing Storm to master and worker nodes

The Storm installations can currently be found at http://storm.apache.org/downloads.html. For this book, we used apache-storm-0.9.3. You should download the Storm release zip file to each node and extract the contents of the zip file somewhere on each of the machines. The location is up to you; something like /opt/storm is one example. Figure 5.5 shows the extracted contents in an /opt/storm directory.

There are two files in this figure that we're particularly interested in for this chapter: /opt/storm/bin/storm and /opt/storm/conf/storm.yaml. Let's discuss storm.yaml and its purpose next.

```
/opt/storm
  bin
    storm
    storm-config.cmd
    storm-local
    storm.cmd
  conf
    storm.yaml
  lib
  logback
  logs
  public
  CHANGELOG.md
  DISCLAIMER
  LICENSE
  NOTICE
  README.markdown
  RELEASE
```

Figure 5.5 Extracted contents of a Storm release zip

5.3.4 Configuring the master and worker nodes via storm.yaml

The Storm release contains a conf/storm.yaml file that configures the Storm daemons. This file overrides configuration settings found in defaults.yaml.[2] It's likely that

---

[2] You can find defaults.yaml at https://github.com/apache/storm/blob/master/conf/defaults.yaml.

you'll want to override at least some of the values; many of the defaults point to "local-host" for a machine name. Table 5.3 lists some of the initial configuration options you may want to override in order to get your Storm cluster up and running.

Table 5.3   storm.yaml properties you may want to override for your Storm installations

Properties	Description	Default value
`storm.zookeeper.servers`	The lists of hosts in the Zookeeper cluster for your Storm cluster.	`storm.zookeeper.servers:` `  - "localhost"`
`storm.zookeeper.port`	Needed if the port your Zookeeper cluster uses is different from the default.	`storm.zookeeper.port:` `2181`
`storm.local.dir`	The directory that the Nimbus and Supervisor daemons will use for storing small amounts of state. You must create these directories and give them proper permissions on each machine that'll be running Nimbus and workers.	`storm.local.dir: "storm-` `local"`

`java.library.path`	The location of the Java installation.	`java.library.path: "/usr/`
		`local/lib:/opt/local/`
		`lib:/usr/lib"`

`nimbus.host`	The hostname of the Nimbus machine.	`nimbus.host: "localhost"`

`supervisor.slots.ports`	For each worker machine, the ports that are used for receiving messages. The number of available ports will determine the number of worker processes Storm runs on each worker machine.	`supervisor.slots.ports:`
		`  – 6700`
		`  – 6701`
		`  – 6702`
		`  – 6703`

You'll need to update the configuration on each node in the cluster. Doing so can become tedious if you have a cluster containing several worker nodes. For this reason, we recommend using an external tool such as Puppet[3] for automating the deployment and configuration of each node.

5.3.5   *Launching Nimbus and Supervisors under supervision*

As mentioned earlier, running daemons under supervision is a critical step in setting up a Storm cluster. The supervisory processes allow our system to be fault-tolerant. What does this mean exactly? Why is it needed?

Storm is a fail-fast system, meaning that any Storm process encountering an unexpected error will stop. Storm is designed so that any process can safely stop at any point and recover when the process is restarted. Running these processes under

---

[3] http://puppetlabs.com/

supervision allows them to be restarted whenever a failure occurs. Thus, your topologies are unaffected by failures in the Storm daemons. To run the Storm daemons under supervision, execute the following commands:

- *Starting Nimbus*—Run `bin/storm nimbus` under supervision on the master machine.
- *Starting Supervisors*—Run `bin/storm supervisor` under supervision on each worker machine.
- *Storm UI*—Run `bin/storm ui` under supervision on the master machine.

Running the Storm daemons is the last step in setting up a Storm cluster. With everything up and running, your cluster is ready to start accepting topologies. Let's see how you go about getting your topology to run on a Storm cluster.

5.4 Getting your topology to run on a Storm cluster

In previous chapters we've run our topologies locally. This approach is fine for learning the fundamentals of Storm. But if one wants to reap the benefits Storm provides (especially along the lines of guaranteed message processing and parallelism), a remote Storm cluster is required. In this section we'll show you how to do this by taking some of the code from the credit card authorization topology in chapter 4 and doing the following:

- Revisit the code for wiring together the topology components
- Show the code for running that topology in local mode
- Show the code for running that topology on a remote Storm cluster
- Show how to package and deploy that code to the remote Storm cluster

5.4.1 Revisiting how to put together the topology components

Before we get into the code for running a topology in both local mode and on a remote cluster, let's quickly rehash the code for wiring together the components for the topology from chapter 4, the credit card authorization topology, to provide some context. We've already presented some of this code in section 5.1.2, but the next listing shows it in a more structured format.

> **Listing 5.2** `CreditCardTopologyBuilder.java` **for building the credit card authorization topology**

```
public class CreditCardTopologyBuilder {
  public static StormTopology build() {
    TopologyBuilder builder = new TopologyBuilder();

    builder.setSpout("rabbitmq-spout", new RabbitMQSpout(), 1);

    builder.setBolt("check-status", new VerifyOrderStatus(), 1)
        .shuffleGrouping("rabbitmq-spout")
        .setNumTasks(2);

    builder.setBolt("authorize-card", new AuthorizeCreditCard(), 1)
        .shuffleGrouping("check-status")
        .setNumTasks(2);
```

```
builder.setBolt("notification", new ProcessedOrderNotification(), 1)
        .shuffleGrouping("authorize-card")
        .setNumTasks(1);

    return builder.createTopology();
    }
}
```

We've encapsulated the code for building the topology in CreditCardTopology-Builder.java because this code doesn't change, regardless of whether we're running in local mode or on a Storm cluster. This is something we started doing in chapter 3 and the advantage of this approach is it allows us to call the code for building the topology from multiple places without having to duplicate code.

Now that we have the code for building the topology, we'll show you how to take this built topology and run it locally.

5.4.2 Running topologies in local mode

Local mode is useful when developing topologies. It allows you to simulate a Storm cluster in process on your local machine so you can quickly develop and test your topologies. This provides the benefit of a quick turnaround between making a change in code and functionally testing that change in a running topology. There are some drawbacks to local mode, though:

- You can't achieve the parallelism you would with a remote Storm cluster. This makes testing parallelism changes difficult, if not impossible in local mode.
- Local mode won't reveal potential serialization issues when Nimbus attempts to serialize instances of spouts and bolts to the individual worker nodes.

The following listing shows the class, `LocalTopologyRunner`, with a `main()` method that takes the topology we built in listing 5.2 and runs it locally.

Listing 5.3 `LocalTopologyRunner.java`, which runs the topology on a local cluster

```
public class LocalTopologyRunner {
  public static void main(String[] args) {
    StormTopology topology = CreditCardTopologyBuilder.build();

    Config config = new Config();
    config.setDebug(true);

    LocalCluster cluster = new LocalCluster();
    cluster.submitTopology("local-credit-card-topology",
                           config,
                           topology);
  }
}
```

Using the CreditCard-Topology-Builder to build the topology

Normally we run in debug mode when running locally to gain insights into the inner workings of the topology.

Simulates a Storm cluster locally in memory

Submit the topology to the local cluster, passing in the topology name, configuration, and topology.

The code in this listing should be familiar to you. What we have yet to address is the code for submitting the topology to a remote Storm cluster. Fortunately, this code isn't that much different. Let's take a look.

5.4.3 Running topologies on a remote Storm cluster

The code for running your topology remotely is similar to running it locally. The only difference is the code for submitting the topology to a cluster. You may also want a slightly different configuration as well, because local mode doesn't support some of the things (parallelism and guaranteed message processing) that a remote cluster supports. The next listing shows this code in a class we call `RemoteTopologyRunner`.

> **Listing 5.4 `RemoteTopologyRunner`, which submits the topology to a remote cluster**

```
public class RemoteTopologyRunner {
    public static void main(String[] args) {
        StormTopology topology = CreditCardTopologyBuilder.build();

        Config config = new Config();
        config.setNumWorkers(2);
        config.setMessageTimeoutSecs(60);

        StormSubmitter.submitTopology("credit-card-topology",
                                       config,
                                       topology);
    }
}
```

Using the CreditCard-Topology-Builder to build the topology

Set the number of worker processes (JVMs) to 2. This is a config item that we usually tweak only when running a topology on a remote cluster.

Using StormSubmitter to submit the topology to the remote cluster, passing in topology name, configuration, and the topology

Configure how long each tuple tree has to complete before it gets failed automatically.

You'll notice that the only differences are a slightly different configuration and using `StormSubmitter.submitTopology` instead of `LocalCluster.submitTopology`.

> **NOTE** We've wrapped the building, running locally, and running remotely of our topology within three different classes (`CreditCardTopologyBuilder`, `LocalTopologyRunner`, and `RemoteTopologyRunner`). Although you can set up your code however you please, we've found this split works well and we use it across all our topologies.

Now that we've written the code for running our topologies on a remote cluster, let's shift our attention to physically getting that code onto the Storm cluster so it can be run.

5.4.4 Deploying a topology to a remote Storm cluster

What does it mean to "deploy" your topology to a Storm cluster? By "deploy," we mean physically copying a JAR containing your topology's compiled code to the cluster so it can be run. You will need to deploy your topology from a machine with a properly-configured Storm installation. Figure 5.6 provides a refresher on the extracted contents of a Storm release zip.

You'll want to make sure you update the /opt/storm/conf/storm.yaml file so the nimbus.host property is set to the proper location. We're also interested in the /opt/storm/bin/storm file for this step: this is the executable you'll run in order to deploy your topology JAR to the remote cluster. Figure 5.7 shows the command you'd run to deploy your topology. You'll notice in the figure that we reference the full location for the storm executable via /opt/storm/bin/storm. If you don't want to do this, put /opt/storm/bin on your PATH and you can directly reference the storm command from anywhere on your machine.

After you execute the command in figure 5.7, your topology will be up and running on the Storm cluster. Once your topology is running, how do you know it's actually working and processing data as expected? This is where you'd look to the Storm UI, which is discussed next.

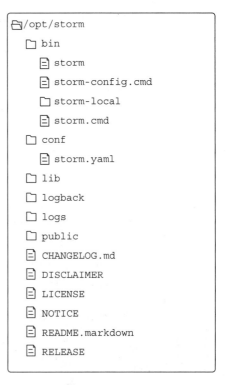

Figure 5.6 Extracted contents of a Storm release zip

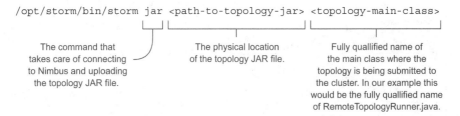

Figure 5.7 The command for deploying your topology to a Storm cluster

5.5   *The Storm UI and its role in the Storm cluster*

The Storm UI is the central place to find diagnostics on the Storm cluster and individual topologies. As mentioned in section 5.3.5, running the command /bin/storm ui on Nimbus will start the Storm UI. Two properties in defaults.yaml affect where to find the Storm UI:

1 nimbus.host—The hostname of the Nimbus machine
2 ui.port—The port number to serve up the Storm UI (defaults to 8080)

Once it's running, enter http://{nimbus.host}:{ui.port} in a web browser to get to the Storm UI.

The Storm UI has several sections:

- The Cluster Summary screen
- The individual topology summary screen
- Screens for each of the spouts and bolts

Each screen shows information related to different parts of the Storm cluster at varying levels of granularity. The Cluster Summary screen is related to the Storm cluster as a whole, as seen in figure 5.8.

Clicking on a particular topology link (such as github-commit-count in figure 5.8) takes you to a topology summary screen. This screen shows information related to the specific topology, as you can see in figure 5.9.

Let's delve into each screen in more detail next.

5.5.1   *Storm UI: the Storm cluster summary*

The Storm Cluster Summary consists of four parts, as shown in figure 5.10.

Each section of this screen is explained in more detail in the following sections.

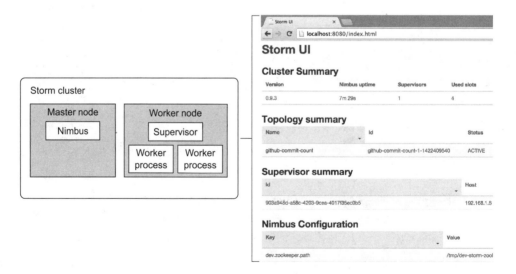

Figure 5.8   The Cluster Summary screen shows details for the entire Storm cluster.

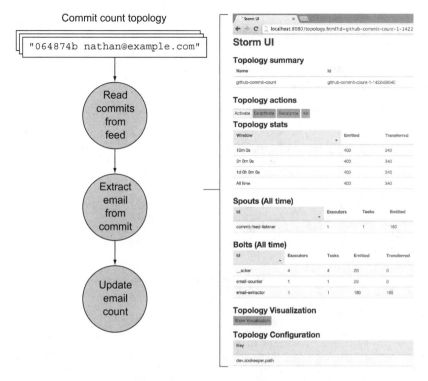

Figure 5.9   The Topology summary screen shows details for a specific topology.

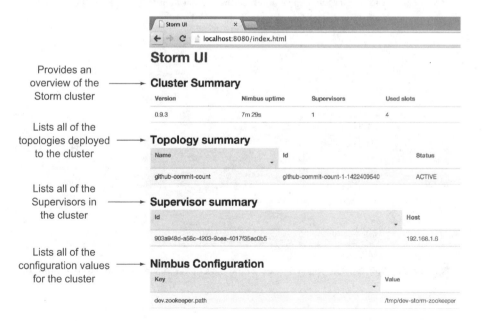

Figure 5.10   The Cluster Summary screen of the Storm UI

CLUSTER SUMMARY

The Cluster Summary section provides a small but useful overview of your Storm cluster. You'll notice the term *slots* in figure 5.11. A slot corresponds to a worker process, so a cluster with two used slots means there are two worker processes running on that cluster. Figure 5.11 provides more detail on each of the columns in this section.

TOPOLOGY SUMMARY

The Topology summary lists all of the topologies deployed to the cluster. Figure 5.12 provides more detail on what information you see in this section.

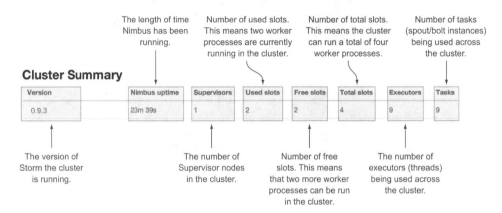

Figure 5.11   The Cluster Summary section on the Cluster Summary screen of the Storm UI

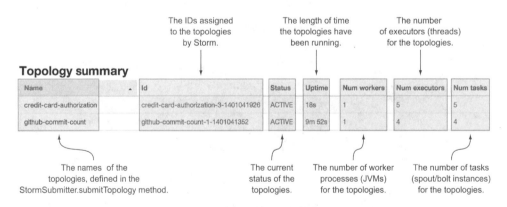

Figure 5.12   The Topology summary section on the Cluster Summary screen of the Storm UI

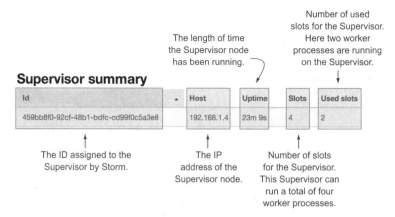

Figure 5.13   The Supervisor summary section on the Cluster Summary screen of the Storm UI

SUPERVISOR SUMMARY

The Supervisor summary lists all the Supervisors in the cluster. Again, you'll notice the term slots in figure 5.13. This corresponds to a worker process on a particular Supervisor node. Figure 5.13 provides more detail on what information you see in this section.

NIMBUS CONFIGURATION

The Nimbus Configuration lists the configuration defined in defaults.yaml and any overridden values in storm.yaml. Figure 5.14 provides more detail on what information you see in this section.

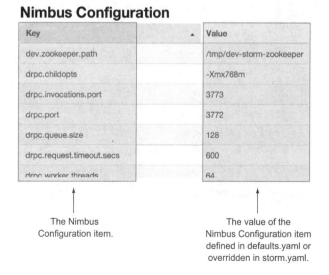

Figure 5.14   The Nimbus Configuration section on the Cluster Summary screen of the Storm UI

Having covered the Cluster Summary screen, let's dive into what the screen for an individual topology looks like. You can access this screen by clicking on a given topology name in the list of topologies.

5.5.2   *Storm UI: individual Topology summary*

The sections of the individual Topology summary screen can be seen in figure 5.15. Each section of this screen is explained in more detail in the following sections.

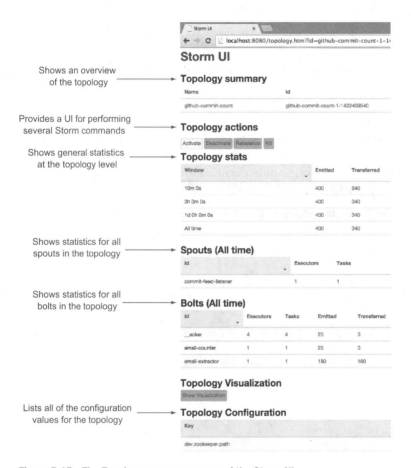

Figure 5.15   The Topology summary screen of the Storm UI

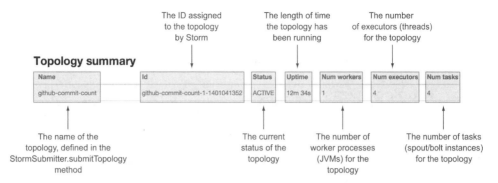

Figure 5.16   The Topology summary section on the Topology summary screen of the Storm UI

TOPOLOGY SUMMARY

The Topology summary provides a small but useful overview of the topology being observed. Figure 5.16 provides more detail on each of the individual columns in this section.

TOPOLOGY ACTIONS

The Topology actions section provides a UI for activating, deactivating, rebalancing, and killing your topology. Figure 5.17 describes these actions in more detail.

TOPOLOGY STATS

The Topology stats section provides some general statistics at the topology level. These statistics can be shown for all time, the past 10 minutes, the past 3 hours, or the past day. The time interval that's selected is also applied to the spout and bolt stats sections, which are described next. Figure 5.18 provides more detail on the information you see in this section.

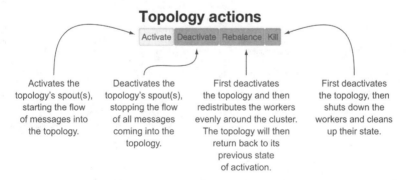

Figure 5.17   The Topology actions section on the Topology summary screen of the Storm UI

Topology stats

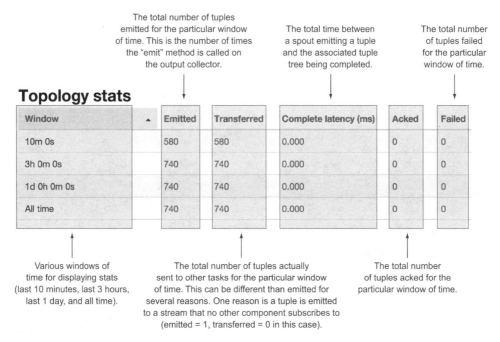

Figure 5.18 The Topology stats section on the Topology summary screen of the Storm UI

SPOUT STATS

The Spouts section shows the statistics for all spouts in the topology. The statistics are for the window of time that's selected in the Topology Stats section (all time, the past 10 minutes, the past 3 hours, or the past day). Figure 5.19 provides more detail on the information you see in this section.

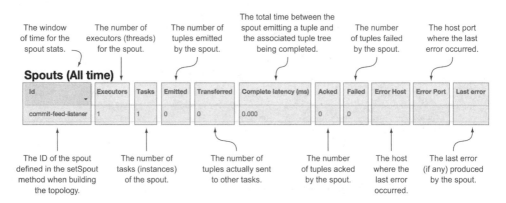

Figure 5.19 The Spouts section on the Topology summary screen of the Storm UI

BOLT STATS

The Bolts section shows the statistics for all bolts in the topology. The statistics are for the window of time that's selected in the Topology Stats section (all time, the past 10 minutes, the past 3 hours, or the past day). Figure 5.20 provides more detail up to the Capacity column. Figure 5.21 offers more detail on the remaining columns.

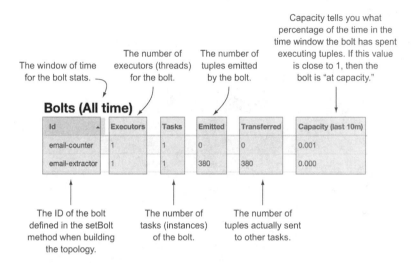

Figure 5.20 The Bolts section on the Topology summary screen of the Storm UI, up to Capacity column

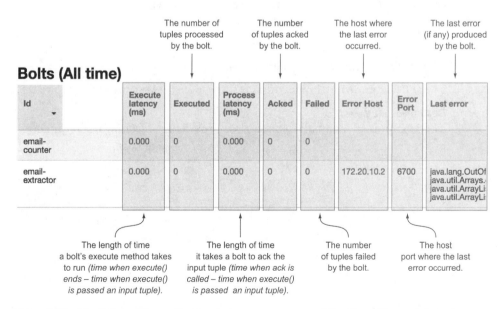

Figure 5.21 The Bolts section on the Topology summary screen of the Storm UI, remaining columns

TOPOLOGY CONFIGURATION

The Topology Configuration lists the configuration defined for the particular topology being viewed. Figure 5.22 provides more detail on what information you see in this section.

From the Topology summary screen, you can dive into one of the individual spouts or bolts. You access an individual spout or bolt by clicking on a spout or bolt name while on the Topology summary screen.

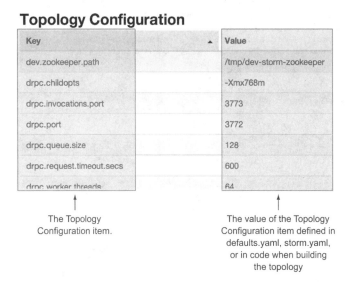

Figure 5.22   The Topology Configuration section on the Topology summary screen of the Storm UI

5.5.3   *Storm UI: individual spout/bolt summary*

In the UI, an individual bolt contains six sections, as you can see in figure 5.23.

COMPONENT SUMMARY

The Component summary section shows some high-level information about the bolt or spout being observed. Figure 5.24 provides more details.

Provides an overview of the component in question, in this case, the email extractor bolt.

Shows general statistics for the bolt.

Shows statistics related to input tuples being processed by the bolt.

Shows statistics related to output tuples being emitted by the bolt.

Shows statistics for the executors (threads) executing the bolt.

Displays errors that have occurred in the bolt.

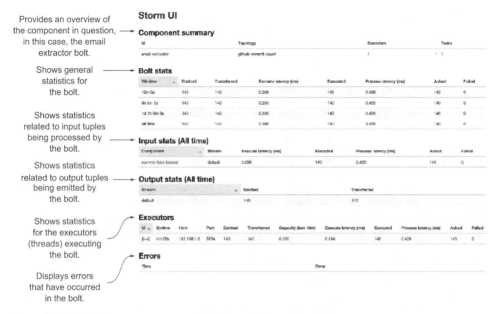

Figure 5.23   The bolt summary screen in the Storm UI

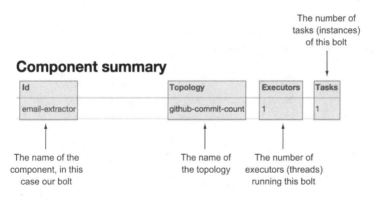

The number of tasks (instances) of this bolt

The name of the component, in this case our bolt

The name of the topology

The number of executors (threads) running this bolt

Figure 5.24   The Component Summary section for a bolt in the Storm UI

BOLT STATS

The Bolt stats section provides much of the same information that you saw in the Bolts section for the Topology summary, but the information is limited to an individual bolt (see figure 5.25).

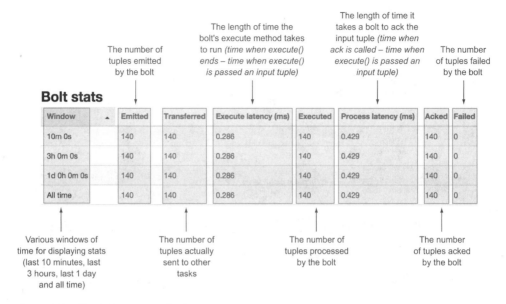

Figure 5.25   The Bolt stats section in the Storm UI

INPUT STATS

The Input stats section shows statistics related to tuples being consumed by the bolt. The statistics are relative to a particular stream; in this case it's the "default" stream. Figure 5.26 goes into more detail about this section.

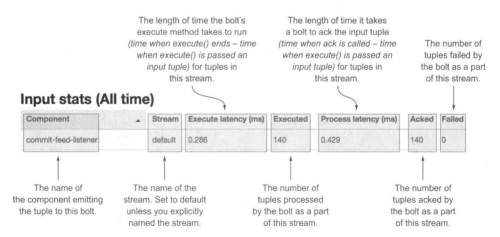

Figure 5.26   The Input stats section for a bolt in the Storm UI

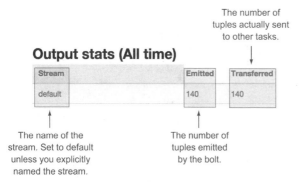

Figure 5.27 The Output stats section for a bolt in the Storm UI

OUTPUT STATS

The Output stats section shows statistics related to tuples being emitted by the bolt (see figure 5.27).

EXECUTORS

The Executors section shows the statistics for all executors running instances of the particular bolt. We've split this section into two figures. Figure 5.28 shows the first part and figure 5.29 shows the second.

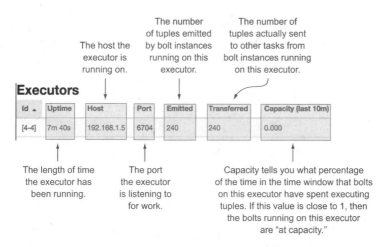

Figure 5.28 The Executors section for a bolt in the Storm UI, through Capacity column

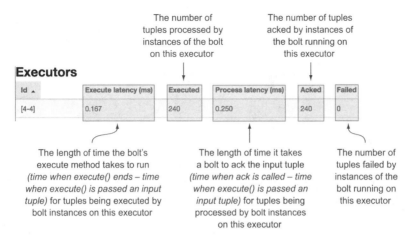

Figure 5.29   The Executors section for a bolt in the Storm UI, remaining columns

ERRORS

The Errors section shows you a history of errors experienced by this bolt, as you can see in figure 5.30.

The Storm UI provides a wealth of information, giving you a clear picture of how your topology is operating in production. With the Storm UI, you can quickly tell if your topology is healthy or if something is amiss. You should easily be able to spot errors your topology is encountering while also being able to quickly identify other issues, such as bottlenecks.

As you can probably imagine, once you deploy your topology to a production Storm cluster, your job as a developer doesn't end. Once it's deployed, you enter a whole new world of making sure your topology is running as efficiently as possible. This is the world of tuning and troubleshooting. We've devoted the next two chapters to those tasks.

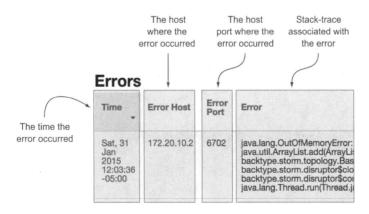

Figure 5.30   The Errors section for a bolt in the Storm UI

This chapter laid the foundation for tuning by explaining the parts of a Storm cluster and what each part of the Storm cluster does. We also provided a thorough explanation of the primary tool you'll use while tuning and troubleshooting: the Storm UI.

5.6 *Summary*

In this chapter you learned the following:

- A Storm cluster consists of Nimbus, which acts as the control center, and Supervisors, which execute the logic in the instances of spouts and bolts.
- A Zookeeper cluster is necessary to run alongside a Storm cluster as it coordinates communication between Nimbus/Supervisors while also maintaining state.
- Supervisors run worker processes (JVMs), which in turn run executors (threads) and tasks (instances of spouts/bolts).
- How to install a Storm cluster, including the key configuration options that must be set in order to get the cluster running.
- How to deploy your topologies to a Storm cluster and how running them on the cluster is really no different than running them locally.
- What the Storm UI is and how the different parts of the Storm ecosystem map to the different screens of the Storm UI.
- What information each section of the Storm UI provides and how these pieces of information may be useful for tuning and troubleshooting your topologies.

Tuning in Storm

So far, we've given you as gentle an introduction to Storm concepts as we can. It's time to kick things up a notch. In this chapter, we'll discuss life as a developer after you've deployed your topology to a Storm cluster. You thought your job was over once the topology was deployed, didn't you? Think again! Once you deploy your topology, you need to make sure it's running as efficiently as possible. That's why we've devoted two chapters to tuning and troubleshooting.

We'll briefly revisit the Storm UI, because this will be the most important tool you'll use to determine whether your topology is running efficiently. Then we'll outline a repeatable process you can use in order to identify bottlenecks and resolve those bottlenecks. Our lesson on tuning doesn't end there—we still need to discuss one of the greatest enemies of fast code: latency. We'll conclude by covering Storm's metrics-collecting API as well as introduce a few custom metrics of our own. After all, knowing exactly what your topology is doing is an important part of understanding how to make it faster.

NOTE In this chapter, we have you check out source code from GitHub when running through the tuning examples. To check out this code, run the following command: `git checkout [tag]`, replacing `[tag]` with a version of the code we specify. The GitHub repository is located at https://github.com/Storm-Applied/C6-Flash-sale-recommender.

Before we get into each of these topics, let's set the stage with a use case that will serve as our example throughout the chapter: Daily Deals! reborn.

6.1 *Problem definition: Daily Deals! reborn*

Here's the story. We work for an up-and-coming flash sale site. Every day, we put a number of items on sale for a short period of time and watch the traffic roll in. Over time, the number of sales per day has been growing and it's become difficult for customers to find sales they're interested in. Another team at our company has built an online "Find My Sale!" recommendation system. Find My Sale! narrows down the number of products customers might be interested in. It starts with some basic information the customer has given but also incorporates purchase history, browsing history, and so forth to try to get sales in which customers will most likely be interested in front of them. Our website interacts with this system via an HTTP API where we pass a customer identifier and get back a list of recommendation identifiers. We can then turn around and look up the details of those sales and display them to the customer on site.

It has been a great boon to the company and has helped fuel excellent growth. At the same time, we have an aging "Daily Deals!" email that has survived from the early days of the company about upcoming sales. In the beginning, its one sale per email was quite effective. Eventually it was changed to use a basic heuristic of getting a decent upcoming sale in our customers' inboxes every day. Over time, the effectiveness of the email has declined. Early testing indicates that the problem is that the contents of the email simply aren't relevant anymore. With many sales every day, the simple heuristic isn't picking highly relevant sales to send; it picks only moderately relevant ones.

We've been tasked with a new initiative: crafting an email to replace Daily Deals! that will be sent to customers once a day with any sales coming the next day that Find My Sales! targets as being of interest to the customer. We want to use the Find My Sale! system to improve relevancy and hopefully the click-through rate and eventual sales on site. There's a caveat or two, though. Find My Sale! is purely an online system where currently the recommending of sales is somewhat tangled up with its external HTTP interface. Before we consider rewriting it, we want to validate our idea that more relevant Daily Deals! emails are going to have a significant impact on business (some members of the team think the current emails are good enough and increased relevancy isn't going to result in more than a small uptick in traffic).

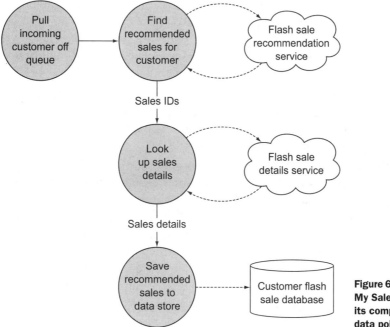

Figure 6.1   The Find My Sale! topology: its components and data points

6.1.1   *Formation of a conceptual solution*

We set about designing a solution that will handle the email creation. It consumes an incoming stream of customer information and makes a real-time call to Find My Sale! to find any upcoming flash sales that would be of interest. (We've had to modify Find My Sale! slightly—normally it only considers active sales, but we've changed it to take a date range of active times to consider.) We then look up information about those sales and finally store it for another process that performs the email sending. Figure 6.1 gives a general overview of this design.

The design is fairly straightforward; it has four components that talk to two external services and one database. With this design in hand, let's turn our focus to how it maps to Storm concepts.

6.1.2   *Mapping the solution to Storm concepts*

This design maps in Storm terms to a fairly simple topology to start. We have a spout that emits customer information, which in turn hands it off to the Find My Sale bolt, which interacts with the external service. Any found sales are emitted along with the customer information to a bolt that looks up information about the sale, which emits that information with the customer information to a persistence bolt that stores the information so another process can pick it up later for sending the email. Figure 6.2 illustrates the design mapped to these Storm concepts.

The mapping of our design to Storm concepts follows a pattern similar to the one found in chapters 2–4. We have a spout acting as the source of tuples, with three bolts

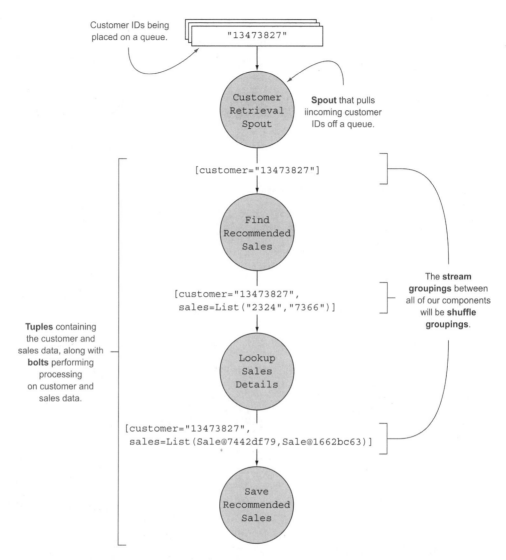

Figure 6.2 The Find My Sale! design mapped to Storm concepts

performing transformations on these tuples. We'll now show you a first-pass implementation of this design in code.

6.2 *Initial implementation*

Before we get into the implementation of the design, it's important to keep in mind a couple of interfaces that will be referenced frequently in the following code:

- `TopologyBuilder`—Exposes the API for specifying a topology for Storm to execute
- `OutputCollector`—The core API for emitting and failing tuples

We'll start with `FlashSaleTopologyBuilder`, which is responsible for connecting our spout and bolts (see the following listing). All work for building the topology is handled in this class, regardless of how we are going to run it: in local mode or deploying to a remote cluster.

Listing 6.1 FlashSaleTopologyBuilder.java

```java
public class FlashSaleTopologyBuilder {
  public static final String CUSTOMER_RETRIEVAL_SPOUT = "customer-retrieval";
  public static final String FIND_RECOMMENDED_SALES = "find-recommended-sales";
  public static final String LOOKUP_SALES_DETAILS = "lookup-sales-details";
  public static final String SAVE_RECOMMENDED_SALES = "save-recommended-sales";

  public static StormTopology build() {
    TopologyBuilder builder = new TopologyBuilder();

    builder.setSpout(CUSTOMER_RETRIEVAL_SPOUT, new CustomerRetrievalSpout())
        .setMaxSpoutPending(250);

    builder.setBolt(FIND_RECOMMENDED_SALES, new FindRecommendedSales(), 1)
        .setNumTasks(1)
        .shuffleGrouping(CUSTOMER_RETRIEVAL_SPOUT);

    builder.setBolt(LOOKUP_SALES_DETAILS, new LookupSalesDetails(), 1)
        .setNumTasks(1)
        .shuffleGrouping(FIND_RECOMMENDED_SALES);

    builder.setBolt(SAVE_RECOMMENDED_SALES, new SaveRecommendedSales(), 1)
        .setNumTasks(1)
        .shuffleGrouping(LOOKUP_SALES_DETAILS);

    return builder.createTopology();
  }
}
```

Now that we've seen how to put all the components in our topology together via the `FlashSaleTopologyBuilder`, we'll go into more detail for each individual component, starting with the spout.

6.2.1 *Spout: read from a data source*

Data will flow into our topology through the spout. This data comes in the form of a single customer ID, as shown in figure 6.3.

But as in other topologies, we're going to cheat in order to get up and running quickly. For now, we'll have the spout generate data whenever its `nextTuple()` method is called rather than being hooked up to a real message queue, as shown in the following listing.

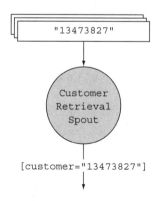

Figure 6.3 The spout emits a tuple for each customer ID that it receives.

Listing 6.2 `CustomerRetrievalSpout.nextTuple` generating customer IDs

```
...
@Override
public void nextTuple() {
  new LatencySimulator(1, 25, 10, 40, 5).simulate(1000);

  int numberPart = idGenerator.nextInt(9999999) + 1;
  String customerId = "customer-" + Integer.toString(numberPart);

  outputCollector.emit(new Values(customerId));
}
...
```

If we released our topology into a real production environment, the customer retrieval spout would be hooked up to a messaging bus like Kafka or RabbitMQ. We'd keep the list of customers we needed to process on a queue, and should our topology completely crash or otherwise come to a halt, we could restart and continue on from where we left off. Our stream of data has a durable home that's separate from the system that'll process it.

In addition, if we decided we didn't want to do this in a batch fashion, we'd have to convert it to a real-time system. With Storm and our design, we're processing our data as a stream but kicking off the run as a batch. We've separated the "how" of stream processing as a stream from the "when" of our batch orientation. Any time we want to, we could take this system from its current form as a batch system to a real-time system without changing anything about our topology.

Before we get to the meat of this chapter, let's step through each of our bolts and identify the important bits of logic.

6.2.2 Bolt: find recommended sales

The bolt that finds recommended sales accepts a customer ID in its input tuple and emits a tuple containing two values: the customer ID and a list of sales IDs. To retrieve the sales IDs, it makes a call to an external service. Figure 6.4 illustrates where we are in the topology.

The implementation of this bolt is seen in the next listing.

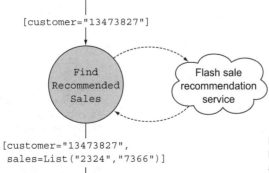

Figure 6.4 The `FindRecommendedSales` bolt accepts a customer ID in its input tuple and emits a tuple containing a customer ID and a list of sales IDs.

Listing 6.3 `FindRecommendedSales.java`

```java
public class FindRecommendedSales extends BaseBasicBolt {
  private final static int TIMEOUT = 200;
  private FlashSaleRecommendationClient client;

  @Override
  public void prepare(Map config,
                         TopologyContext context) {
    client = new FlashSaleRecommendationClient(TIMEOUT);
  }

  @Override
  public void execute(Tuple tuple,
                         BasicOutputCollector outputCollector) {
    String customerId = tuple.getStringByField("customer");

    try {
      List<String> sales = client.findSalesFor(customerId);
      if (!sales.isEmpty()) {
        outputCollector.emit(new Values(customerId, sales));
      }
    } catch (Timeout e) {
      throw new ReportedFailedException(e);
    }
  }
  ...
}
```

Instantiate a client for communicating with the flash sales recommendation service, timing out if a request to this service takes over 200 ms.

Retrieve recommended sales for the customer.

If we find recommended sales for the customer, emit the entire list in one tuple.

This exception is thrown if the call to the flash sales recommendation service takes over 200 ms.

Throwing this type of exception will allow us to see the latest error in the Storm UI.

All we're getting back from our `client.findSalesFor` call is a list of sales identifiers. To send our email, we'll need some additional information about the product and sale. This is where our next bolt comes into play.

6.2.3   *Bolt: look up details for each sale*

To send a meaningful email with details about each sale, we need to look up the details for each of the recommended sales. The bolt that does this accepts a tuple containing the customer ID and list of sales IDs, looks up the details for each sale by making a call to an external service, and emits a tuple containing the customer ID and a list of `Sale` objects containing the details for each sale (see figure 6.5).

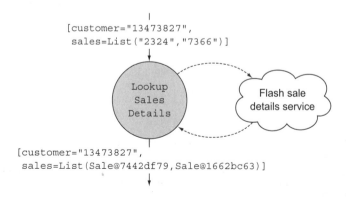

Figure 6.5   The bolt for looking up sales details accepts a customer ID and list of sales IDs in its input tuple and emits a tuple containing a customer ID and list of `Sale` objects containing the details of each sale.

The following listing shows the implementation for the `LookupSalesDetails` bolt.

Listing 6.4   `LookupSalesDetails.java`

```
public class LookupSalesDetails extends BaseRichBolt {
  private final static int TIMEOUT = 100;
  private FlashSaleClient client;
  private OutputCollector outputCollector;

  @Override
  public void prepare(Map config,
                      TopologyContext context,
                      OutputCollector outputCollector) {
    this.outputCollector = outputCollector;
    client = new FlashSaleClient(TIMEOUT);
  }

  @Override
  public void execute(Tuple tuple) {
    String customerId = tuple.getStringByField("customer");
    List<String> saleIds = (List<String>) tuple.getValueByField("sales");

    List<Sale> sales = new ArrayList<Sale>();
    for (String saleId: saleIds) {
      try {
        Sale sale = client.lookupSale(saleId);
        sales.add(sale);
      } catch (Timeout e) {
        outputCollector.reportError(e);
      }
    }

    if (sales.isEmpty()) {
      outputCollector.fail(tuple);
    } else {
      outputCollector.emit(new Values(customerId, sales));
      outputCollector.ack(tuple);
    }
  }
  ...
}
```

Assign an instance of the output collector so we have more control over reporting individual failures, failing the input tuple and acking the input tuple.

Instantiate a client for communicating with the flash sales service that times out if a request to this service takes over 100ms.

Look up the details for an individual recommended sale.

Iterate over each of the recommended sales for the particular customer.

This exception is thrown if the call to the flash sales service takes over 100ms.

If a timeout occurs for a single sale lookup, report the error but continue processing the other recommended sales.

If we couldn't look up any sales details, then we fail the input tuple.

Otherwise we emit a new tuple containing the customer ID and sales details ...

... and ack the input tuple.

The one big difference between this bolt and the previous one is that this one can both succeed and fail at the same time. We could attempt to look up ten sales, get nine, and not get one. To handle this more complicated definition of success, we extend `BaseRichBolt` and manually ack tuples ourselves. As long as we can look up at least one of the sales from the sale IDs obtained from our input tuple, we'll call it a success and move on. Our main priority is to get as many emails out on time as possible.

This leads us to our last bolt, where we'll save the results to a database for sending via another process.

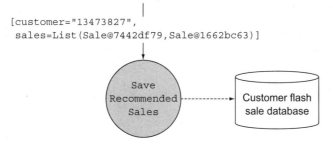

```
[customer="13473827",
 sales=List(Sale@7442df79,Sale@1662bc63)]
```

Figure 6.6 The save recommended sales bolt accepts an input tuple containing the customer ID and a list of Sale objects and persists that information to a database.

6.2.4 Bolt: save recommended sales

The bolt that saves the recommended sales accepts an input tuple containing a customer ID and a list of Sale objects with the details for each sale. It then persists that data to a database for later processing, emitting no tuples because this is the last bolt in our topology (see figure 6.6).

The next listing shows the implementation for SaveRecommendedSales.

Listing 6.5 SaveRecommendedSales.java

```
public class SaveRecommendedSales extends BaseBasicBolt {
  private final static int TIMEOUT = 50;
  private DatabaseClient dbClient;

  @Override
  public void prepare(Map config,
                      TopologyContext context) {
    dbClient = new DatabaseClient(TIMEOUT);
  }

  @Override
  public void execute(Tuple tuple,
                      BasicOutputCollector outputCollector) {
    String customerId = tuple.getStringByField("customer");
    List<Sale> sales = (List<Sale>) tuple.getValueByField("sales");

    try {
      dbClient.save(customerId, sales);
    } catch (Timeout e) {
      throw new ReportedFailedException(e);
    }
  }

  ...
}
```

Instantiate a client for communicating with the database, timing out if a request to the database takes over 50 ms.

Attempt to save the customer and their associated sales details to the database.

This exception is thrown if the call to the database takes over 50 ms.

Throwing this type of exception will allow us to see the latest error in the Storm UI.

The same patterns we used in the previous two bolts are used here as well. There's our logic. It all looks sound. Imagine we've done some testing of our topology and its working but it's far from ready to be released into production. Is it going to be fast enough? It's hard to tell. Let's see how we would go about finding out.

6.3   *Tuning: I wanna go fast*

How does one go about tuning their topologies? It may seem like a daunting task at first, but Storm provides us with tools that can be used to quickly identify bottlenecks, allowing us to take steps to alleviate those bottlenecks. Using the Storm UI and metrics-collecting API, you have tools at your disposal to establish a repeatable process you can use for tuning your topologies.

6.3.1   *The Storm UI: your go-to tool for tuning*

An understanding of the Storm UI is essential because it's the primary tool that will give us feedback on whether your tuning efforts are having any effect. Figure 6.7 gives a quick refresher on the Topology summary screen of the Storm UI.

As you'll recall, there are seven sections in the UI for a single topology:

- *Topology summary*—Shows the status, uptime, and the number of workers, executors and tasks assigned to the entire topology.
- *Topology actions*—Allows you to deactivate, rebalance, or kill your topology straight from the UI.
- *Topology stats*—Shows high-level statistics for the entire topology across four time windows; one of those windows is All Time.
- *Spouts (All time)*—Shows the statistics for your spout(s) across all time. This includes the number of executors and tasks; the number of tuples that have been emitted, acked, and failed by the spout(s); and the last error (if there has been one) associated with the spout(s).

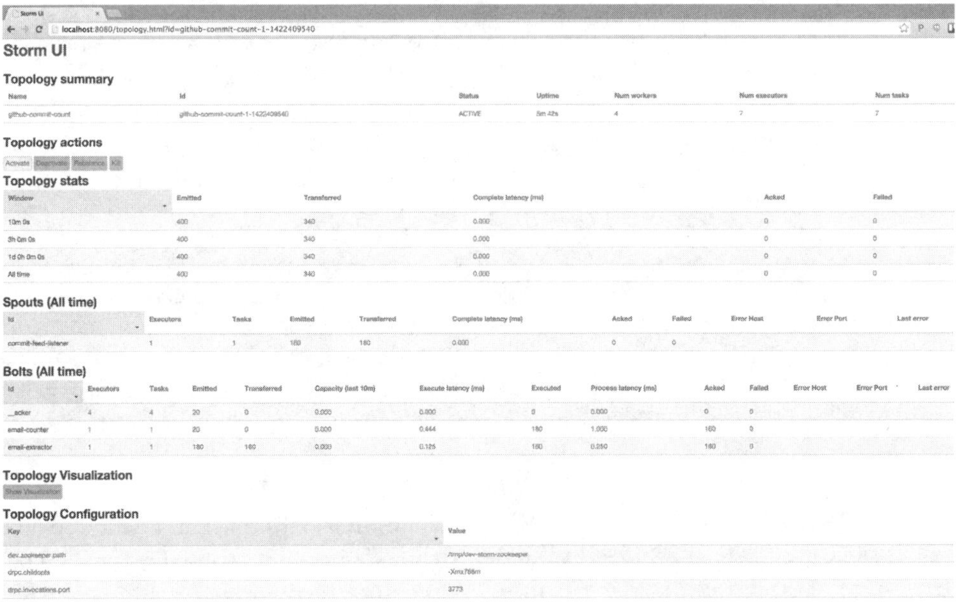

Figure 6.7   Topology summary screen of the Storm UI

- *Bolts (All time)*—Shows your statistics for your bolt(s) across all time. This includes the number of executors and tasks; the number of tuples that have been emitted, acked, and failed by the bolt(s); some metrics related to latency and how busy the bolt(s) are; and the last error (if there has been one) associated with the bolt(s).
- *Visualization*—Shows a visualization of the spouts, bolts, how they are connected, and the flow of tuples between all of the streams.
- *Topology Configuration*—Shows all the configuration options that have been set for your topology.

We'll focus on the Bolts section of the UI for our tuning lesson. Before we get into figuring out what needs to be tuned and how, we need to define a set of baseline numbers for our topology.

Defining your service level agreement (SLA)

Before you start analyzing whether your topology is a finely tuned machine, ask yourself what *fast enough* means to you. What velocity do you need to hit? Think of Twitter's trending topics for a moment. If it took eight hours to process every tweet, those topics wouldn't be anywhere near as trending as they are on the site. A SLA could be fairly flexible in regard to time "within an hour" but rigid according to data flow. Events can't back up beyond a certain point; there's a queue out there somewhere, holding onto all the data that's going to be processed. After a certain high watermark is set, we need to be consuming data as fast as it's going on, lest we hit a queue limit or, worse, cause an out-of-memory error.

For our use case, where we're processing a stream in a batch-like fashion, our SLA is different. We need to have fully processed all our data in time for our email to go out. *Fast enough* has a couple of simple metrics: 1) Did it finish on time? 2) As we process more data each day, will it continue to finish on time?

Let's make our SLA a little more real. It takes a while to process all these emails (say 60 minutes) before sending. And we want to start sending at 8 a.m. every morning. Deals for the coming day can be entered until 11 p.m. and we can't start processing until after that. This gives us eight hours from the time we start to when we have to finish. Currently we have 20 million customers—which means that to barely hit our mark we need to process some 695 customers per second. That's cutting it pretty close; we decide for our first pass we need to feel confident in finishing in seven hours. That's 794 customers a second, and, given our growth, we want to rapidly ramp up to being done within three hours so we don't have to worry about tuning for a while. To do that, we need to process 1,852 customers a second.

6.3.2   *Establishing a baseline set of performance numbers*

Time to dive into developing basic Storm tuning skills that can be used to take a topology and make it progressively faster. In our source code, you'll find version 0.0.1 of the Find My Sale! topology. To check out that specific version, use this command:

```
git checkout 0.0.1
```

While we're tuning, we need to pay attention to one primary class: FlashSaleTopology-Builder. This is where we build our topology and set the parallelism of each component. Let's take a look at its build method again to refresh your memory:

```
public static StormTopology build() {
  TopologyBuilder builder = new TopologyBuilder();

  builder.setSpout(CUSTOMER_RETRIEVAL_SPOUT, new CustomerRetrievalSpout())
      .setMaxSpoutPending(250);

  builder.setBolt(FIND_RECOMMENDED_SALES, new FindRecommendedSales(), 1)
      .setNumTasks(1)
      .shuffleGrouping(CUSTOMER_RETRIEVAL_SPOUT);

  builder.setBolt(LOOKUP_SALES_DETAILS, new LookupSalesDetails(), 1)
      .setNumTasks(1)
      .shuffleGrouping(FIND_RECOMMENDED_SALES);

  builder.setBolt(SAVE_RECOMMENDED_SALES, new SaveRecommendedSales(), 1)
      .setNumTasks(1)
      .shuffleGrouping(LOOKUP_SALES_DETAILS);

  return builder.createTopology();
}
```

Note that we're creating one executor (in the call to setBolt) and one task for each bolt (in setNumTasks). This will give us a basic baseline of how our topology is performing. Next we'll take it, deploy it to a remote cluster, and then run it with some customer data for 10–15 minutes, collecting basic data from the Storm UI. Figure 6.8 shows what we have at this point, with the important parts highlighted and annotated.

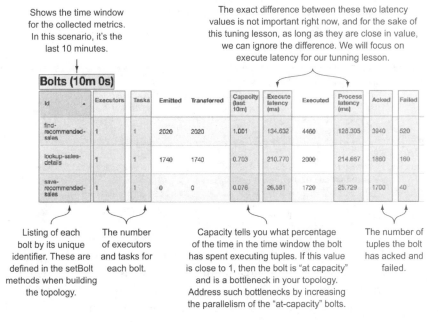

Figure 6.8   Identifying the important parts of the Storm UI for our tuning lesson

We now have a useful interface for displaying the metrics related to our topology along with a baseline set of performance numbers. The next step in the tuning process is to identify the bottlenecks in our topology and do something about them.

6.3.3   *Identifying bottlenecks*

What can we see from these metrics after our first run? Let's zero in on capacity. For two of our bolts, it's fairly high. The find-recommended-sales bolt is at 1.001 and the lookup-sales-details bolt is hovering around .7. The value of 1.001 indicates a bottleneck for find-recommended-sales. We're going to need to increase its parallelism. Given that lookup-sales-details is at .7, it's highly likely that opening up find-recommended-sales without also opening up lookup-sales-details will just turn it into a new bottleneck. Our intuition says they should be tuned in tandem. save-recommended-sales, on the other hand, is really low at 0.07 and probably won't be a bottleneck for quite some time.

Next, we'll guess how high we might want to take our parallelism, set our number of tasks to that, and release again. We'll show you the stats from that run as well so you can see that changing the number of tasks without changing the number of executors makes no difference.

You can check out version 0.0.2 of the code by executing this command:

```
git checkout 0.0.2
```

The only important change is in FlashSaleTopologyBuilder:

```
public static StormTopology build() {
  TopologyBuilder builder = new TopologyBuilder();

  builder.setSpout(CUSTOMER_RETRIEVAL_SPOUT, new CustomerRetrievalSpout())
        .setMaxSpoutPending(250);

  builder.setBolt(FIND_RECOMMENDED_SALES, new FindRecommendedSales(), 1)
        .setNumTasks(32)
        .shuffleGrouping(CUSTOMER_RETRIEVAL_SPOUT);

  builder.setBolt(LOOKUP_SALES_DETAILS, new LookupSalesDetails(), 1)
        .setNumTasks(32)
        .shuffleGrouping(FIND_RECOMMENDED_SALES);

  builder.setBolt(SAVE_RECOMMENDED_SALES, new SaveRecommendedSales(), 1)
        .setNumTasks(8)
        .shuffleGrouping(LOOKUP_SALES_DETAILS);

  return builder.createTopology();
}
```

Why 32, 32, and 8 for bolt tasks? We probably won't need more than 16, 16, and 4 when we're done, but it's smart to go with double that as a first pass. With this change in place, we don't need to release the topology multiple times. We can release just version 0.0.2 and use the rebalance command on our Nimbus node to adjust the parallelism of our running topology.

After release, we let it run for about 10–15 minutes. As you can see, the only meaningful change in the UI is the number of tasks per bolt.

What do we do next? Let's start by quadrupling the parallelism for both the `find-recommended-sales` and `lookup-sales-details` bolts by running the `rebalance` command.

> **NOTE** The `rebalance` command used throughout this chapter takes the form `storm rebalance topology-name -e [bolt-name]=[number-of-executors]`. This command will redistribute executors for the given bolt, allowing us to increase the parallelism for the given bolt on the fly. All `rebalance` commands assume we're running on our Nimbus node and that we have the Storm command in our `PATH`.

We'll run one `rebalance`, wait for the change to appear in the UI, and then run the second `rebalance` command:

```
storm rebalance flash-sale -e find-recommended-sales=4
storm rebalance flash-sale -e lookup-sales-details=4
```

Okay, our rebalance is done. It's 10 minutes later—let's see what we got (figure 6.9).

Here's something that might surprise you. We increased the parallelism of our `find-recommended-sales` bolt but there's no change in capacity. It's just as busy as it was before. How can that be possible? The flow of tuples coming in from the

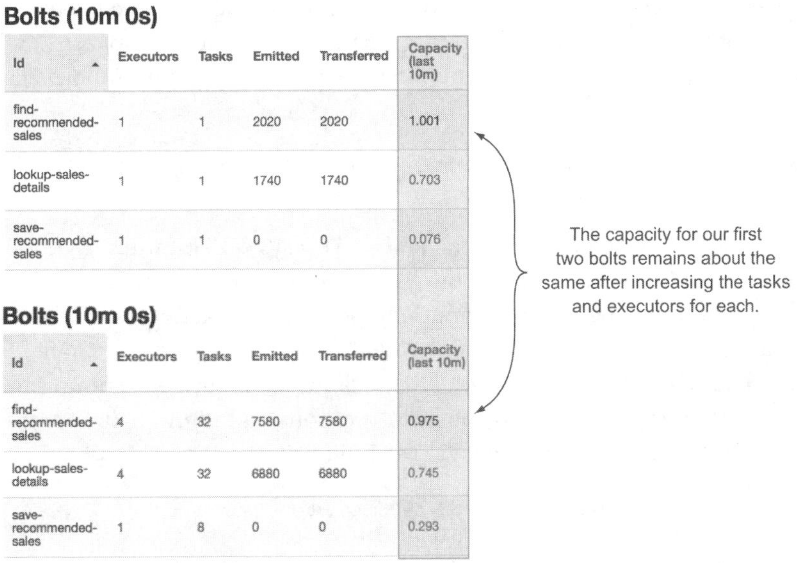

Bolts (10m 0s)

Id	Executors	Tasks	Emitted	Transferred	Capacity (last 10m)
find-recommended-sales	1	1	2020	2020	1.001
lookup-sales-details	1	1	1740	1740	0.703
save-recommended-sales	1	1	0	0	0.076

The capacity for our first two bolts remains about the same after increasing the tasks and executors for each.

Bolts (10m 0s)

Id	Executors	Tasks	Emitted	Transferred	Capacity (last 10m)
find-recommended-sales	4	32	7580	7580	0.975
lookup-sales-details	4	32	6880	6880	0.745
save-recommended-sales	1	8	0	0	0.293

Figure 6.9   Storm UI shows a minimal change in capacity after a first attempt at increasing parallelism for our first two bolts.

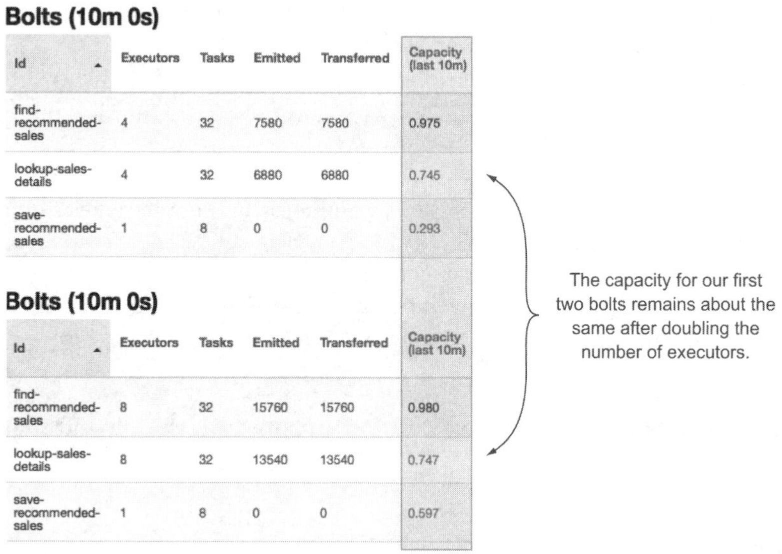

Bolts (10m 0s)

Id	Executors	Tasks	Emitted	Transferred	Capacity (last 10m)
find-recommended-sales	4	32	7580	7580	0.975
lookup-sales-details	4	32	6880	6880	0.745
save-recommended-sales	1	8	0	0	0.293

Bolts (10m 0s)

Id	Executors	Tasks	Emitted	Transferred	Capacity (last 10m)
find-recommended-sales	8	32	15760	15760	0.980
lookup-sales-details	8	32	13540	13540	0.747
save-recommended-sales	1	8	0	0	0.597

The capacity for our first two bolts remains about the same after doubling the number of executors.

Figure 6.10 Storm UI showing minimal change in capacity after doubling the number of executors for our first two bolts

spout was unaffected; our bolt was/is a bottleneck. If we were using a real queue, messages would've backed up on that queue as a result. Note the capacity metrics of the `save-recommended-sales` bolt has gone up to about 0.3 as well. That's still fairly low, so we don't have to worry about that becoming a bottleneck yet.

Let's try that again, this time doubling the parallelism of both bolts. That has to make a dent in that queue:

```
storm rebalance flash-sale -e find-recommended-sales=8
storm rebalance flash-sale -e lookup-sales-details=8
```

Let's pretend the rebalances are done and we've waited 10 minutes (figure 6.10).

The capacity is unchanged for both `find-recommended-sales` and `lookup-sales-details`. That queue behind our spout must be really backed up. `save-recommended-sales` capacity has just about doubled, though. If we ratchet up the parallelism on our first two bolts, that might become a bottleneck for us, so let's bring it up some as well. Again, double the parallelism for our first two bolts and then quadruple the parallelism used for the `save-recommended-sales` bolt:

```
storm rebalance flash-sale -e find-recommended-sales=16
storm rebalance flash-sale -e lookup-sales-details=16
storm rebalance flash-sale -e save-recommended-sales=4
```

Three rebalancing commands and 10 minutes later we have figure 6.11.

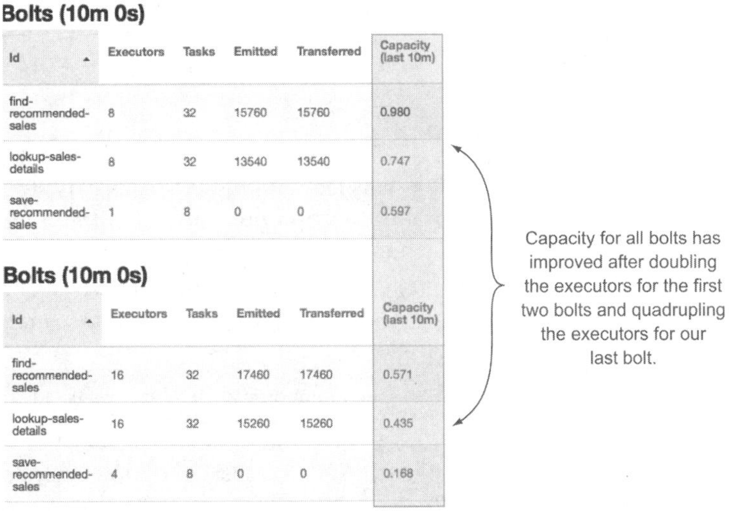

Bolts (10m 0s)

Id	Executors	Tasks	Emitted	Transferred	Capacity (last 10m)
find-recommended-sales	8	32	15760	15760	0.980
lookup-sales-details	8	32	13540	13540	0.747
save-recommended-sales	1	8	0	0	0.597

Bolts (10m 0s)

Id	Executors	Tasks	Emitted	Transferred	Capacity (last 10m)
find-recommended-sales	16	32	17460	17460	0.571
lookup-sales-details	16	32	15260	15260	0.435
save-recommended-sales	4	8	0	0	0.168

Capacity for all bolts has improved after doubling the executors for the first two bolts and quadrupling the executors for our last bolt.

Figure 6.11 Storm UI showing improved capacity for all three bolts in our topology

Excellent! We've finally made a dent, and a decent one in terms of capacity. The number of spouts (one) might now be our limiting factor. In a topology where we're hooked up to a real message queue, we'd check to make sure the flow of messages met whatever our SLA was. In our use case, we don't care about messages backing up but we're concerned with time to get through all messages. If our job from start to finish would take too long, we could increase the parallelism of our spout and go through the tuning steps we just showed you. Faking out spout parallelism is beyond the realm of our little test topology, but feel free to go about trying to emulate it. It might be a rewarding exercise.

Increasing parallelism at executor vs. worker level

So far, we haven't touched the parallelism of workers at all. Everything is running on a single worker and with a single spout, and we don't need more than one worker. Our advice is to scale on a single worker with executors until you find increasing executors doesn't work anymore. The basic principle we just used for scaling our bolts can be applied to spouts and workers.

6.3.4 *Spouts: controlling the rate data flows into a topology*

If we still aren't meeting our SLAs at this point in tuning, it's time to start looking at how we can control the rate that data flows into our topology: controls on spout parallelism. Two factors come into play:

- The number of spouts
- The maximum number of tuples each spout will allow to be live in our topology

NOTE Before we get started, remember in chapter 4 when we discussed guaranteed message processing and how Storm uses tuple trees for tracking whether or not a tuple emitted from a spout is fully processed? Here when we mention a tuple being unacked/live, we're referring to a tuple tree that hasn't been marked as fully processed.

These two factors, the number of spouts and maximum number of live tuples, are intertwined. We'll start with the discussion of the second point because it's more nuanced. Storm spouts have a concept called *max spout pending*. Max spout pending allows you to set a maximum number of tuples that can be unacked at any given time. In the `FlashSaleTopologyBuilder` code, we're setting a max spout pending value of 250:

```
builder
    .setSpout(CUSTOMER_RETRIEVAL_SPOUT, new CustomerRetrievalSpout())
    .setMaxSpoutPending(250);
```

By setting that value to 250, we ensure that, per spout task, 250 tuples can be unacked at a given time. If we had two instances of the spout, each with two tasks, that would be:

2 spouts x 2 tasks x 250 max spout pending = 1000 unacked tuples possible

When setting parallelism in your topology, it's important to make sure that max spout pending isn't a bottleneck. If the number of possible unacked tuples is lower than the total parallelism you've set for your topology, then it could be a bottleneck. In this case, we have the following

- 16 `find-recommended-sales` bolts
- 16 `lookup-sales-details` bolts
- 4 `saved-recommended-sales` bolts

which yields 36 tuples at a time we can process.

In this example, with a single spout, our maximum possible unacked tuples, 250, is greater than the maximum number of tuples we can process based on our parallelization, 36, so we can feel safe saying that max spout pending isn't causing a bottleneck (figure 6.12).

If max spout pending can cause bottlenecks, why would you set it at all? Without it, tuples will continue to flow into your topology whether or not you can keep up with processing them. Max spout pending allows us to control our ingest rate. Without controlling our ingest rate, it's possible to swamp our topology so that it collapses under the weight of incoming data. Max spout pending lets us erect a dam in front of our topology, apply back pressure, and avoid being overwhelmed. We recommend that, despite the optional nature of max spout pending, you always set it.

When attempting to increase performance to meet an SLA, we'd increase the rate of data ingest by either increasing spout parallelism or increasing the max spout pending. If we made a fourfold increase in the maximum number of active tuples allowed, we'd expect to see the speed of messages leaving our queue increase (maybe

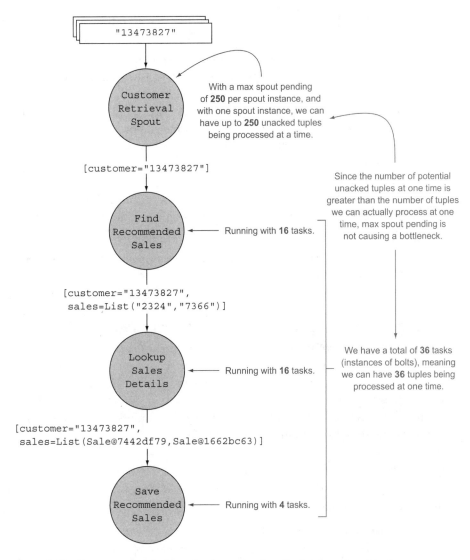

Figure 6.12 Because max spout pending is greater than the total number of tuples we can process at one time, it's not a bottleneck.

not by a factor of four, but it'd certainly increase). If that caused the capacity metric for any of our bolts to return to one or near it, we'd tune the bolts again and repeat with the spout and bolt until we hit our SLA. If adjusting spout and bolt parallelism failed to provide additional benefits, we'd play with the number of workers to see if we were now bound by the JVM we were running on and needed to parallelize across JVMs. This basic method can be applied over and over, and in many cases, we can meet our SLAs based on this.

Keep the following points in mind if you're working with external services from a topology you're tuning:

1   It's easy when interacting with external services (such as a SOA service, database, or filesystem) to ratchet up the parallelism to a high enough level in a topology that limits in that external service keep your capacity from going higher. Before you start tuning parallelism in a topology that interacts with the outside world, be positive you have good metrics on that service. We could keep turning up the parallelism on our `find-recommended-sales` bolt to the point that it brings the Find My Sales! service to its knees, crippling it under a mass of traffic that it's not designed to handle.

2   The second point is about latency. This is a bit more nuanced and requires a longer explanation and some background information, so before we get to that, let's take our parallelism changes and check them in.

You can check out the version of the code we have at this point in our tuning example by executing this command:

```
git checkout 0.0.3
```

6.4   *Latency: when external systems take their time*

Let's talk about one of the greatest enemies of fast code: latency. Latency is generally defined as the period of time one part of your system spends waiting on a response from another part of your system. There's latency accessing memory on your computer, accessing the hard drive, and accessing another system over the network. Different interactions have different levels of latency, and understanding the latency in your system is one of the keys to tuning your topology.

6.4.1   *Simulating latency in your topology*

If you look at the code for this topology, you'll find something that looks like this inside code from Database.java:

```
private final LatencySimulator latency = new LatencySimulator(
    20, 10, 30, 1500, 1);

public void save(String customerId, List<Sale> sale, int timeoutInMillis) {
    latency.simulate(timeoutInMillis);
}
```

Don't worry if you haven't gone through the code. We'll cover all the important parts here. The LatencySimulator is our way of making this topology behave something like a real one would when interacting with external services. Anything you interact with exhibits latency, from main memory on your computer to that networked filesystem you have to read from. Different systems will display different latency characteristics that our LatencySimulator attempts to emulate in a simple fashion.

Let's break down its five constructor arguments (see figure 6.13).

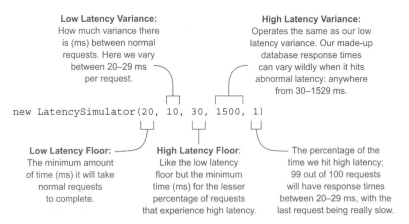

Figure 6.13 `LatencySimulator` constructor arguments explained

Note that we're not expressing latency in terms of a basic average that we vary from. That's rarely how latency works. You'll usually get fairly consistent response times and all of the sudden those response times will vary wildly because of any number of factors:

- The external service is having a garbage collection event.
- A network switch somewhere is momentarily overloaded.
- Your coworker wrote a runaway query that's currently hogging most of the database's CPU.

NOTE At our day job, almost all our systems run on the JVM and we use Coda Hale's excellent Metrics library[1] as well as Netflix's great Hystrix library[2] to measure the latency of our systems and adjust accordingly.

Table 6.1 shows the latency of the various systems our topology is interacting with. Looking at the table, we can see there's a lot of variance from the best request to the worst in each of these services. But what really stands out is how often we get hit by latency. On occasion, the database takes longer than any other service, but it rarely happens when compared to the `FlashSaleRecommendationService`, which hits a high latency period an order of magnitude more. Perhaps there's something we can address there.

Table 6.1 Latency of external services

System	Low floor	Low variance	High floor	High variance	High %
FlashSaleRecommendationService	100	50	150	1000	10
FlashSaleService	50	50	100	200	5
Database	20	10	30	1500	1

---

[1] https://github.com/dropwizard/metrics
[2] https://github.com/Netflix/Hystrix

When you look in the `FindRecommendedSales` bolt, you'll see this:

```
private final static int TIMEOUT = 200;

...

@Override
public void prepare(Map config, TopologyContext context) {
  client = new FlashSaleRecommendationClient(TIMEOUT);
}
```

We've set a timeout of 200 ms for looking up recommendations per client. It's a nice number, 200, but how did we settle on that? It probably seemed right when we were trying to get the topology working. In figure 6.14, look at the Last Error column. You'll see that all our bolts are experiencing timeouts. That makes sense. We wait only 200 ms to get recommendations, yet according to table 6.1, one out of ten requests hits a higher-than-normal latency that could take anywhere from 150 to 1049 ms to return a result and nine out of ten requests will return less than 150 ms. There are two primary types of reasons this could happen: extrinsic and intrinsic.

Id		Last error
find-recommended-sales	...	backtype.storm.topology.ReportedFailedException: stormapplied.flashsale.services.Timeout: Timeout after 200ms at stormapplied.flashsale.topology.FindRecommendedSales.execute(FindRecommendedSales.java
lookup-sales-details	...	backtype.storm.topology.ReportedFailedException: stormapplied.flashsale.services.Timeout: Timeout after 100ms at stormapplied.flashsale.topology.LookupSalesDetails.execute(LookupSalesDetails.java:44)
save-recommended-sales	...	backtype.storm.topology.ReportedFailedException: stormapplied.flashsale.services.Timeout: Timeout after 50ms at stormapplied.flashsale.topology.SaveRecommendedSales.execute(SaveRecommendedSales.java:

Figure 6.14   Storm UI showing the last error for each of our bolts

6.4.2   *Extrinsic and intrinsic reasons for latency*

An *extrinsic* reason is one that has little to nothing to do with the data. We hit high latency because of network issues or a garbage collection event or something that should pass with time. The next time we retry that request, our situation might be different.

An *intrinsic* reason is related to something about the data that's likely to cause the delay. In our example, it may take longer to come up with recommended sales for certain customers. No matter how many times we fail the tuple in this bolt and try again, we won't get recommended sales for those customers. It's just going to take too long. Intrinsic reasons can combine with extrinsic ones; they aren't mutually exclusive.

That's all well and good, but what does it have to do with our topology? Well, as we are interacting with external services, we can account for latency and attempt to increase our throughput without increasing our parallelism. Let's be smarter about our latency.

All right, we're making recommendations here, so we're declaring that after investigation, we've discovered that our variance with the FlashSaleRecommendationService is based on the customer. Certain customers are going to be slower to look up:

- We can generate recommendations for 75% of them in less than 125 ms.
- For another 15%, it takes about 125–150 ms.
- The last 10% usually take at least 200 ms, sometimes as long as 1500 ms.

Those are intrinsic variances in latency. Sometimes one of those "fast" lookups might end up taking longer due to an extrinsic event. One strategy that has worked well for us with services that exhibit this problem is to perform initial lookup attempts with a hard ceiling on timeouts. In this example, we could use 150 ms, and, if that fails, send it to a less parallelized instance of the same bolt that will take longer with its timeout. The end result is that our time to process a large number of messages goes down—we're effectively declaring war on extrinsic latency. If 90% of requests take longer than 150 ms, it's probably either because

1. It's a customer with intrinsic issues.
2. Extrinsic issues such as stop-the-world garbage collection are having an effect.

Your mileage will vary with this strategy, so test before you use it. Caveats aside, let's look at one way you can pull this off. Check out version 0.0.4 of our code

```
git checkout 0.0.4
```

and see the following listing for the changes in FindRecommendedSales and FlashSaleTopologyBuilder.

> **Listing 6.6 FindRecommendedSales.java with retry logic**

```java
public class FindRecommendedSales extends BaseBasicBolt {
  public static final String RETRY_STREAM = "retry";
  public static final String SUCCESS_STREAM = "success";

  private FlashSaleRecommendationClient client;

  @Override
  public void prepare(Map config,
                      TopologyContext context) {
    long timeout = (Long)config.get("timeout");
    client = new FlashSaleRecommendationClient((int)timeout);
  }

  @Override
  public void execute(Tuple tuple,
                      BasicOutputCollector outputCollector) {
    String customerId = tuple.getStringByField("customer");
    try {
      List<String> sales = client.findSalesFor(customerId);
      if (!sales.isEmpty()) {
        outputCollector.emit(SUCCESS_STREAM,
                             new Values(customerId, sales));
```

The timeout is no longer a hardcoded value; we're getting it from the topology configuration.

If we successfully get results without timing out, we're emitting new values as before but to a new **SUCCESS_STREAM**.

```
      }
    } catch (Timeout e) {
      outputCollector.emit(RETRY_STREAM, new Values(customerId));    ←┐
    }
  }
  ...
}
```

We're no longer throwing a ReportedFailedException if we encounter a timeout; we're now taking the customerId and emitting it to a separate RETRY_STREAM.

Check out what's going on in FlashSaleTopologyBuilder:

```
builder
  .setSpout(CUSTOMER_RETRIEVAL_SPOUT, new CustomerRetrievalSpout())
  .setMaxSpoutPending(250);

builder
  .setBolt(FIND_RECOMMENDED_SALES_FAST, new FindRecommendedSales(), 16)
  .addConfiguration("timeout", 150)
  .setNumTasks(16)
  .shuffleGrouping(CUSTOMER_RETRIEVAL_SPOUT);

builder
  .setBolt(FIND_RECOMMENDED_SALES_SLOW, new FindRecommendedSales(), 16)
  .addConfiguration("timeout", 1500)
  .setNumTasks(16)
  .shuffleGrouping(FIND_RECOMMENDED_SALES_FAST,
                   FindRecommendedSales.RETRY_STREAM)
  .shuffleGrouping(FIND_RECOMMENDED_SALES_SLOW,
                   FindRecommendedSales.RETRY_STREAM);

builder
  .setBolt(LOOKUP_SALES_DETAILS, new LookupSalesDetails(), 16)
  .setNumTasks(16)
  .shuffleGrouping(FIND_RECOMMENDED_SALES_FAST,
                   FindRecommendedSales.SUCCESS_STREAM)
  .shuffleGrouping(FIND_RECOMMENDED_SALES_SLOW,
                   FindRecommendedSales.SUCCESS_STREAM);

builder
  .setBolt(SAVE_RECOMMENDED_SALES, new SaveRecommendedSales(), 4)
  .setNumTasks(4)
  .shuffleGrouping(LOOKUP_SALES_DETAILS);
```

Where we previously had a single FindRecommendedSales bolt, we now have two: one for "fast" lookups and the other for "slow." Let's take a closer look at the fast one:

```
builder
  .setBolt(FIND_RECOMMENDED_SALES_FAST, new FindRecommendedSales(), 16)
  .addConfiguration("timeout", 150)
  .setNumTasks(16)
  .shuffleGrouping(CUSTOMER_RETRIEVAL_SPOUT);
```

It's identical to our previous FindRecommendedSales bolt except that it has one addition:

```
.addConfiguration("timeout", 150)
```

This is the timeout value (in ms) that we're using in the bolt's prepare() method to initialize the FindRecommendationSalesClient's timeout value. Every tuple through the fast bolt will time out after 150 ms and be emitted on the retry stream. Here's the "slow" version of the FindRecommendedSales bolt:

```
builder
  .setBolt(FIND_RECOMMENDED_SALES_SLOW, new FindRecommendedSales(), 16)
    .addConfiguration("timeout", 1500)
    .setNumTasks(16)
    .shuffleGrouping(FIND_RECOMMENDED_SALES_FAST,
                    FindRecommendedSales.RETRY_STREAM)
    .shuffleGrouping(FIND_RECOMMENDED_SALES_SLOW,
                    FindRecommendedSales.RETRY_STREAM);
```

Note that it has a timeout of 1500 ms:

```
.addConfiguration("timeout", 1500)
```

That's the maximum we decided we should ever need to wait based on reasons that are intrinsic to that customer.

What's going on with those two shuffle groupings?

```
.shuffleGrouping(FIND_RECOMMENDED_SALES_FAST,
                FindRecommendedSales.RETRY_STREAM)
.shuffleGrouping(FIND_RECOMMENDED_SALES_SLOW,
                FindRecommendedSales.RETRY_STREAM);
```

We've hooked up the slow FindRecommendedSales bolt to two different streams: the retry streams from both the fast and slow versions of the FindRecommendedSales bolts. Whenever a timeout occurs in any version of the bolt, it'll be emitted on the retry stream and retried at a slower speed.

We have to make one more big change to our topology to incorporate this. Our next bolt, the LookupSalesDetails, has to get tuples from the success stream of both FindRecommendedSales bolts, slow and fast:

```
builder.setBolt(LOOKUP_SALES_DETAILS, new LookupSalesDetails(), 16)
      .setNumTasks(16)
      .shuffleGrouping(FIND_RECOMMENDED_SALES_FAST,
                      FindRecommendedSales.SUCCESS_STREAM)
      .shuffleGrouping(FIND_RECOMMENDED_SALES_SLOW,
                      FindRecommendedSales.SUCCESS_STREAM);
```

We could also consider applying this pattern to other bolts further downstream. It's important to weigh the additional complexity this creates against possible performance increases. As always, it's all about trade-offs.

Let's go back to a previous decision. Remember the code in LookupSalesDetails that can result in some sales details not being looked up?

```
@Override
public void execute(Tuple tuple) {
  String customerId = tuple.getStringByField("customer");
  List<String> saleIds = (List<String>) tuple.getValueByField("sales");
```

```
List<Sale> sales = new ArrayList<Sale>();
for (String saleId: saleIds) {
  try {
    Sale sale = client.lookupSale(saleId);
    sales.add(sale);
  } catch (Timeout e) {
    outputCollector.reportError(e);
  }
}

if (sales.isEmpty()) {
  outputCollector.fail(tuple);
} else {
  outputCollector.emit(new Values(customerId, sales));
  outputCollector.ack(tuple);
}
}
```

We made a trade-off to get speed. We're willing to accept the occasional loss of fidelity in the number of recommended sales to each customer versus emailing them to make sure we hit our SLA. But what kind of impact is this decision having? How many sales aren't being sent to customers? Currently, we have no insight. Thankfully, Storm ships with some built-in metrics capabilities we can leverage.

6.5   Storm's metrics-collecting API

Prior to the Storm 0.9.x series of releases, metrics were the Wild West. You had topology-level metrics available in the UI, but if you wanted business-level or JVM-level metrics, you needed to roll your own. The Metrics API that now ships with Storm is an excellent way to get access to metrics that can be used to solve our current quandary: understanding how much fidelity we're losing in our LookupSalesDetails bolt.

6.5.1   Using Storm's built-in CountMetric

To follow along in the source code, run the following command:

```
git checkout 0.0.5
```

The next listing shows the changes we've made to our LookupSalesDetail bolt.

Listing 6.7   `LookupSalesDetails.java` **with metrics**

```
public class LookupSalesDetails extends BaseRichBolt {
  ...

  private final int METRICS_WINDOW = 60;
  private transient CountMetric salesLookedUp;        ◁─── Variable for keeping
  private transient CountMetric salesLookupFailures;  ◁───    a running count of
                                                                sales lookups
  @Override
  public void prepare(Map config,                     ◁─── Variable for keeping
                      TopologyContext context,             a running count of
                      OutputCollector outputCollector) {   sales lookup
                                                           failures
    ...
```

```
    salesLookedUp = new CountMetric();
    context.registerMetric("sales-looked-up",
                            salesLookedUp,
                            METRICS_WINDOW);
    salesLookupFailures = new CountMetric();
    context.registerMetric("sales-lookup-failures",
                            salesLookupFailures,
                            METRICS_WINDOW);
}

@Override
public void execute(Tuple tuple) {
    String customerId = tuple.getStringByField("customer");
    List<String> saleIds = (List<String>) tuple.getValueByField("sales");

    List<Sale> sales = new ArrayList<Sale>();
    for (String saleId: saleIds) {
        try {
            Sale sale = client.lookupSale(saleId);
            sales.add(sale);
        } catch (Timeout e) {
            outputCollector.reportError(e);
            salesLookupFailures.incr();
        }
    }

    if (sales.isEmpty()) {
        outputCollector.fail(tuple);
    } else {
        salesLookedUp.incrBy(sales.size());
        outputCollector.emit(new Values(customerId, sales));
        outputCollector.ack(tuple);
    }
}
}
```

Register the sales lookup metric, reporting the count for the past 60 seconds.

Register the sales lookup failures metric, reporting the count for the past 60 seconds.

Increment the number of sales lookup failures by one if a Timeout exception occurs.

Increase the number of sales lookups by the size of the sales list.

We've created and registered two `CountMetric` instances in our `prepare()` method: one to keep a running count of the number of sales for which we've successfully looked up details and the other for tracking the number of failures.

6.5.2 Setting up a metrics consumer

Now we have some basic raw data that we're going to record, but to get at it, we must set up a consumer. A metrics consumer implements the interface `IMetricsConsumer`, which acts as a bridge between Storm and an external system such as Statsd or Riemann. In this example, we'll use the provided `LoggingMetricsConsumer`. When a topology is run in local mode, `LoggingMetricsConsumer` ends up being directed to standard output (stdout) along with other log output. We can set this up by adding the following to our `LocalTopologyRunner`:

```
Config config = new Config();
config.setDebug(true);
config.registerMetricsConsumer(LoggingMetricsConsumer.class, 1);
```

Let's say we succeeded in looking up 350 sales over the time window:

```
244565 [Thread-16-__metricsbacktype.storm.metric.LoggingMetricsConsumer]
INFO  backtype.storm.metric.LoggingMetricsConsumer - 1393581398
localhost:1      22:lookup-sales-details      sales-looked-up      350
```

On a remote cluster, the `LoggingMetricsConsumer` writes info-level messages to a file called metrics.log in the Storm logs directory. We've also enabled metrics logging for when we deploy to a cluster with the following addition:

```
public class RemoteTopologyRunner {
  ...
  private static Config createConfig(Boolean debug) {
    ...

    Config config = new Config();
    ...
    config.registerMetricsConsumer(LoggingMetricsConsumer.class, 1);
    ...
  }
}
```

Storm's built-in metrics are useful. But what if you need more than what's built-in? Fortunately, Storm provides the ability to implement custom metrics so you can create metrics tailored to a specific need.

6.5.3 Creating a custom SuccessRateMetric

We have the raw metrics, but we want to aggregate them and then do the math ourselves to determine the success rate. We care less about the raw successes and failures and more about just the success rate. Storm has no built-in metric that we can use to get that, but it's easy to create a class that will record that for us. The following listing introduces the `SuccessRateMetric`.

Listing 6.8 SuccessRateMetric.java

```
public class SuccessRateMetric implements IMetric {
  double success;
  double fail;

  public void incrSuccess(long incrementBy) {      <-- Custom method for incrementing the number of successes
    success += Double.valueOf(incrementBy);
  }

  public void incrFail(long incrementBy) {      <-- Custom method for incrementing the number of failures
    fail += Double.valueOf(incrementBy);
  }

  @Override
  public Object getValueAndReset() {      <-- Only method that must be implemented by anything implementing the IMetric interface
    double rate = (success / (success + fail)) * 100.0;      <-- Calculate the success percentage for the return value for the metric.
```

```
    success = 0;                    ◁──┐  Reset the
    fail = 0;                          │  metric values.

    return rate;
  }
}
```

Changing the code to use this new custom metric is simple (see the next listing).

Listing 6.9 `LookupSalesDetails.java` using our new custom metric

```
public class LookupSalesDetails extends BaseRichBolt {
  ...

  private final int METRICS_WINDOW = 15;
  private transient SuccessRateMetric successRates;      ◁──┐  The new
                                                            │  success rate
  @Override                                                 │  metric
  public void prepare(Map config,
                      TopologyContext context,
                      OutputCollector outputCollector) {
    ...

    successRates = new SuccessRateMetric();
    context.registerMetric("sales-lookup-success-rate",
                           successRates,
                           METRICS_WINDOW);      ◁──┐  Register the success
  }                                                 │  rate metric, reporting
                                                    │  the success rate for the
  @Override                                         │  past 15 seconds.
  public void execute(Tuple tuple) {
    ...

    List<Sale> sales = new ArrayList<Sale>();
    for (String saleId: saleIds) {
      try {
        Sale sale = client.lookupSale(saleId);
        sales.add(sale);                          Increment the
      } catch (Timeout e) {                       failure count by I if
        successRates.incrFail(1);              ◁──┘  a timeout occurs.
        outputCollector.reportError(e);
      }
    }

    if (sales.isEmpty()) {                        Increase the success
      outputCollector.fail(tuple);                count by the number
    } else {                                      of sales retrieved.
      successRates.incrSuccess(sales.size());  ◁──┘
      outputCollector.emit(new Values(customerId, sales));
      outputCollector.ack(tuple);
    }
  }

  ...
}
```

Everything is pretty much as it was. We register a metric (just of a different type) and report our successes and failures to it. The logged output is much closer to what we want to know:

```
124117 [Thread-16-__metricsbacktype.storm.metric.LoggingMetricsConsumer]
INFO  backtype.storm.metric.LoggingMetricsConsumer - 1393581964
localhost:1    32:lookup-sales-details    sales-lookup-success-rate
98.13084112149532
```

You can try it out yourself:

```
git checkout 0.0.5
mvn clean compile -P local-cluster
```

Beware! It's a lot of output.

6.5.4   *Creating a custom MultiSuccessRateMetric*

At this point, we've moved to production and the business folks are happy for a couple days—until they want to know the distribution of fidelity across customers. In other words, we need to record success and failure on a per-customer basis.

Luckily, there's a Storm metric called MultiCountMetric that does exactly that—except it uses CountMetrics, not SuccessRateMetrics. But that's easy enough to deal with—we'll just create a new metric of our own from it:

```
git checkout 0.0.6
```

The following listing shows the new metric: MultiSuccessRateMetric.

Listing 6.10   MultiSuccessRateMetric.java

```
public class MultiSuccessRateMetric implements IMetric {
  Map<String, SuccessRateMetric> rates = new HashMap();

  public SuccessRateMetric scope(String key) {
    SuccessRateMetric rate = rates.get(key);

    if (rate == null) {
      rate = new SuccessRateMetric();
      rates.put(key, rate);
    }

    return rate;
  }

  @Override
  public Object getValueAndReset() {
    Map ret = new HashMap();

    for(Map.Entry<String, SuccessRateMetric> e : rates.entrySet()) {
      ret.put(e.getKey(), e.getValue().getValueAndReset());
    }
```

Annotations:

Store individual SuccessRateMetric instances in a hash with customer ID as the key so we can keep track of success rates per customer.

Return the SuccessRateMetric for the given "key" (customer ID), creating a new SuccessRateMetric if one doesn't exist for that customer.

Return the map of success rates per customer, while resetting both the individual success rates for each customer and clearing our map.

```
      rates.clear();

      return ret;
   }
}
```

The class is straightforward; we store individual `SuccessRateMetrics` in a hash. We'll use customer IDs as a key and be able to keep track of successes and failures per customer. As you can see in the next listing, the changes we need to do this are minor.

Listing 6.11 `LookupSalesDetails.java` **with the new** `MultiSuccessRateMetric`

```java
public class LookupSalesDetails extends BaseRichBolt {
   ...

   private transient MultiSuccessRateMetric successRates;          ◁——  New
                                                                         MultiSuccessRateMetric
   @Override
   public void prepare(Map config,
                       TopologyContext context,
                       OutputCollector outputCollector) {

      ...

      successRates = new MultiSuccessRateMetric();
      context.registerMetric("sales-lookup-success-rate",
                       successRates,
                       METRICS_WINDOW);                    ◁——
   }
```

Register MultiSuccessRateMetric, reporting the success rate for the past 15 seconds.

```java
   @Override
   public void execute(Tuple tuple) {
      String customerId = tuple.getStringByField("customer");
      List<String> saleIds = (List<String>) tuple.getValueByField("sales");

      List<Sale> sales = new ArrayList<Sale>();
      for (String saleId: saleIds) {
         try {
            Sale sale = client.lookupSale(saleId);
            sales.add(sale);
         } catch (Timeout e) {
            successRates.scope(customerId).incrFail(1);      ◁——
            outputCollector.reportError(e);
         }
      }
```

Increment the number of failures by one for the given customer ID.

```java
      if (sales.isEmpty()) {
         outputCollector.fail(tuple);
      } else {
         successRates.scope(customerId).incrSuccess(sales.size());   ◁——
         outputCollector.emit(new Values(customerId, sales));
         outputCollector.ack(tuple);
      }
   }
}
```

Increase the success count by the number of sales retrieved for the given customer ID.

Now we're recording metrics in a fashion useful to the business folks:

```
79482 [Thread-16-__metricsbacktype.storm.metric.LoggingMetricsConsumer]
INFO  backtype.storm.metric.LoggingMetricsConsumer - 1393582952
localhost:4    24:lookup-sales-details    sales-lookup-success-rate
{customer-7083607=100.0, customer-7461335=80.0, customer-2744429=100.0,
customer-3681336=66.66666666666666, customer-8012734=100.0,
customer-7060775=100.0, customer-2247874=100.0, customer-3659041=100.0,
customer-1092131=100.0, customer-6121500=100.0, customer-1886068=100.0,
customer-3629821=100.0, customer-8620951=100.0, customer-8381332=100.0,
customer-8189083=80.0, customer-3720160=100.0, customer-845974=100.0,
customer-4922670=100.0, customer-8395305=100.0,
customer-2611914=66.66666666666666, customer-7983628=100.0,
customer-2312606=100.0, customer-8967727=100.0,
customer-552426=100.0, customer-9784547=100.0, customer-2002923=100.0,
customer-6724584=100.0, customer-7444284=80.0, customer-5385092=100.0,
customer-1654684=100.0, customer-5855112=50.0, customer-1299479=100.0}
```

The log message provides a sample of what we may see with the new metric: a list of customer IDs, each with an associated success rate. Here's a lucky customer in that list with a 100% success rate:

```
customer-2247874=100.0
```

With this data, we have a much deeper insight into how many customers are receiving their full set of potential flash sales.

6.6   *Summary*

In this chapter, you learned that

- All basic timing information for a topology can be found in the Storm UI.
- Establishing a baseline set of performance numbers for your topology is the essential first step in the tuning process.
- Bottlenecks are indicated by a high capacity for a spout/bolt and can be addressed by increasing parallelism.
- Increasing parallelism is best done in small increments so that you can gain a better understanding of the effects of each increase.
- Latency that is both related to the data (intrinsic) and not related to the data (extrinsic) can reduce your topology's throughput and may need to be addressed.
- Metrics (both built-in and custom) are essential if you want to have a true understanding of how your topology is operating.

Resource contention

This chapter covers

- Contention for worker processes in a Storm cluster
- Memory contention within a worker process (JVM)
- Memory contention on a worker node
- Worker node CPU contention
- Worker node network/socket input/output (I/O) contention
- Worker node disk I/O contention

In chapter 6, we discussed tuning at the individual topology level. Tuning is an important skill to master and will serve you well when you're deploying topologies to production. But it's only a small part of a bigger picture. Your topology is going to have to coexist on a Storm cluster with a variety of other topologies. Some of those topologies will burn CPU doing heavy mathematical calculations, some will consume large amounts of network bandwidth, and so on and so forth with a variety of resources.

In this chapter, we'll present the various types of resources that can come under contention in a Storm cluster and explain how to address each of them. We hope that no single Storm cluster would have so many contention issues, so we've eschewed our usual case study format for a more appropriate cookbook approach. Take a quick skim through this chapter to gain a general understanding of the types of contention and then refer back to whatever section is relevant to you when you start encountering problems.

The first three recipes in this chapter focus on common solutions for addressing several types of contention presented later. We recommend reading through these three recipes first because they will give you a better understanding of what we're talking about when we discuss a solution to a particular type of contention.

Throughout the chapter we use certain terminology when addressing the resources that can come under contention. It's important to understand what part of a Storm deployment we're referencing when you see certain terms. Figure 7.1 highlights these resources, with the key terms in bold. Most of this should already be familiar to you,

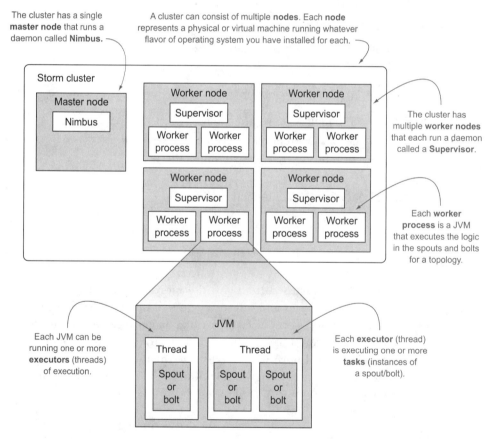

Figure 7.1 The various types of nodes in a Storm cluster and worker nodes broken down as worker processes and their parts

but if not, make sure you take the time to study the terms and relationships between the various components before moving forward.

With the terminology defined, let's get started with the first of our "common solution" recipes in our cookbook approach, changing the number of worker processes (JVMs) running on a worker node. Addressing these "common solution" recipes now will provide a nice reference for later and allow us to focus on why each is a good solution for a particular scenario.

Choosing an operating system when discussing OS-level contentions

Everyone's experience administering, maintaining, and diagnosing issues in a Storm cluster will vary. We've tried to cover the major issues and some of the tools you'll need. But your situation may vary from any we've encountered. The configuration of your cluster may vary in the number of machines, number of JVMs per machine, and so forth. No one can give you the answers for how to set up your cluster. The best we can do is present you with guidelines for adjusting to problems that arise. Because we're addressing so many issues that exist at the operating system level and because there are so many operating systems that you could be running Storm on, we've decided to focus on one specific family of operating systems: Linux-based.

The OS-level tools discussed in this chapter should be available in every variation of Linux. Further, these tools should either exist or have an equivalent in any Unix-type OS such as Solaris or FreeBSD. For those of you considering using Windows, you're going to have to do more work to translate the ideas over to your OS, but the general principles apply. It's important to note that our discussion of tool usage is far from exhaustive—it's intended to provide a basis for you to build on. To administer and diagnose problems in a production cluster, you'll be required to learn more about the tools and the OS you're running on. Man pages, search engines, the Storm mailing list, IRC channels, and your friendly neighborhood operations person are all excellent resources that you should lean on to learn more.

7.1 Changing the number of worker processes running on a worker node

In several of the recipes throughout this chapter, one of the solutions for addressing the contention in question is changing the number of worker processes running on a worker node (figure 7.2).

In some cases, this means increasing worker processes and in others it means decreasing worker processes. It's such a common solution that we've decided to break it into its own recipe so you can refer back to this section whenever we come across it as a solution.

7.1.1 Problem

You're experiencing a contention where you need to either increase or decrease the number of worker processes running on a worker node.

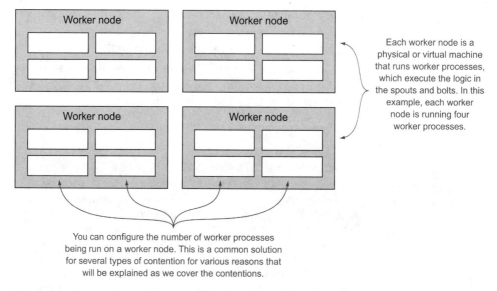

Figure 7.2 Many worker processes running on a worker node

7.1.2 Solution

The number of worker processes running on a worker node is defined by the supervisor.slots.ports property in each worker node's storm.yaml configuration file. This property defines the ports that each worker process will use to listen for messages. The next listing shows the default settings for this property.

> **Listing 7.1 Default settings for supervisor.slots.ports**

```
supervisor.slots.ports
 - 6701
 - 6702
 - 6703
 - 6704
```

To increase the number of worker processes that can be run on a worker node, add a port to this list for each worker process to be added. The opposite holds true for decreasing the number of worker processes: remove a port for each worker process to be removed.

After updating this property, you'll need to restart the Supervisor process on the worker node to effect the change. If you installed Storm to /opt/storm, as we did in our installation run-through in chapter 5, this would require killing the Supervisor process and starting again with the following command:

```
/opt/storm/bin storm supervisor
```

Upon restarting, Nimbus will be aware of the updated configuration and send messages to only the ports defined in this list.

7.1.3   *Discussion*

Storm defaults to four worker processes per worker node, with each worker process listening on ports 6701, 6702, 6703, and 6704, respectively. This is usually good enough when you're first starting to build a cluster, so don't worry about trying to figure out the best configuration right away. But if you do need to add ports, be sure to check whether the ports you want to add are already in use by using a tool such as netstat on Linux.

Another thing to consider is the number of worker nodes you have in your cluster. If widespread changes are needed, updating the configuration and restarting the Supervisor process across hundreds or even tens of nodes is a tedious and time-consuming task. So we recommend a tool such as Puppet (http://puppetlabs.com) for automating the deployment and configuration of each node.

7.2   *Changing the amount of memory allocated to worker processes (JVMs)*

In a few of the recipes throughout this chapter, one of the solutions for addressing the contention in question is changing the amount of memory allocated to worker processes (JVMs) on a worker node.

In some cases this means increasing the amount of memory allocated and in others it means decreasing memory. Whatever the reason for the solution, the steps for changing this setting are the same, which is why we've dedicated a separate recipe to it.

7.2.1   *Problem*

You're experiencing a contention where you need to either increase or decrease the amount of memory being used by the worker processes on a worker node.

7.2.2   *Solution*

The amount of memory allocated to all worker processes (JVMs) on a worker node can be changed in the worker.childopts property in each worker node's storm.yaml configuration file. This property accepts any valid JVM startup option, providing the ability to set the startup options for the initial memory allocation pool (-Xms) and maximum memory allocation pool (-Xmx) for the JVMs on the worker node. The following listing shows what this would look like, focusing only on the memory-related arguments.

Listing 7.2   Setting worker.childopts in storm.yaml

```
worker.childopts: "...
-Xms512m
-Xmx1024m
..."
```

It's important to be aware that changing this property will update all the worker processes on a particular worker node. After updating this property, you'll need to restart the Supervisor process on the worker node to effect the change. If you installed Storm to /opt/storm, as we did in our installation run-through in chapter 5, this would require killing the Supervisor process and starting again with the following command:

```
/opt/storm/bin storm supervisor
```

Upon restarting, all of the worker processes (JVMs) on the worker node should be running with the updated memory settings.

7.2.3 Discussion

One thing to keep in mind when increasing JVM sizes is to make sure the worker node (machine/VM) itself has the resources for such size increases. If the worker node doesn't have enough memory to support whatever you set the –Xmx value to, you'll need to change the sizing of the actual machines/VMs before changing the amount of memory allocated to the JVM.

Another tip we highly recommend following is setting –Xms and –Xmx to the same value. If these values are different, the JVM will manage the heap, sometimes increasing and sometimes decreasing the heap size, depending on heap usage. We find the overhead of this heap management to be unnecessary and therefore recommend setting both to the same value to eliminate any heap management overhead. Along with being more efficient, this strategy has the added benefit of making it easier to reason about JVM memory usage, because the heap size is a fixed constant for the life of the JVM.

7.3 Figuring out which worker nodes/processes a topology is executing on

Many of the recipes in this chapter involve contentions at both the worker node and worker process level. Often these contentions will manifest themselves in the form of a topology throwing errors in the Storm UI, experiencing reduced throughput, or having no throughput at all. In all these scenarios, you'll most likely need to identify which worker nodes and worker processes that particular topology is executing on.

7.3.1 Problem

You have a problematic topology and need to identify the worker nodes and worker processes that topology is executing on.

7.3.2 Solution

The way to do this is by looking at the Storm UI. You want to start out by looking at the UI for the specific topology in question. We suggest checking out the Bolts section to see if anything looks amiss. As figure 7.3 shows, one of the bolts is having issues.

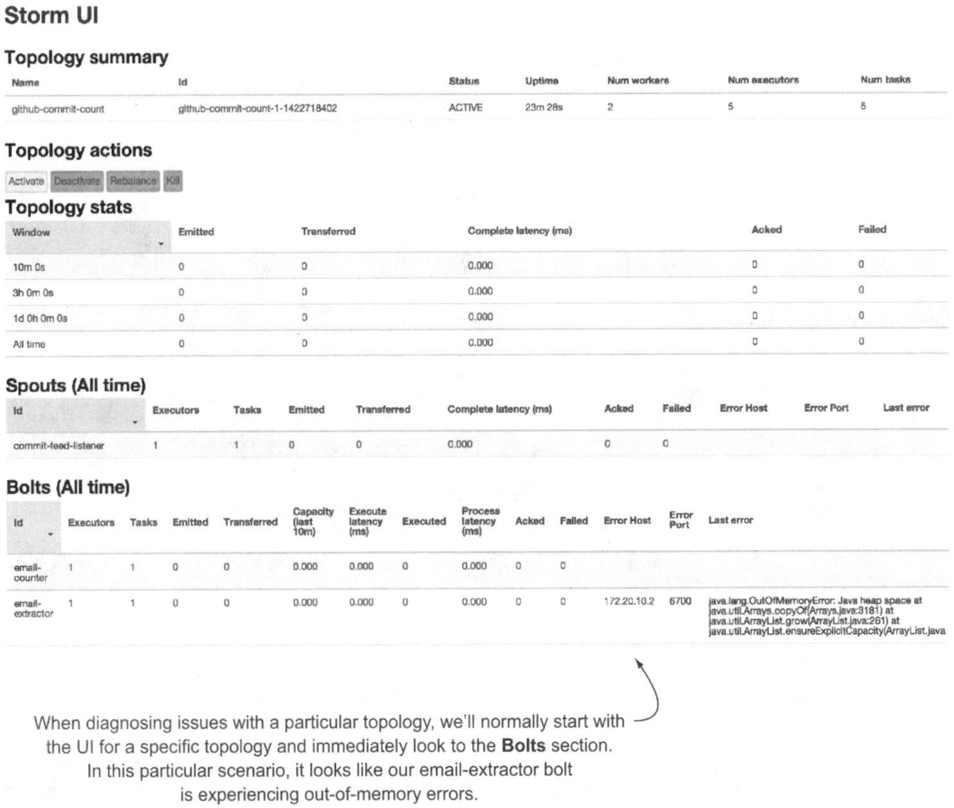

Storm UI

Topology summary

Name	Id	Status	Uptime	Num workers	Num executors	Num tasks
github-commit-count	github-commit-count-1-1422718402	ACTIVE	23m 28s	2	5	5

Topology actions

Activate Deactivate Rebalance Kill

Topology stats

Window	Emitted	Transferred	Complete latency (ms)	Acked	Failed
10m 0s	0	0	0.000	0	0
3h 0m 0s	0	0	0.000	0	0
1d 0h 0m 0s	0	0	0.000	0	0
All time	0	0	0.000	0	0

Spouts (All time)

Id	Executors	Tasks	Emitted	Transferred	Complete latency (ms)	Acked	Failed	Error Host	Error Port	Last error
commit-feed-listener	1	1	0	0	0.000	0	0			

Bolts (All time)

Id	Executors	Tasks	Emitted	Transferred	Capacity (last 10m)	Execute latency (ms)	Executed	Process latency (ms)	Acked	Failed	Error Host	Error Port	Last error
email-counter	1	1	0	0	0.000	0.000	0	0.000	0	0			
email-extractor	1	1	0	0	0.000	0.000	0	0.000	0	0	172.20.10.2	6700	java.lang.OutOfMemoryError: Java heap space at java.util.Arrays.copyOf(Arrays.java:3181) at java.util.ArrayList.grow(ArrayList.java:261) at java.util.ArrayList.ensureExplicitCapacity(ArrayList.java

When diagnosing issues with a particular topology, we'll normally start with
the UI for a specific topology and immediately look to the **Bolts** section.
In this particular scenario, it looks like our email-extractor bolt
is experiencing out-of-memory errors.

Figure 7.3   Diagnosing issues for a particular topology in the Storm UI

Having identified the problematic bolt, you now want to see more details about what's happening with that bolt. To do so, click on that bolt's name in the UI to get a more detailed view for that bolt. From here, turn your attention to the Executors and Errors section for the individual bolt (figure 7.4).

The Executors section for an individual bolt is of particular interest; this tells you which worker nodes and worker processes the bolt is executing on. From here, given the type of contention being experienced, you can take the necessary steps to identify and solve the problem at hand.

7.3.3   Discussion

The Storm UI is your friend. Become familiar with its various screens. It's normally the first place we look when diagnosing any type of contention. Being able to quickly identify a problematic topology, bolt, worker node, and worker process has been extremely valuable in our experience.

Though a great tool, the Storm UI may not always show you what you need. This is where additional monitoring can help. This can come in the form of monitoring the

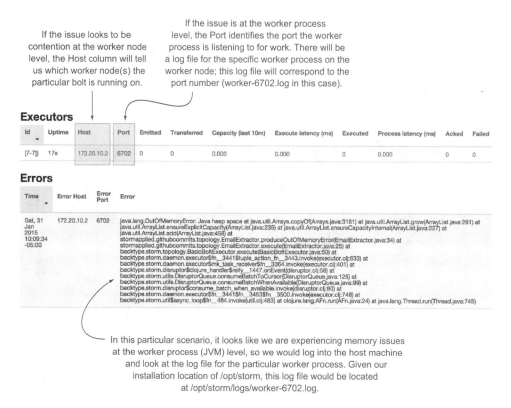

If the issue looks to be contention at the worker node level, the Host column will tell us which worker node(s) the particular bolt is running on.

If the issue is at the worker process level, the Port identifies the port the worker process is listening to for work. There will be a log file for the specific worker process on the worker node; this log file will correspond to the port number (worker-6702.log in this case).

Executors

Id	Uptime	Host	Port	Emitted	Transferred	Capacity (last 10m)	Execute latency (ms)	Executed	Process latency (ms)	Acked	Failed
[7-7])	17s	172.20.10.2	6702	0	0	0.000	0.000	0	0.000	0	0

Errors

Time	Error Host	Error Port	Error
Sat, 31 Jan 2015 10:09:34 -05:00	172.20.10.2	6702	java.lang.OutOfMemoryError: Java heap space at java.util.Arrays.copyOf(Arrays.java:3181) at java.util.ArrayList.grow(ArrayList.java:261) at java.util.ArrayList.ensureExplicitCapacity(ArrayList.java:235) at java.util.ArrayList.ensureCapacityInternal(ArrayList.java:227) at java.util.ArrayList.add(ArrayList.java:458) at stormapplied.githubcommits.topology.EmailExtractor.produceOutOfMemoryError(EmailExtractor.java:34) at stormapplied.githubcommits.topology.EmailExtractor.execute(EmailExtractor.java:25) at backtype.storm.topology.BasicBoltExecutor.execute(BasicBoltExecutor.java:50) at backtype.storm.daemon.executor$fn__3441$tuple_action_fn__3443.invoke(executor.clj:633) at backtype.storm.daemon.executor$mk_task_receiver$fn__3364.invoke(executor.clj:401) at backtype.storm.disruptor$clojure_handler$reify__1447.onEvent(disruptor.clj:58) at backtype.storm.utils.DisruptorQueue.consumeBatchToCursor(DisruptorQueue.java:125) at backtype.storm.utils.DisruptorQueue.consumeBatchWhenAvailable(DisruptorQueue.java:99) at backtype.storm.disruptor$consume_batch_when_available.invoke(disruptor.clj:80) at backtype.storm.daemon.executor$fn__3441$fn__3453$fn__3500.invoke(executor.clj:748) at backtype.storm.util$async_loop$fn__484.invoke(util.clj:463) at clojure.lang.AFn.run(AFn.java:24) at java.lang.Thread.run(Thread.java:745)

In this particular scenario, it looks like we are experiencing memory issues at the worker process (JVM) level, so we would log into the host machine and look at the log file for the particular worker process. Given our installation location of /opt/storm, this log file would be located at /opt/storm/logs/worker-6702.log.

Figure 7.4   Looking at the Executors and Errors portion of the Storm UI for a particular bolt to determine the type of issue the bolt is having while also determining the worker nodes and worker processes that bolt is executing on

health of individual worker nodes or custom metrics in your bolt's code to give you a deeper insight into how well the bolt is performing. The bottom line here is you shouldn't rely solely on the Storm UI. Put other measures in place to make sure you have coverage everywhere. After all, it's not a matter of *if* something will break; it's a matter of *when*.

7.4   *Contention for worker processes in a Storm cluster*

When you install a Storm cluster, you install it with a fixed number of available worker processes across all your worker nodes. Each time you deploy a new topology to the cluster, you specify how many worker processes that topology should consume. It's easy to get yourself into a situation where you deploy a topology that requires a certain number of worker processes but you can't obtain those worker processes because they've all been assigned to existing topologies. This renders the topology in question useless, because it can't process data without worker processes. Figure 7.5 illustrates this point.

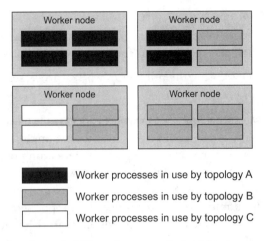

Attempting to deploy a new topology to this cluster will result in the new topology having zero worker processes. This is because all of the worker processes are already in use by existing topologies.

Figure 7.5 Example Storm cluster where all of the worker processes have been assigned to topologies.

Figure 7.5 illustrates a problem we've experienced firsthand several times. Fortunately, this problem is easy to detect; it can be found by looking at the cluster summary page of the Storm UI (figure 7.6).

7.4.1 Problem

You notice a topology isn't processing any data or has a sudden drop in throughput and zero free slots are available, according to the Storm UI.

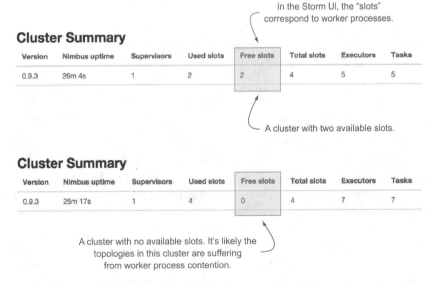

Figure 7.6 Storm UI: Zero free slots could mean your topologies are suffering from slot contention.

7.4.2   Solution

The bottom line is you have a fixed number of worker processes that can be allocated to the topologies requesting them. You can address this problem with these strategies:

- Decreasing the number of worker processes in use by existing topologies
- Increasing the total number of worker processes in the cluster

DECREASING THE NUMBER OF WORKER PROCESSES IN USE BY EXISTING TOPOLOGIES

This is the quickest and easiest way to free up slots for other topologies in your cluster. But this may or may not be possible depending on the SLAs for your existing topologies. If you can reduce the number of worker processes being used by a topology without violating the SLA, we recommend this approach.

The number of worker processes a topology requests is specified in the code for building and submitting your topology to the Storm cluster. The next listing shows this code.

> **Listing 7.3   Configuring the number of worker processes for a topology**

```
import backtype.storm.Config;
import backtype.storm.StormSubmitter;
import backtype.storm.topology.TopologyBuilder;

...

TopologyBuilder builder = new TopologyBuilder();
// build the various pieces of your topology here

Config config = new Config();                        Set the number of
config.setNumWorkers(2);                             worker processes
                                                     for the topology.
...

StormSubmitter.submitTopology("topology-name",
                    config,
                    builder.createTopology());
```

If your SLAs don't allow you to reduce the number of slots being used by any of the topologies in your cluster, you'll have to add new worker processes to the cluster.

INCREASING THE TOTAL NUMBER OF WORKER PROCESSES IN THE CLUSTER

There are two ways to increase the total number of worker processes in the cluster. One is by adding more worker processes to your worker nodes via the steps listed in section 7.1. But this won't work if your worker nodes don't have the resources to support additional JVMs. If this is the case, you'll need to add more worker nodes to your cluster, thus adding to the pool of worker processes.

We recommend adding new worker nodes if you can. This approach has the least impact on existing topologies, because adding worker processes to existing nodes has the potential to cause other types of contention that must then be addressed.

7.4.3　*Discussion*

Worker process contention can have a variety of causes, some of which are self-inflicted and some of which aren't. Scenarios include the following:

- You deploy a topology that's configured to consume more worker processes than there are slots available in the cluster.
- You deploy a topology to your cluster that has no available slots.
- A worker node goes down, thus decreasing the number of available slots, possibly causing contention among existing topologies.

It's important to always be aware of the resources available in your cluster when deploying new topologies. If you ignore what's available within your cluster, you can easily affect every topology in your cluster by deploying something that consumes too many resources.

7.5　*Memory contention within a worker process (JVM)*

Just as you install a Storm cluster with a fixed number of worker processes, you also set up each worker process (JVM) with a fixed amount of memory it can grow to use. The amount of memory limits the number of threads (executors) that can be launched on that JVM— each thread takes a certain amount of memory (the default is 1 MB on a 64-bit Linux JVM).

JVM contention can be a problem on a per-topology basis. The combination of memory used by your bolts, spouts, threads, and so forth might exceed that allocated to the JVMs they're running on (figure 7.7).

JVM contention usually manifests itself as out-of-memory (OOM) errors and/or excessively long garbage collection (GC) pauses. OOM errors will appear in the Storm logs and Storm UI, usually as a stack trace starting with `java.lang.OutOfMemory-Error: Java heap space`.

Gaining visibility into GC issues requires a little more setup, but it's something that's easily supported by both the JVM and Storm configuration. The JVM offers startup options for tracking and logging GC usage, and Storm provides a way to specify JVM startup options for your worker processes. The `worker.childopts` property in storm.yaml is where you'd specify these JVM options. The following listing shows a sample storm.yaml configuration in a worker node.

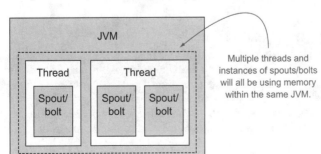

Multiple threads and instances of spouts/bolts will all be using memory within the same JVM.

Figure 7.7　Worker processes, executors and tasks mapping to the JVM, threads and instances of spouts/bolts, and the threads/instances contending for memory in the same JVM

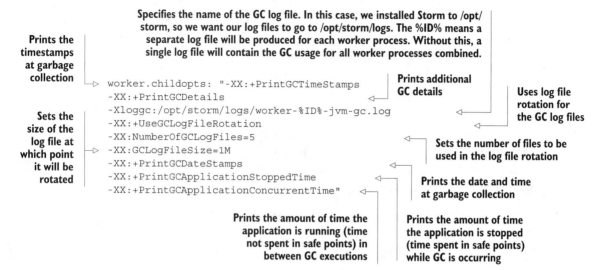

Listing 7.4 Setting up GC logging for worker processes

Prints the timestamps at garbage collection

Sets the size of the log file at which point it will be rotated

Specifies the name of the GC log file. In this case, we installed Storm to /opt/storm, so we want our log files to go to /opt/storm/logs. The %ID% means a separate log file will be produced for each worker process. Without this, a single log file will contain the GC usage for all worker processes combined.

```
worker.childopts: "-XX:+PrintGCTimeStamps
-XX:+PrintGCDetails
-Xloggc:/opt/storm/logs/worker-%ID%-jvm-gc.log
-XX:+UseGCLogFileRotation
-XX:NumberOfGCLogFiles=5
-XX:GCLogFileSize=1M
-XX:+PrintGCDateStamps
-XX:+PrintGCApplicationStoppedTime
-XX:+PrintGCApplicationConcurrentTime"
```

Prints additional GC details

Uses log file rotation for the GC log files

Sets the number of files to be used in the log file rotation

Prints the date and time at garbage collection

Prints the amount of time the application is running (time not spent in safe points) in between GC executions

Prints the amount of time the application is stopped (time spent in safe points) while GC is occurring

One interesting item to note is the value for the -Xloggc setting. Remember you can have multiple worker processes per worker node. The worker.childopts property applies to all worker processes on a node, so specifying a regular log filename would produce one log file for all the worker processes combined. A separate log file per worker process would make tracking GC usage per JVM easier. Storm provides a mechanism for logging a specific worker process; the ID variable is unique for each worker process on a worker node. Therefore, you can add a "%ID%" string to the GC log filename and you'll get a separate GC log file for each worker process.

Reading GC logs can be a little daunting at first, so we're going to run through a quick tutorial outlining what the options in listing 7.4 will produce in the associated logs. This listing shows example output for a GC cycle that included both a minor (young generation) and major collection (tenured generation). It's entirely possible that not every single GC log statement will include major collection statistics, because major collections don't occur during every GC cycle. But for the sake of completeness, we wanted to include both.

Java generational garbage collection

Java uses what's called generational garbage collection. This means memory is divided into different "generations," and as objects survive enough GC events, they get promoted to older generations. Objects will start out in what's called the young generation and eventually get promoted to the tenured generation if they survive enough GC events while in young generation. A collection of young generation object references is called a minor collection; a collection of tenured generation objects is called a major collection.

Listing 7.5   Sample GC log output

```
2014-07-27T16:29:29.027+0500: 1.342: Application time: 0.6247300 seconds

2014-07-27T16:29:29.027+0500: 1.342: [GC 1.342: [DefNew: 8128K->8128K(8128K),
    0.0000505 secs] 1.342: [Tenured: 18154K->2311K(24576K), 0.1290354 secs]
    26282K->2311K(32704K), 0.1293306 secs]

2014-07-27T16:29:29.037+0500: 1.353: Total time for which application threads
    were stopped: 0.0107480 seconds
```

Let's break down each of the parts in this output. Figure 7.8 shows the first line, containing the length of time the application has been running since the last GC.

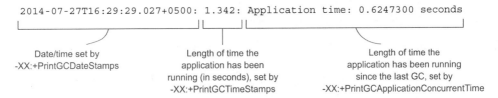

Figure 7.8   GC log output showing the output for `-XX:+PrintGCDateStamps`, `-XX:+PrintGCTimeStamps`, and `-XX:+PrintGCApplicationConcurrentTime`

The next line is the result of the `-XX:+PrintGCDetails` option and is broken down into several figures in order to better explain what's being represented. We've excluded the date/timestamps for the sake of keeping the figures simpler. Figure 7.9 shows the GC details for the minor collection of the young generation.

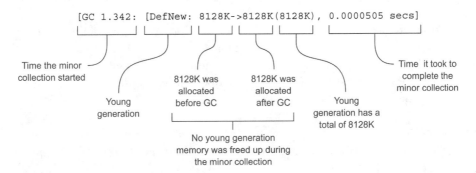

Figure 7.9   GC log output showing details of a minor garbage collection of young generation memory

The GC details for the major collection of the tenured generation are shown in Figure 7.10. Figure 7.11 shows the final part of the `-XX:+PrintGCDetails` output, which shows the overall heap values along with how long the entire GC cycle took.

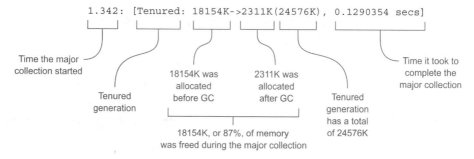

Figure 7.10 GC log output showing details of a major garbage collection of tenured generation memory

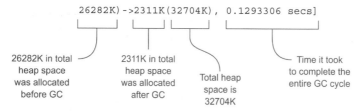

Figure 7.11 GC log output showing entire heap values and complete GC time

With the first and second lines of the GC output covered, the last line of the output is simple; the `-XX:+PrintGCApplicationStoppedTime` option results in a line like the following: `2014-07-27T16:29:29.037+0500: 1.353: Total time for which application threads were stopped: 0.0107480 seconds`. This provides a more summary-level description of how long the application was paused due to GC.

And that's it. What looks daunting at first is easily explained when you break it down into smaller pieces. Being able to read these logs will help you tremendously when debugging JVM contention issues not only in Storm, but in any application running on a JVM. With an understanding of how to set up and read GC logs along with knowing how to find OOM errors, you'll be able to identify whether your topologies are experiencing JVM contention.

7.5.1 *Problem*

Your spouts and/or bolts are attempting to consume more memory than what has been allocated to the JVM, resulting in OOM errors and/or long GC pauses.

7.5.2 *Solution*

You can address the problem in a couple of ways:

- By increasing the number of worker processes being used by the topology in question
- By increasing the size of your JVMs

INCREASING THE NUMBER OF WORKER PROCESSES BEING USED BY THE TOPOLOGY IN QUESTION

See section 7.1 for steps on doing this. By adding a worker process to a topology, you'll decrease the average load across all worker processes for that topology. This should result in a smaller memory footprint for each worker process (JVM), hopefully eliminating the JVM memory contention.

INCREASING JVM (WORKER PROCESS) SIZE

See section 7.2 for steps on how to do this. Because increasing the size of your JVMs could require you to change the size of the machines/VMs they're running on, we recommend the "increase worker processes" solution if you can.

7.5.3 *Discussion*

Swapping and balancing memory across JVMs has been one of our biggest challenges with Storm. Different topologies will have different memory usage patterns. Over time, we've gone from having four worker processes per worker node, each using 500 MB of memory, to two worker processes per worker node, each using 1 GB of memory.

Our topologies had high enough parallelism that the cost of memory per thread was making tuning at 500 MB problematic. At 1 GB per worker process, we have plenty of headroom for most topologies. Some get close to that limit, so we start spreading out the load more across multiple worker nodes.

Don't worry if you don't get it right initially. We've been running Storm in production for a couple of years now and are still tweaking the amount of memory per worker process and worker processes per machine as our topologies change, grow, and expand. Just remember, this is a never-ending process as the shape of your cluster and topologies changes.

Beware when increasing the memory allocated to a JVM; as a rule of thumb, when you cross certain key points you'll notice a change in how long garbage collection takes—500 MB, 1 GB, 2 GB, and 4 GB are all around the points when our GC time has taken a jump. It's more art than science, so bring your patience with you. There's nothing more frustrating than addressing OOM issues by increasing JVM memory size only to have it noticeably impact GC times.

7.6 *Memory contention on a worker node*

Much like how an individual JVM has a limited amount of available memory, so does a worker node as a whole. In addition to the memory needed to run your Storm worker processes (JVMs), you need memory to run the Supervisor process and any other processes on your worker node without swapping (figure 7.12).

If a worker node is experiencing memory contention, that worker node will be swapping. *Swapping* is the little death and needs to be avoided if you care about latency and throughput. This is a problem when using Storm; each worker node needs to have enough memory so that the worker processes and OS don't swap. If you want to maintain consistent performance, you must avoid swapping with Storm's JVMs.

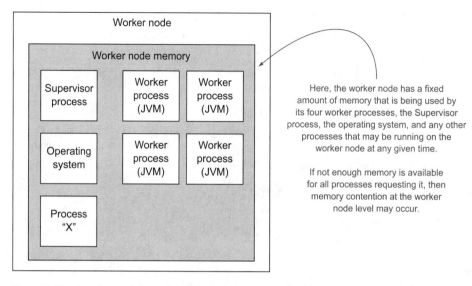

Figure 7.12   A worker node has a fixed amount of memory that's being used by its worker processes along with any other processes running on that worker node.

One way to keep an eye on this in Linux is with the `sar` (System Activity Reporter) command. This is a Linux-based system statistics command that collects and displays all system activities and statistics. We run this command in the format of `sar [option] [interval [count]]` (figure 7.13).

Various options can be passed in to display specific types of statistics. For diagnosing worker node memory contention, we use the `-S` option for reporting swap space utilization statistics. Figure 7.14 illustrates the output for swap space utilization.

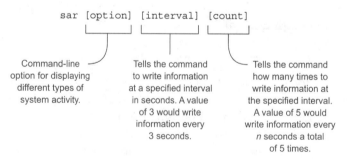

Figure 7.13   `sar` command breakdown

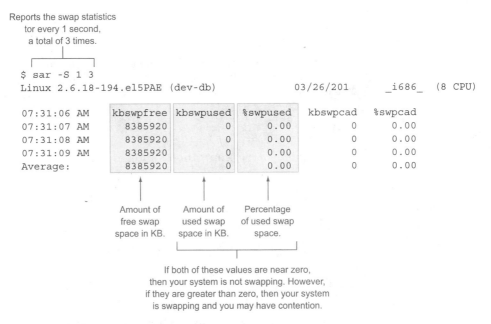

Figure 7.14 Output of `sar -S 1 3` **for reporting swap space utilization**

A note on operating system contentions

The only way to avoid contention at the OS level is to sidestep it entirely! What do we mean by that? Well, let's explain.

If you run a single worker process per worker node, it's impossible to run into contention between workers on that node. This can make maintaining consistent performance within a cluster much easier. We know of more than one development team that has opted for this approach. If possible, we advise you to seriously consider going this route.

This is a nonstarter if you aren't running in a virtualized environment. The cost is simply too high to do this if you're running on "bare metal" with a single OS instance per physical machine. Within a virtualized environment, you'll use more resources by doing this. Assume for a moment that your OS install requires n GB of disk space and uses 2 GB of memory to run effectively. If you have eight workers running on your cluster and you assign four workers per node, you'd use $n * 2$ GB of disk and 4 GB of memory to run the OS on your cluster nodes. If you were to run a single worker per node, that would skyrocket to $n * 8$ GB of disk and 16 GB of memory. That's a four-fold increase in a rather small cluster. Imagine the additional usage that would result if you had a cluster that was 16, 32, 128, or more nodes in size. If you're running in an environment such as Amazon Web Services (AWS) where you pay per node, the costs can add up quickly. Therefore, we suggest this approach only if you're running in a private virtualized environment where the cost of hardware is relatively fixed and you have disk and memory resources to spare.

> **(continued)**
> If that limited scenario doesn't describe you, don't worry; we have plenty of tips in the following pages to help you out as well. And even if it does describe you, you're going to want to familiarize yourself with the following material anyway because a single topology can still run up against these problems.

7.6.1 *Problem*

Your worker node is swapping due to contention for that node's memory.

7.6.2 *Solution*

Here's how you can address this problem:

- Increase the memory available to each worker node. This would mean giving more memory to the physical machine or VM, depending on how you configured your cluster.
- Lower the collective memory used by worker processes.

LOWERING THE COLLECTIVE MEMORY USED BY WORKER PROCESSES

Lowering the collective memory used by worker processes can be done in one of two ways. The first is by reducing the number of worker processes per worker node. See section 7.1 for the appropriate steps. Reducing the total number of worker processes will lower the overall memory footprint of the combined remaining processes.

The second way is by reducing the size of your JVMs. See section 7.2 for those steps. Be careful when lowering memory allocated to existing JVMs, though, to avoid introducing memory contention within the JVM.

7.6.3 *Discussion*

Our solution is to always go the route of increasing the memory available to each machine. It's the simplest solution and its resulting ramifications are the easiest to understand. If you are tight on memory, lowering memory usage can work, but you open yourself up to all the problems we discussed concerning GC and OOM on a per-JVM basis. Long story short, if you have the memory to spare, go with increasing memory on each machine.

7.7 *Worker node CPU contention*

Worker node CPU contention occurs when the demand for CPU cycles outstrips the amount available. This is a problem when using Storm and is one of the primary sources of contention in a Storm cluster. If your Storm topology's throughput is lower than what you expect it to be, you may want to check the worker node(s) running your topology to see if CPU contention exists.

One way to keep an eye on this in Linux is with the sar command, passing in the option –u for displaying real-time CPU usage of all CPUs. Figure 7.15 illustrates the output for CPU usage along with the columns you'll want to keep an eye on.

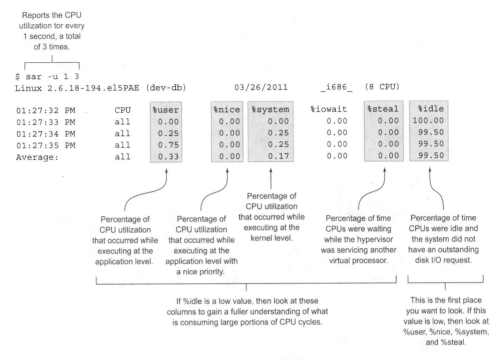

Figure 7.15 Output of sar –u 1 3 for reporting CPU utilization

7.7.1 Problem

The throughput of your topologies is low, and based on running the sar command, you see that CPU contention exists.

7.7.2 Solution

To address the problem, you have the following options:

- Increasing the number of CPUs available to the machine. This is only possible in a virtualized environment.
- Upgrading to a more powerful CPU (Amazon Web Services (AWS) type of environment).
- Spreading the JVM load across more worker nodes by lowering the number of worker processes per worker node.

SPREADING JVM LOAD ACROSS MORE WORKER NODES

To spread worker process (JVM) load across more worker nodes, you need to reduce the number of worker processes running on each worker node (see section 7.1 for those steps). Reducing the number of worker processes per worker node results in less processing (CPU requests) being done on each worker node. There are two scenarios you may find yourself in when attempting this solution. The first is you have unused worker processes in your cluster and can therefore reduce the number of worker processes on your existing nodes, thus spreading the load (figure 7.16).

The second scenario is where you don't have any unused worker processes and therefore need to add worker nodes in order to reduce the number of worker processes per worker node (figure 7.17).

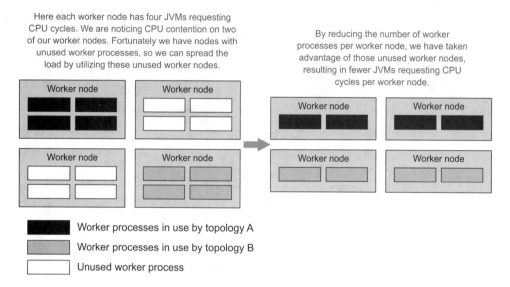

Figure 7.16   Reducing the number of worker processes per worker node in a cluster where there are unused worker processes

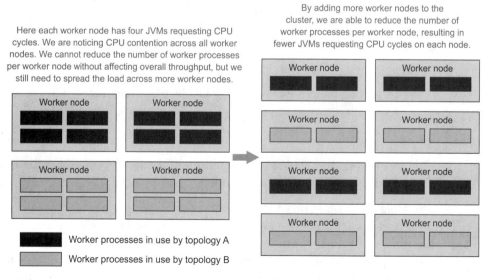

Figure 7.17   Reducing the number of worker processes per worker node in a cluster where there are no unused worker processes, resulting in more worker nodes being added

Reducing the number of worker processes per worker node is a good way to reduce the number of CPU cycles being requested on each node. You just need to be aware of what resources are available and in use and act appropriately in your given scenario.

7.7.3   *Discussion*

If you're like us and run your own private cloud, the first option is a great one. Your Storm nodes are running across different host machines with *x* number of CPUs available (in our case, 16). When we first started using Storm, our computational needs were much lower, and we assigned a max of two cores to each node. Eventually that became problematic and we moved to four and then eight. Most of the time, each node isn't using all the CPU, but it's there when needed.

You can follow the same pattern in AWS and other hosted solutions by upgrading to a more powerful CPU and/or number of available cores. But you're going to hit a limit. There's only so much CPU time to go around among all those guest machines running on a single physical box. If you hit that point or can't scale up CPUs, distributing the load across more machines is your only option.

So far, we've never had to solve CPU usage issues in this way (but we've solved others' issues in such a fashion). And sometimes, we've solved the problem entirely differently. It turned out that one time our issue was a bug that caused a topology to burn CPU needlessly over and over in a tight loop. That's always what you should check for first, but leading with "Are you sure you didn't mess up?" seemed like a less than friendly way to start the discussion.

7.8   *Worker node I/O contention*

I/O contention on a worker node can fall under one of two categories:

- Disk I/O contention, reading from and writing to the file system
- Network/socket I/O contention, reading from and writing to a network via a socket

Both types of contention are regularly an issue for certain classes of Storm topologies. The first step in determining if you're experiencing either of these contentions is to establish whether a worker node is experiencing I/O contention in general. Once you do, you can dive down into the exact type of I/O contention your worker node is suffering from.

One way to determine if a worker node in your cluster is experiencing I/O contention is by running the sar command with the -u option for displaying real-time CPU usage. This is the same command we ran for CPU contention in section 7.7, but this time we'll focus on a different column in the output (figure 7.18).

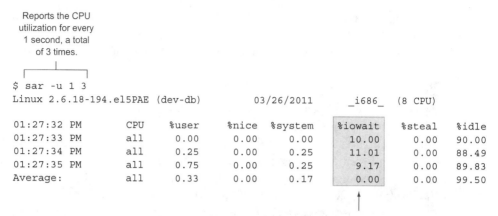

Reports the CPU
utilization for every
1 second, a total
of 3 times.

```
$ sar -u 1 3
Linux 2.6.18-194.el5PAE (dev-db)        03/26/2011        _i686_   (8 CPU)

01:27:32 PM      CPU    %user    %nice   %system   %iowait   %steal   %idle
01:27:33 PM      all     0.00     0.00      0.00     10.00     0.00   90.00
01:27:34 PM      all     0.25     0.00      0.25     11.01     0.00   88.49
01:27:35 PM      all     0.75     0.00      0.25      9.17     0.00   89.83
Average:         all     0.33     0.00      0.17      0.00     0.00   99.50
```

Figure 7.18 Output of sar -u 1 3 for reporting CPU utilization and, in particular, I/O wait times

Percentage of time the CPUs were idle, during which the system had an outstanding disk I/O request. If this value is above 10.00, you are most likely experiencing performance degradation due to I/O contention. With a value above 25.00, you're most definitely in a world of pain.

A healthy topology that uses a lot of I/O shouldn't spend a lot of time waiting for the resources to become available. That's why we use 10.00% as the threshold at which you start experiencing performance degradation.

You might think distinguishing between socket/network and disk I/O contention is a difficult task, but you'd be surprised at how often your own intuition will lead you to the correct choice. Let's explain.

If you know what topologies are running on a given worker node (section 7.3 discusses determining this), you know that they use a lot of network resources or disk I/O, and you see iowait problems, you can probably safely assume which of the two is your issue. Here's a simple test to help you with that: if you're seeing troubling I/O contention signs, first attempt to determine if you're suffering from socket/network I/O contention. If you aren't, assume that you're suffering from disk I/O contention. Although this might not always be the case, it can take you a long way as you learn the tools of the trade.

Let's dive a little deeper into each of the I/O contentions to give you a fuller understanding of what we're talking about.

7.8.1 Network/socket I/O contention

If your topologies interact over a network with external services, network/socket I/O contention is bound to be a problem for your cluster. In our experience, the main cause for this type of contention is that all of the ports allocated for opening sockets are being used.

Most Linux installs will default to 1024 maximum open files/sockets per process. In an I/O-intensive topology, it's easy to hit that limit quickly. We've written topologies that open several thousand sockets per worker node. To determine the limits of your

OS, you can examine the /proc filesystem to check your processes limits. In order to do this, you'll first need to know your process ID. Once you do that, you can get a listing of all limits for that process. The following listing shows you how to use the ps and grep commands to find your process ID (aka PID) and then how to get your process limits from the /proc filesystem.

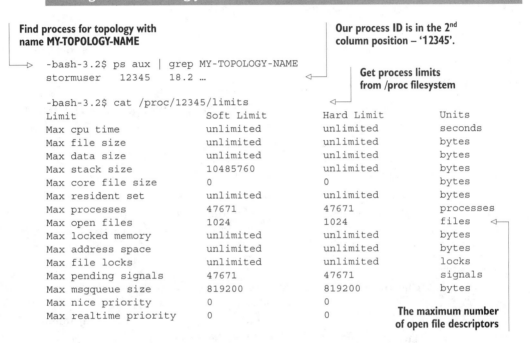

Listing 7.6 Determining your resource limits

Find process for topology with name MY-TOPOLOGY-NAME

Our process ID is in the 2nd column position – '12345'.

```
-bash-3.2$ ps aux | grep MY-TOPOLOGY-NAME
stormuser    12345    18.2 ...
```

Get process limits from /proc filesystem

```
-bash-3.2$ cat /proc/12345/limits
```

Limit	Soft Limit	Hard Limit	Units
Max cpu time	unlimited	unlimited	seconds
Max file size	unlimited	unlimited	bytes
Max data size	unlimited	unlimited	bytes
Max stack size	10485760	unlimited	bytes
Max core file size	0	0	bytes
Max resident set	unlimited	unlimited	bytes
Max processes	47671	47671	processes
Max open files	1024	1024	files
Max locked memory	unlimited	unlimited	bytes
Max address space	unlimited	unlimited	bytes
Max file locks	unlimited	unlimited	locks
Max pending signals	47671	47671	signals
Max msgqueue size	819200	819200	bytes
Max nice priority	0	0	
Max realtime priority	0	0	

The maximum number of open file descriptors

If you're hitting this limit, the Storm UI for your topology should display an exception in the "Last Error" column that the max open files limit has been reached. This will most likely be a stack trace starting with java.net.SocketException: Too many open files.

Dealing with a saturated network link and network/socket I/O-intensive topologies

We've never seen a saturated network link, but we know it's theoretically possible, so we mention it here instead of devoting an entire recipe to it. Depending on your operating system, you can use various tools to determine whether your network link is saturated. For Linux, we recommend iftop.

There are two things you can do for a saturated network link: 1) get a faster network or 2) lower the number of worker processes per worker node in order to spread the load across more machines; this will work as long as you're overloading your local network and not the entire network in general.

PROBLEM

Your topology is experiencing reduced throughput or no throughput at all, and you're seeing errors for hitting the limit of open sockets.

SOLUTION

A couple of ways to address this problem are as follows:

- Increasing the number of available ports on the worker node
- Adding more worker nodes to the cluster

For increasing the number of available ports, you'll need to edit the `/etc/security/limits.conf` file on most Linux distributions. You can add lines such as the following:

```
* soft nofile 128000
* hard nofile 25600
```

These settings will set the hard and soft limit on open files per user. The value we're concerned with as a Storm user is the soft limit. We don't advise going higher than 128k. If you do, then as a rule of thumb (until you learn more about soft/hard limits for number of files open on Linux), we suggest setting the hard limit to two times the value of the soft limit. Note that you need super-user access to change `limits.conf` and you're going to need to reboot the system to make sure they take effect.

Increasing the number of worker nodes in the cluster will give you access to more ports. If you don't have the resources to add more physical machines or VMs, you'll have to try the first solution.

DISCUSSION

The first real contention issue we hit was the number of sockets available per machine. We use a lot of them because a number of our topologies make lots of calls to external services to look up additional information that isn't available from our initial incoming data. Having a high number of sockets available is a must. Don't add more workers on other machines until you've increased available sockets on each node as much as you can. Once you've done that, you should also look at your code.

Are you opening and closing sockets all the time? If you can keep connections open, do that. There's this wonderful thing called TCP_WAIT. It's where a TCP connection will stay open after you close it waiting for any stray data. If you're on a slow network link (like many were when TCP was first designed), this is a wonderful idea that helps prevent data corruption. If you're on a fast modern LAN, it'll drive you insane. You can tune your TCP stack via various OS-specific means to lower how long you linger in TCP_WAIT, but when you're making tons of network calls, even that won't be enough. Be smart: open and close connections as little as possible.

7.8.2   *Disk I/O contention*

Disk I/O contention affects how quickly you can write to disk. This could be a problem with Storm but should be exceedingly rare. If you're writing large volumes of data to your logs or storing the output of calculations to files on the local filesystem, it might be an issue, but that should be unlikely.

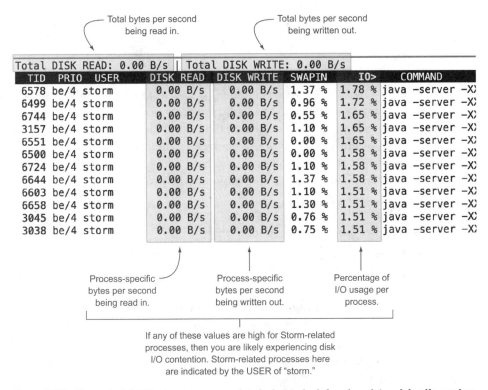

Figure 7.19   The output for the `iotop` command and what to look for when determining if a worker node is experiencing disk I/O contention

If you have a topology that's writing data to disk and notice its throughput is lower than what you're expecting, you should check to see if the worker nodes it's running on are experiencing disk I/O contention. For Linux installations, you can run a command called `iotop` to get a view of the disk I/O usage for the worker nodes in question. This command displays a table of current I/O usage by processes/threads in the system, with the most I/O-intensive processes/threads listed first. Figure 7.19 shows the command and its associated output, along with the parts of the output we're interested in.

PROBLEM

You have a topology that reads/writes to/from disk, and it looks like the worker nodes it's running on are experiencing disk I/O contention.

SOLUTION

To address this problem

- Write less data to disk. This can mean cutting back within your topology. It can also mean putting fewer worker processes on each worker node if multiple worker processes are demanding disk on the same worker node.
- Get faster disks. This could include using a RAM disk.

- If you're writing to NFS or some other network filesystem, stop immediately. Writing to NFS is slow and you're setting yourself up for disk I/O contention if you do.

DISCUSSION

Slow disk I/O sucks. It drives us insane. The worst part is fast disks aren't cheap. The disks that we run our Storm workers on are fairly slow. We save our fast disks for stuff where we really need speed: Elasticsearch, Solr, Riak, RabbitMQ, and similar write-heavy parts of our infrastructure. If you're writing large amounts of data to disk and you don't have fast disks, you're going to have to accept it as a bottleneck. There's not much you can do without throwing money at the problem.

7.9   Summary

In this chapter, you learned the following:

- Several types of contention exist above the topology level, so it's helpful to be able to monitor things like CPU, I/O, and memory usage for the operating system your worker nodes are running on.
- It is important to have some level of familiarity with monitoring tools for the operating system of the machines/VMs in your cluster. In Linux, these include `sar`, `netstat`, and `iotop`.
- There's value in knowing common JVM startup options, such as `-Xms`, `-Xmx`, and those related to GC logging.
- Although the Storm UI is a great tool for the initial diagnosis of many types of contention, it's smart to have other types of monitoring at the machine/VM level to let you know if something is awry.
- Including custom metrics/monitoring in your individual topologies will give you valuable insights that the Storm UI may not be able to.
- Be careful when increasing the number of worker processes running on a worker node because you can introduce memory and/or CPU contention at the worker node level.
- Be careful when decreasing the number of worker processes running on a worker node because you can affect your topologies' throughput while also introducing contention for worker processes across your cluster.

Storm internals
8

This chapter covers

- How an executor works under the covers
- How tuples are passed between executors
- Storm's internal buffers
- Overflow and tuning of Storm's internal buffers
- Routing and tasks
- Storm's debug log output

Here we are, four chapters into covering Storm in production. We've explained how you can use the Storm UI to understand what's going on in your topologies, how to use that information to tune your topologies, and how to diagnose and treat cross-topology contention issues. We've explored a number of tools you can put to good use. In this chapter, we'll introduce you to one more: a deeper understanding of Storm's internals.

Why do we think this is important? Well, in the previous three chapters we've given you the tools and strategies for handling issues you're likely to encounter, but we can't know every possible problem you will encounter. Each Storm cluster is unique; your combination of hardware and code is bound to encounter issues we've never seen and, perhaps, that other people haven't seen either. The deeper the understanding you have of how Storm works, the better equipped you'll be to handle such issues. The intent of this chapter, unlike the previous chapter, isn't to provide solutions to specific problems.

To become a master of tuning Storm, debugging Storm issues, designing your topologies for maximum efficiency, and all the other myriad tasks that are part of running a production system, you need to have a deep understanding of the tool you're using. We aim in this chapter to take you deep into the abstractions that make up Storm. We aren't going to take you all the way down to the bottom, because Storm is a living project that's actively being developed and a lot of that development is going on at the core. But there's a level of abstraction deeper than any we've covered so far, and it's this level of abstraction that we'll endeavor to familiarize you with. How you'll deploy the knowledge you get from this chapter we can't say, but we know you won't master Storm until you have a firm grasp of the internals that are the subject of this chapter.

> **NOTE** Some of the terminology we use throughout this chapter doesn't map directly to the verbiage in the Storm source code but is true to the spirit. This is intentional, because the focus should be on how the internals work, not necessarily how they're named.

To focus on Storm's internals rather than the details of a new use case, we're going to bring back an old friend, the commit count topology from chapter 2. Let's go through a quick rundown of this topology just in case you've forgotten.

8.1   *The commit count topology revisited*

The commit count topology provides a simple topology (one spout and two bolts) we can use to explain Storm's internals within the context of a particular use case but without getting bogged down with the details of the use case. Having said that, there are a few additional qualifiers we'll add to this topology for teaching purposes. But before we get to those qualifiers, let's quickly rehash the topology itself.

8.1.1   *Reviewing the topology design*

As you'll recall from chapter 2, the commit count topology is broken down into (1) one spout that'll read commits from a feed, and (2) two bolts that'll extract the email from the commit message and store counts for each email, respectively. This can all be seen in figure 8.1.

This design is straightforward and easy to understand. As such, it provides us with a nice scenario to delve into the internals of Storm. One thing we'll do differently in this chapter is present the topology deployed to a remote Storm cluster, as opposed to having it run in local mode. Let's discuss why this is needed and how our topology may look when deployed to a remote cluster with multiple worker nodes.

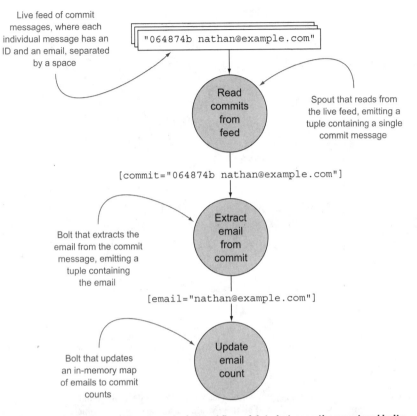

Live feed of commit messages, where each individual message has an ID and an email, separated by a space

"064874b nathan@example.com"

Read commits from feed

Spout that reads from the live feed, emitting a tuple containing a single commit message

[commit="064874b nathan@example.com"]

Extract email from commit

Bolt that extracts the email from the commit message, emitting a tuple containing the email

[email="nathan@example.com"]

Update email count

Bolt that updates an in-memory map of emails to commit counts

Figure 8.1   Commit count topology design and flow of data between the spout and bolts

8.1.2   *Thinking of the topology as running on a remote Storm cluster*

Presenting the topology as running on a remote Storm cluster is essential for this chapter, because the Storm internals we want to cover exist only in a remote cluster setup. For this, we'll say our topology is running across two worker nodes. Doing this allows us to explain what happens when tuples are passed between components within the same worker process (JVM) as well as across worker processes (from one JVM to another). Figure 8.2 illustrates the two worker nodes along with specifics on where each spout and bolt is executing. This diagram should look familiar, as we presented something similar in chapter 5 when providing a hypothetical configuration of the credit card authorization topology.

8.1.3   *How data flows between the spout and bolts in the cluster*

Let's trace the flow of a tuple through the topology, much as we did in chapter 2. But rather than showing the data flow from the viewpoint of figure 8.1, we'll show it from the viewpoint of data being passed between instances of our spout and bolts across executors and worker processes (figure 8.3).

Our topology is executing across two worker nodes
(physical or virtual machines), where each worker node
is running a single worker process (JVM).

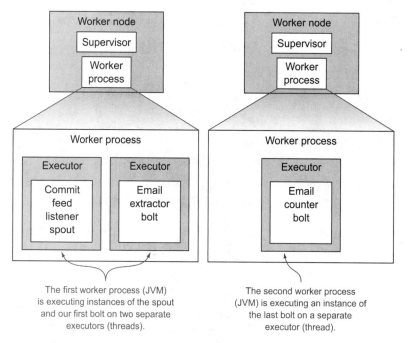

Figure 8.2   **Commit count topology running across two worker nodes, with one worker process executing a spout and bolt and another worker process executing a bolt**

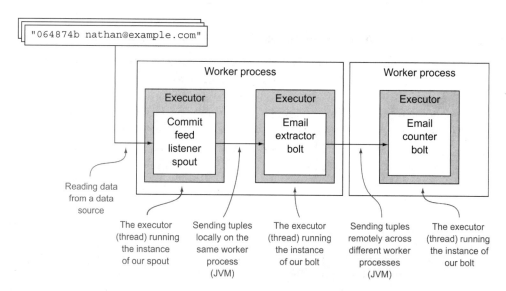

Figure 8.3   **Breaking down the flow of data through the topology into six sections, each of which highlights something different within an executor or how data is passed between executors**

Figure 8.3 illustrates nicely how the tuples will flow between instances of our spout and bolts across threads (executors) within a single JVM (worker process) along with data flowing between worker nodes to a completely separate JVM (worker process). Think of figure 8.3 as the 10,000-foot view of how tuples are being passed between components. The goal of this chapter is to dive down much deeper into what's happening in figure 8.3, so let's do exactly that, following the flow of data within and between executors in our scenario.

8.2 Diving into the details of an executor

In previous chapters, we've described executors as a single thread running on a JVM. That has served us well until now. In our day-to-day reasoning about our own topologies, we usually think of an executor at that level of abstraction as well. But an executor is more than a single thread. Let's discuss what we mean by this, starting with the executor running our spout instance that reads data from a data source.

8.2.1 Executor details for the commit feed listener spout

Data enters the commit count topology via the commit feed listener spout that listens to a feed of data containing individual commit messages. Figure 8.4 illustrates where we are in our data flow for the topology.

There's a bit more to this executor than a single thread. It's actually two threads and one queue. The first thread is what we call the *main thread* and is primarily responsible for running user-supplied code; in this instance, it's the code we wrote in `nextTuple`. The second thread is what we'll call the *send thread*, which we'll talk about shortly in the next section, and it handles transferring tuples to the next bolt in the topology.

In addition to the two threads, we have a single queue for transferring emitted tuples out of the executor. Think of this queue as a post-execute-spout function.

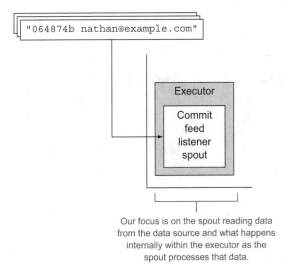

Our focus is on the spout reading data
from the data source and what happens
internally within the executor as the
spout processes that data.

**Figure 8.4 Focusing on
data flowing into the spout**

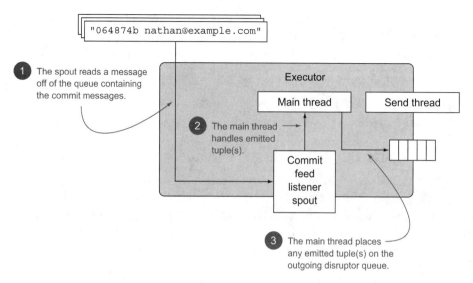

Figure 8.5   The spout reads messages off the queue containing commit messages and converts those messages into tuples. The main thread on the executor handles emitted tuples, passing them to the executor's outgoing queue.

This queue is designed for high-performance messaging between executors. It's achieved by having the queue implementation rely on a library known as the *LMAX Disruptor.*[1] All you need to know about a disruptor queue for now is that Storm uses it for the internal executor queue implementations. Figure 8.5 illustrates this more detailed understanding of the executor for our spout, with two threads and one queue.

The illustration in figure 8.5 covers data being read in by the spout instance and the main thread taking the tuple emitted by the spout and placing it on the outgoing queue. What hasn't been covered is what happens once the emitted tuple has been placed on the outgoing queue. This is where the send thread comes into play.

8.2.2   Transferring tuples between two executors on the same JVM

Our tuple has been placed on the spout's outgoing disruptor queue. Now what? Before we get into what happens here, let's take a look at figure 8.6, which shows where we are in our topology's data flow.

---

[1] The LMAX Disruptor is a high-performance inter-thread messaging library. It's an open source project available at http://lmax-exchange.github.io/disruptor.

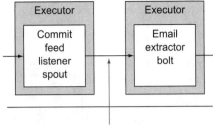

Focusing on what happens when tuples are
sent between executors (threads) running
on the same worker process (JVM)

**Figure 8.6   Focusing on passing
tuples within the same JVM**

Once the data has been placed on the spout's outgoing disruptor queue, the send
thread will read that tuple off the outgoing disruptor queue and send it to the appropriate executor(s) via a *transfer function*.

Because the commit feed listener spout and email extractor bolt are both on the
same JVM, this transfer function will execute a *local transfer* between executors. When a
local transfer occurs, the executor's send thread publishes outgoing tuples to the next
executor directly. Both executors here are on the same JVM, so there's little to no overhead during the send, making this an extremely fast type of transfer function. This is
illustrated in more detail in figure 8.7.

How exactly does the executor for our first bolt receive tuples directly? This is
covered in the next section, where we break down the executor for the email extractor bolt.

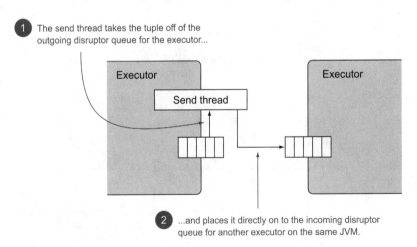

**Figure 8.7   A more detailed look at a local transfer of tuples between the commit
feed listener spout and the email extractor bolt**

8.2.3 *Executor details for the email extractor bolt*

So far we've covered our spout reading a commit message from a feed of data and emitting a new tuple for each individual commit message. We're at the point where our first bolt, the email extractor, is ready to process an incoming tuple. Figure 8.8 highlights where we are in our data flow.

You probably have some idea of what the executors for our bolts look like given that we've already covered the executor for a spout. The only real difference between executors for spouts and for bolts is that an executor for a bolt has an additional queue: the queue for handling incoming tuples. This means our bolt's executor has an incoming disruptor queue and a main thread that reads a tuple off the incoming disruptor queue and processes that tuple, resulting in zero or more tuples to be emitted. These emitted tuples are placed on the outgoing disruptor queue. Figure 8.9 breaks down the details.

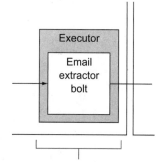

Our focus is on what happens within an executor that is running an instance of a bolt that accepts an input tuple from some other component and emits an output tuple.

Figure 8.8 Focusing on a bolt that emits a tuple

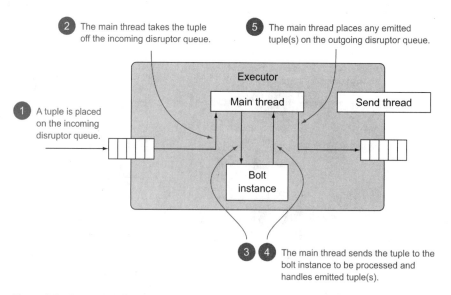

Figure 8.9 The executor for our bolt, with two threads and two queues

Once the email extractor bolt has processed the tuple, it's ready to be sent to the next bolt down the line, the commit counter bolt. We've already discussed what happens when a tuple is sent between the commit feed listener spout and the email extractor bolt. This happens with a local transfer. But we're in a different situation when sending data between the email extractor bolt and the commit counter bolt. The bolt instances are running on different JVMs. Let's discuss what happens in this scenario next.

8.2.4 *Transferring tuples between two executors on different JVMs*

As we mentioned previously, the email extractor and commit counter bolts are running on separate JVMs. Figure 8.10 shows you exactly where we are in the data flow for our topology.

When a tuple is emitted to an executor running on a separate JVM, the sending executor's send thread will execute a *transfer function* that performs what we call a *remote transfer*. A remote transfer is more involved than a local transfer. What happens when Storm needs to send tuples from one JVM to another? The first step in the process is to serialize our tuple for transport. Depending on your tuple, this could be a rather expensive operation. When serializing tuples, Storm attempts to look up a Kryo serializer for that object and ready it for transport. Lacking a Kryo serializer, Storm will fall back on standard Java object serialization. Kryo serialization is far more efficient than Java serialization, so if you care about pulling every last bit of performance out of your topologies, you'll want to register custom serializers for your tuples.

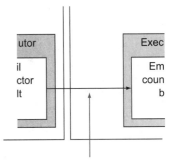

Focusing on what happens when tuples are sent between executors (threads) running on different worker processes (JVMs)

Figure 8.10 Focusing on sending tuples between JVMs

Once a tuple has been serialized for inter-JVM transport, our executor's send/transfer thread publishes it to yet another disruptor queue. This queue is the transfer queue for our entire JVM. Any time an executor on this JVM needs to transfer tuples to executors on other JVMs, those serialized tuples will be published to this queue.

Once a tuple is on this queue, another thread, the worker process's send/transfer thread, picks it up and, via TCP, sends it over the network to its destination JVM.

At the destination JVM, another thread, the worker process's receive thread, is waiting to receive tuples that it in turn passes off to yet another function, the receive function. The worker receive function, much like an executor's transfer function, is responsible for routing the tuple to the correct executor. The receive thread publishes our tuple to the incoming disruptor queue where it's available to be picked up by the executor's primary thread for processing. This entire process can be seen in figure 8.11.

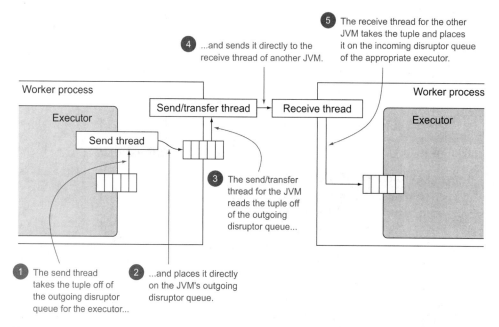

Figure 8.11   The steps that occur during a remote transfer of a tuple between executors on different JVMs

In our commit counter example, an email address such as sean@example.com was extracted from a commit by our email extractor bolt and placed on the executor's transfer queue, where the executor's send thread picked it up and passed it to the transfer function. There it was serialized for transport and placed on the worker's transfer queue. Another thread then picked up the transfer and sent it via TCP to our second worker, where the receive thread accepted it and, via the receive function, routed it to the correct executor by placing it on that executor's incoming disruptor queue.

A word about Netty

In this section, we've used the term *TCP* to discuss connections between JVMs that make up a Storm cluster. As of the current version of Storm, network transport is provided by Netty, a powerful framework designed to make it easy to build high-performance asynchronous network applications. It has a wealth of settings that allow you to tune its performance.

For a standard Storm installation, you shouldn't need to tweak any Netty settings exposed by Storm. If you find yourself running into Netty performance issues, as with any other settings, be prepared to measure before and after changes.

Providing enough information to allow you to confidently wade into tuning Netty is beyond the scope of this book. If you're interested in learning more about Netty, we urge you to get *Netty in Action* (Manning, 2015) by Netty committer Norman Maurer.

8.2.5 *Executor details for the email counter bolt*

The executor for this bolt is similar to the executor for our previous bolt, but because this bolt doesn't emit a tuple, no work needs to be done by the executor's send thread. Figure 8.12 highlights where we are in our flow of a tuple between executors.

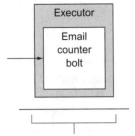

Focusing on what happens within an executor that is running an instance of a bolt that accepts an input tuple from some other component but does not emit an output tuple.

The details of what happens within this executor can be seen in figure 8.13. Notice that the number of steps is reduced, because we aren't emitting tuples in this bolt.

Figure 8.12 Focusing on a bolt that does not emit a tuple

Our data has now managed to flow from the spout where it started through the email counter bolt. Its life cycle is almost done. It'll be deserialized and processed, and the count for that email address will be updated. Our email counter bolt doesn't emit a new tuple—it acks its incoming tuple.

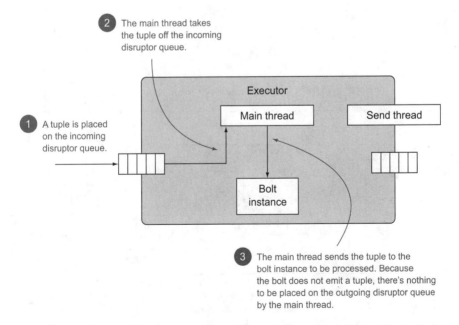

Figure 8.13 The executor for the email counter bolt with a main thread that pulls a tuple off the incoming disruptor queue and sends that tuple to the bolt to be processed

8.3   *Routing and tasks*

A few times in the book, we've explained something only to later admit we lied via omission in order to explain the basics of a concept. And so it is again with our explanation that we've given so far in this chapter. We've omitted a very important part of the conversation. But don't worry; now that you have a handle on the core parts of Storm, we can discuss *tasks and routing*.

Way back in chapter 3, we introduced executors and tasks. Figure 8.14 should look familiar—it's the figure breaking down a worker node as a JVM running an executor with a task (spout/bolt instance), but updated with your current understanding of how an executor works.

Let's dig a little bit more into tasks. As we stated in chapter 3, an executor can have one or more tasks, where the executor is responsible for "executing" the user logic that's in the task. How does this work when an executor has multiple tasks (figure 8.15)?

This is where routing comes into the picture. *Routing* in this context means how a worker process's receive thread (remote transfer) or an executor's send thread (local transfer) sends a tuple to its correct next location (task). It's a multistep process

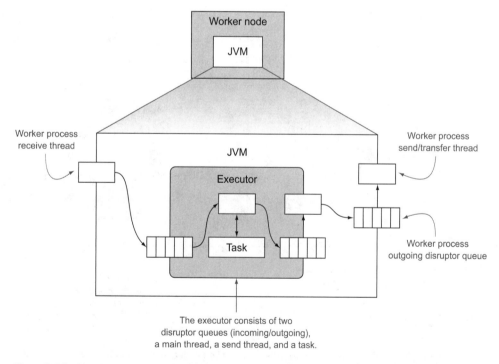

Figure 8.14   **A worker process broken down with its internal threads and queue along with an executor and its internal threads, queues, and a task**

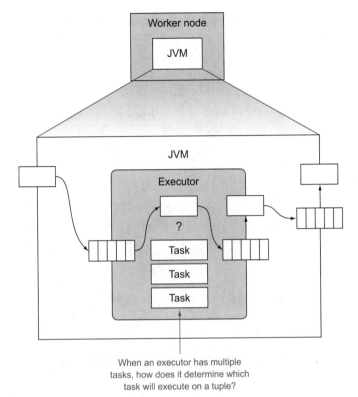

When an executor has multiple
tasks, how does it determine which
task will execute on a tuple?

**Figure 8.15   An executor
with multiple tasks**

that'll be easier with a concrete example. We'll use the email extractor as an example. Figure 8.16 illustrates what happens after the email extractor's main thread has run its `execute` method and a tuple has been emitted.

Figure 8.16 should look somewhat familiar. It includes some of the internal queues and threads we've been discussing along with annotations for the steps that are taken when determining which task is supposed to execute an emitted tuple. The figure references a task ID and tuple pair, which comes in the form of an object of type `TaskMessage`:

```
public class TaskMessage {
  private int _task;
  private byte[] _message;
  ...
}
```

This brings our explanation of Storm's internal queues to a close. We'll now move on to how these queues may overflow and some ways to address such overflow.

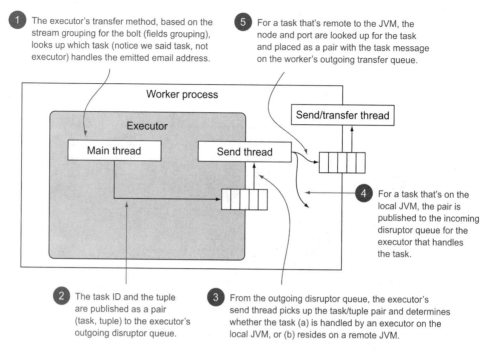

1 The executor's transfer method, based on the stream grouping for the bolt (fields grouping), looks up which task (notice we said task, not executor) handles the emitted email address.

5 For a task that's remote to the JVM, the node and port are looked up for the task and placed as a pair with the task message on the worker's outgoing transfer queue.

Worker process

Send/transfer thread

Executor

Main thread   Send thread

4 For a task that's on the local JVM, the pair is published to the incoming disruptor queue for the executor that handles the task.

2 The task ID and the tuple are published as a pair (task, tuple) to the executor's outgoing disruptor queue.

3 From the outgoing disruptor queue, the executor's send thread picks up the task/tuple pair and determines whether the task (a) is handled by an executor on the local JVM, or (b) resides on a remote JVM.

Figure 8.16   Mapping out the steps taken when determining the destination task for an emitted tuple

8.4   Knowing when Storm's internal queues overflow

We've covered an awful lot in a relatively short period of time. By now, you should have a decent grasp of what constitutes an executor. But before we get into the details of debug logs, we want to bring you back to the three queues internal to Storm we've discussed so far.

8.4.1   The various types of internal queues and how they might overflow

In our discussion of executors, we identified three queues that are internal to Storm:

- An executor's incoming queue
- An executor's outgoing queue
- The outgoing queue that exists on a worker node

We love to talk about troubleshooting and what can go wrong, so we pose the question: *What would it take to overflow each of those queues?*

Go ahead. Take a minute. We'll wait. For a queue to overflow, anything producing data that goes on to the queue has to be generating that data faster than it can be consumed. It's the relationship between producers and consumers that we want to focus on. We'll start by looking at the executor's incoming queue.

EXECUTOR'S INCOMING QUEUE

This queue receives tuples from the spout/bolt preceding it in the topology. If the preceding spout/bolt is producing tuples at a faster rate than the consuming bolt can process them, you're going to have an overflow problem.

The next queue a tuple will encounter is the executor's outgoing transfer queue.

EXECUTOR'S OUTGOING TRANSFER QUEUE

This one is a bit trickier. This queue sits between an executor's main thread, executing user logic, and the transfer thread that handles routing the tuple to its next task. In order for this queue to get backed up, you'd need to be processing incoming tuples faster than they can be routed, serialized, and so forth. That's a pretty tall order—one we've never actually experienced ourselves—but we're sure someone has had it happen.

If we're dealing with a tuple that's being transferred to another JVM, we'll run into the third queue, the worker process's outgoing transfer queue.

WORKER PROCESS'S OUTGOING TRANSFER QUEUE

This queue receives tuples from all executors on the worker that are bound for another, different worker process. Given enough executors within the worker process producing tuples that need to be sent over the network to other worker processes, it's quite possible that you could overflow this buffer. But you're probably going to have to work hard to do it.

What happens if you start to overflow one of these buffers? Storm places the overflowing tuples in a (hopefully) temporary overflow buffer until there's space on a given queue. This will cause a drop in throughput and can cause a topology to grind to a halt. If you're using a shuffle grouping where tuples are distributed evenly among tasks, this should present a problem that you'd solve using the tuning techniques from chapter 6 or the troubleshooting tips from chapter 7.

If you aren't distributing tuples evenly across your tasks, issues will be harder to spot at a macro level and the techniques from chapters 6 and 7 are unlikely to help you. What do you do then? You first need to know how to tell whether a buffer is overflowing and what can be done about it. This is where Storm's debug logs can help.

8.4.2 Using Storm's debug logs to diagnose buffer overflowing

The best place to see whether any of Storm's internal buffers are overflowing is the debug log output in Storm's logs. Figure 8.17 shows a sample debug entry from a Storm log file.

The ID of the particular bolt instance that is specified
in the `TopologyBuilder.setBolt` method.

```
2014-09-28 07:03:05 b.s.d.task [INFO] Emitting: my-bolt __metrics
[#<TaskInfo backtype.storm.metric.api.IMetricsConsumer$TaskInfo@8394a98>
 [#<DataPoint [__ack-count = {}]>
 #<DataPoint [__sendqueue = {write_pos=1, read_pos=-1, capacity=1024, population=0}]>
 #<DataPoint [__receive = {write_pos=54, read_pos=53, capacity=1024, population=1}]>
 #<DataPoint [__process-latency = {}]>
 #<DataPoint [__transfer-count = {__metrics=0}]>
 #<DataPoint [__execute-latency = {}]>
 #<DataPoint [__fail-count = {}]>
 #<DataPoint [__emit-count = {__metrics=0}]>
 #<DataPoint [__execute-count = {}]>]]
```

Metrics around the send/receive queues
for the particular bolt. These are the metrics
we are interested in for this chapter.

Figure 8.17   Snapshot of a debug log output for a bolt instance

In figure 8.17 we've highlighted the lines related to the send/receive queues, which present metrics about each of those queues respectively. Let's take a more detailed look at each of those lines.

The example in figure 8.18 shows two queues that are nowhere near overflowing, but it should be easy to tell if they are. Assuming you're using a shuffle grouping to distribute tuples evenly among bolts and tasks, checking the value for any task of a given bolt should be enough to determine how close you are to capacity. If you're using a grouping that doesn't evenly distribute tuples among bolts and tasks, you may have a harder time quickly spotting the problem. A little automated log analysis should get you where you need to be, though. The pattern of the log entries is well established, and pulling out each entry and looking for population values that are at or near capacity would be a matter of constructing and using an appropriate tool.

Now that you know how to determine whether one of Storm's internal queues is overflowing, we're going to show you some ways to stop the overflow.

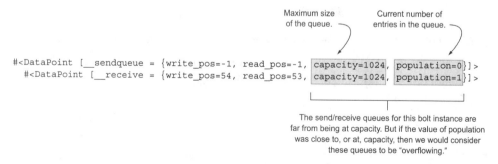

Maximum size
of the queue.

Current number of
entries in the queue.

```
#<DataPoint [__sendqueue = {write_pos=-1, read_pos=-1, capacity=1024, population=0}]>
 #<DataPoint [__receive = {write_pos=54, read_pos=53, capacity=1024, population=1}]>
```

The send/receive queues for this bolt instance are
far from being at capacity. But if the value of population
was close to, or at, capacity, then we would consider
these queues to be "overflowing."

Figure 8.18   Breaking down the debug log output lines for the send/receive queue metrics

8.5 *Addressing internal Storm buffers overflowing*

You can address internal Storm buffers overflowing in one of four primary ways. These aren't all-or-nothing options—you can mix and match as needed in order to address the problem:

- Adjust the production-to-consumption ratio
- Increase the size of the buffer for all topologies
- Increase the size of the buffer for a given topology
- Set max spout pending

Let's cover them one at a time, starting with adjusting the production-to-consumption ratio.

8.5.1 *Adjust the production-to-consumption ratio*

Producing tuples slower or consuming them faster is your best option to handle buffer overflows. You can decrease the parallelism of the producer or increase the parallelism of the consumer until the problem goes away (or becomes a different problem!). Another option beyond tweaking parallelism is to examine your user code in the consuming bolt (inside the execute method) and find a way to make it go faster.

For executor buffer-related problems, there are many reasons why tweaking parallelism isn't going to solve the problem. Stream groupings other than shuffle grouping are liable to result in some tasks handling far more data than others, resulting in their buffers seeing more activity than others. If the distribution is especially off, you could end up with memory issues from adding tons of consumers to handle what is in the end a data distribution problem.

When dealing with an overflowing worker transfer queue, "increasing parallelism" means adding more worker processes, thereby (hopefully) lowering the executor-to-worker ratio and relieving pressure on the worker transfer queue. Again, however, data distribution can rear its head. If most of the tuples are bound for tasks on the same worker process after you add another worker process, you haven't gained anything.

Adjusting the production-to-consumption ratio can be difficult when you aren't evenly distributing tuples, and any gains you get could be lost by a change in the shape of the incoming data. Although you might get some mileage out of adjusting the ratio, if you aren't relying heavily on shuffle groupings, one of our other three options is more likely to help.

8.5.2 *Increase the size of the buffer for all topologies*

We'll be honest with you: this is the cannon-to-kill-a-fly approach. The odds of every topology needing an increased buffer size are low, and you probably don't want to change buffer sizes across your entire cluster. That said, maybe you have a really good reason. You can change the default buffer size for topologies by adjusting the following values in your storm.yaml:

- The default size of all executors' incoming queue can be changed using the value `topology.executor.receive.buffer.size`
- The default size of all executors' outgoing queue can be changed using the value `topology.executor.send.buffer.size`
- The default size of a worker process's outgoing transfer queue can be changed using the value `topology.transfer.buffer.size`

It's important to note that any value you set the size of a disruptor queue buffer to has to be set to a power of 2—for example, 2, 4, 8, 16, 32, and so on. This is a requirement imposed by the LMAX disruptor.

If changing the buffer size for all topologies isn't the route you want to go, and you need finer-grained control, increasing the buffer sizes for an individual topology may be the option you want.

8.5.3   *Increase the size of the buffer for a given topology*

Individual topologies can override the default values of the cluster and set their own size for any of the disruptor queues. This is done via the `Config` class that gets passed into the `StormSubmitter` when you submit a topology. As with previous chapters, we've been placing this code in a `RemoteTopologyRunner` class, which can be seen in the following listing.

> **Listing 8.1   `RemoteTopologyRunner.java` with configuration for increased buffer sizes**

```
publc class RemoteTopologyRunner {
  public static void main(String[] args) {
    ...

    Config config = new Config();
    ...
    config.put(Config.TOPOLOGY_EXECUTOR_RECEIVE_BUFFER_SIZE,
               new Integer(16384));
    config.put(Config.TOPOLOGY_EXECUTOR_SEND_BUFFER_SIZE,
               new Integer(16384));
    config.put(Config.TOPOLOGY_TRANSFER_BUFFER_SIZE,
               new Integer(32));

    StormSubmitter.submitTopology("topology-name",
                                  config,
                                  topology);
  }
}
```

This brings us to our final option (one that should also be familiar): setting max spout pending.

8.5.4 *Max spout pending*

We discussed max spout pending in chapter 6. As you may recall, *max spout pending* caps the number of tuples that any given spout will allow to be live in the topology at one time. How can this help prevent buffer overflows? Let's try some math:

- A single spout has a max spout pending of 512.
- The smallest disruptor has a buffer size of 1024.

  512 < 1024

Assuming all your bolts don't create more tuples than they ingest, it's impossible to have enough tuples in play within the topology to overflow any given buffer. The math for this can get complicated if you have bolts that ingest a single tuple but emit a variable number of tuples. Here's a more complicated example:

- A single spout has a max spout pending of 512.
- The smallest disruptor has a buffer size of 1024.

One of our bolts takes in a single tuple and emits 1 to 4 tuples. That means the 512 tuples that our spout will emit at a given point in time could result in anywhere from 512 to 2048 tuples in play within our topology. Or put another way, we could have a buffer overflow issue. Buffer overflows aside, setting a spout's max spout pending value is a good idea and should always be done.

Having addressed four solutions for handling buffers overflowing, we're going to turn our attention to tweaking the sizes of these buffers in order to get the best performance possible in your Storm topologies.

8.6 *Tweaking buffer sizes for performance gain*

Many blog posts are floating around that detail performance metrics with Storm that are based in part on changing the sizes of internal Storm disruptor buffers. We'd be remiss not to address this performance-tuning aspect in this chapter. But first, a caveat: Storm has many internal components whose configuration is exposed via storm.yaml and programmatic means. We touched on some of these in section 8.5. If you find a setting and don't know what it does, don't change it. Do research first. Understand in general what you're changing and think through how it might impact throughput, memory usage, and so forth. Don't change anything until you're able to monitor the results of your change and can verify you got your desired result.

Lastly, remember that Storm is a complicated system and each additional change builds on previous ones. You might have two different configuration changes—let's call them A and B—that independently result in desirable performance changes but when combined result in a degenerate change. If you applied them in the order of A and then B, you might assume that B is a poor change. But that might not be the case. Let's present a hypothetical scenario to show you what we mean:

- Change A results in 5% throughput improvement.
- Change B results in 10% throughput improvement.
- Change A and B result in a 2% drop in throughput.

Ideally, you should use change B, not change A, for your best performance. Be sure to test changes independently. Be prepared to test in both an additive fashion, applying change B to an existing configuration that already involves A, as well as applying B to a "stock" Storm configuration.

All of this assumes that you need to wring every last bit of performance out of your topology. We'll let you in on a secret: we rarely do that. We spend enough time to get acceptable performance in a given topology and then call it a day and move on to other work. We suspect most of you will as well. It's a reasonable approach, but we still feel it's important, if you're ramping up your Storm usage, to learn about the various internals and start tweaking, setting, and understanding how they impact performance. Reading about it is one thing—experiencing it firsthand is entirely different.

That concludes our chapter on Storm's internals. We hope you've found some value in knowing a bit more about what happens "under the covers" with Storm's internal buffers, how those buffers might overflow, how to handle the overflow, and some thoughts on how to approach performance tuning. Next we'll switch gears and cover a high-level abstraction for Storm: Trident.

8.7   Summary

In this chapter, you learned that

- Executors are more than just a single thread and consist of two threads (main/sender) along with two disruptor queues (incoming/outgoing).
- Sending tuples between executors on the same JVM is simple and fast.
- Worker processes have their send/transfer thread, outgoing queue, and receive thread for handling sending tuples between JVMs.
- Each of the internal queues (buffers) can overflow, causing performance issues within your Storm topologies.
- Each of the internal queues (buffers) can be configured to address any potential overflow issues.

Trident

This chapter covers

- Trident and why it's useful
- Trident operations and streams as a series of batched tuples
- Kafka, its design, and how it aligns with Trident
- Implementing a Trident topology
- Using Storm's distributed remote procedure call (DRPC) functionality
- Mapping native Storm components to Trident operations via the Storm UI
- Scaling a Trident topology

We've come a long way in *Storm Applied*. Way back in chapter 2 we introduced Storm's primitive abstractions: bolts, spouts, tuples, and streams. Over the course of the first six chapters, we dug into those primitives, covering higher-level topics such as guaranteed message processing, stream groupings, parallelism, and so much more. Chapter 7 provided a cookbook approach to identifying various types of resource contention, whereas chapter 8 took you to a level of abstraction below Storm's primitive abstractions. Understanding all of these concepts is essential to mastering Storm.

In this chapter we'll introduce Trident, the high-level abstraction that sits on top of Storm's primitives, and discuss how it allows you to express a topology in terms of the "what" instead of the "how." We'll explain Trident within the context of a final use case: an internet radio application. But rather than start with the use case as we have in previous chapters, we'll start by explaining Trident. Because Trident is a higher-level abstraction, we feel understanding that abstraction before designing a solution for the use case makes sense, as that understanding may influence the design for our internet radio topology.

This chapter will start with an explanation of Trident and its core operations. We'll then talk about how Trident handles streams as a series of batches, which is different than native Storm topologies, and why Kafka is a perfect match for Trident topologies. At that point we'll break out a design for our internet radio application followed by its associated implementation, which will include Storm's DRPC functionality. Once we have the implementation, we'll discuss scaling a Trident topology. After all, Trident is simply an abstraction that still results in a topology that must be tweaked and tuned for maximum performance.

Without further ado, we'll introduce you to Trident, the abstraction that sits on top of Storm's primitives.

9.1   *What is Trident?*

Trident is an abstraction on top of Storm primitives. It allows you to express a topology in terms of the "what" (declarative) as opposed to the "how" (imperative). To achieve this, Trident provides operations such as joins, aggregations, groupings, functions, and filters, along with providing primitives for doing stateful, incremental processing on top of any database or persistence store. If you're familiar with high-level batch-processing tools like Pig or Cascading, the concepts of Trident will be familiar to you.

What does it mean to express computations using Storm in terms of *what* you want to accomplish rather than *how?* We'll answer this question by taking a look at how we built the GitHub commit count topology in chapter 2 and comparing it to a Trident version of this same topology. As you may remember from chapter 2, the goal of the GitHub commit count topology was to read in a stream of commit messages, where each message contained an email, and keep track of the count of commits for each email.

Chapter 2 described the GitHub commit count topology in terms of how to count commit messages per email. It was a mechanical, imperative process. The following listing shows the code for building this topology.

Listing 9.1 Building a GitHub commit count Storm topology

```
TopologyBuilder builder = new TopologyBuilder();            1

builder.setSpout("commit-feed-listener", new CommitFeedListener());
                                                            2
builder.setBolt("email-extractor", new EmailExtractor())
      .shuffleGrouping("commit-feed-listener");             3

builder.setBolt("email-counter", new EmailCounter())        4
      .fieldsGrouping("email-extractor", new Fields("email"));
                                                            5
```

Looking at how this topology is built, you can see that we ❶ assign a spout to the topology to listen for commit messages, ❷ define our first bolt to extract emails from each commit message, ❸ tell Storm how tuples are sent between our spout and first bolt, ❹ define our second bolt that keeps a running count of the number of emails, and end with ❺, where we tell Storm how tuples are sent between our two bolts.

Again, this is a mechanical process, one that's specific to "how" we're solving the commit count problem. The code in the listing is easy to follow because the topology itself isn't complicated. But that may not be the case when looking at more complicated Storm topologies; understanding what's being done at a higher level can become difficult.

This is where Trident helps. With its various concepts of "join," "group," "aggregate," and so forth, we express computations at a higher level than bolts or spouts, making it easier to understand what's being done. Let's show what we mean by taking a look at a Trident version of the GitHub commit count topology. Notice how the code is expressed more in terms of the "what" we're doing rather than "how" it's being done in the following listing.

Listing 9.2 Building a GitHub commit count Trident topology

```
TridentTopology topology = new TridentTopology();
TridentState commits =                                      1
  topology.newStream("spout1", spout)                                2
          .each(new Fields("commit"), new Split(), new Fields("email"))
          .groupBy(new Fields("email"))
          .persistentAggregate(new MemoryMapState.Factory(),
                               new Count(),                  3
                               new Fields("count"))
          .parallelismHint(6);                              4
```

Once you understand Trident's concepts, it's much easier to understand our computation than if we expressed it in terms of spouts and bolts. Even without a great deal of understanding of Trident, we can see that we ❶ create a stream coming from a spout, and for each entry in the stream ❷, we split the field commit into a number of email field entries, group like emails together ❸, and persist a count of the emails ❹.

If we were to come across the code in this listing, we'd have a much easier time understanding what was going on compared to the equivalent code using the Storm primitives we have so far. We're expressing our computation at much closer to a pure "what" level with far less "how" mixed in.

The code in this listing touches on a few of Trident's abstractions that help you write code that expresses the "what" instead of the "how." Let's take a look at the full range of the operations Trident provides.

9.1.1   *The different types of Trident operations*

We have a vague idea of what it means to use Trident to express our code in terms of the "what" instead of the "how." In the code in the previous section, we had a Trident spout emit a stream to be transformed by a series of Trident operations. The combination of these operations adds up to form a Trident topology.

This sounds similar to a Storm topology built on top of Storm's primitives (spouts and bolts), except that we've replaced a Storm spout with a Trident spout and Storm bolts with Trident operations. This intuition isn't true. It's important to understand that Trident operations don't directly map to Storm primitives. In a native Storm topology, you write your code within a bolt that performs your operation(s). You're given a unit of execution that's a bolt and you're afforded the freedom to do whatever you see fit within that. But with Trident, you don't have that flexibility. You're provided with a series of stock operations and need to figure out how to map your problem onto one or more of these stock operations, most likely chaining them together.

Many different Trident operations are available that you can use to implement your functionality. From a high level, they can be listed as follows:

- *Functions*—Operate on an incoming tuple and emit one or more corresponding tuples.
- *Filters*—Decide to keep or filter out an incoming tuple from the stream.
- *Splits*—Splitting a stream will result in multiple streams with the same data and fields.
- *Merges*—Streams can be merged only if they have the same fields (same field names and same number of fields).
- *Joins*—Joining is for different streams with mostly different fields, except for one or more common field(s) to join on (similar to a SQL join).
- *Grouping*—Group by specific field(s) within a partition (more on partitions later).
- *Aggregation*—Perform calculations for aggregating sets of tuples.
- *State updater*—Persist tuples or calculated values to a datastore.
- *State querying*—Query a datastore.
- *Repartitioning*—Repartition the stream by hashing on specific field(s) (similar to a fields grouping) or in a random manner (similar to a shuffle grouping). Repartitioning by hashing on some specific field(s) is different from grouping in that repartitioning happens across all partitions whereas grouping happens within a single partition.

Representing your problem as a series of these operations allows you to think and reason at a much higher level than what the native Storm primitives allow. It also makes the Trident API for wiring in these different operations together feel much like a domain-specific language (DSL). For example, let's say you have a step where you need to save your calculated results to a datastore. At that step, you'd wire in a *state updater* operation. Whether that state updater operation is writing to Cassandra, Elasticsearch, or Redis is completely irrelevant. In fact, you can have a state updater operation that writes to Redis and share that among different Trident topologies.

Hopefully you're starting to gain an understanding of the types of abstractions Trident provides. Don't worry about how these various operations are implemented right now. We'll cover that soon when we dig into the design and implementation of our internet radio topology. But before we get into designing that topology, we need to cover one more topic: how Trident handles streams. This is fundamentally different from how a native Storm topology handles streams and will influence the design of our internet radio topology.

9.1.2 *Trident streams as a series of batches*

One fundamental difference between a Trident topology and a native Storm topology is that within a Trident topology, streams are handled as batches of tuples, whereas in a native Storm topology, streams are handled as a series of individual tuples. This means that each Trident operation processes a batch of tuples whereas each native Storm bolt executes on a single tuple. Figure 9.1 provides an illustration of this.

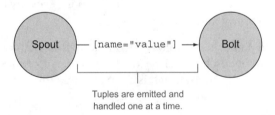

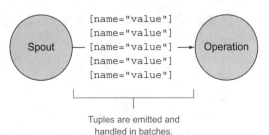

Figure 9.1 Trident topologies operate on streams of batches of tuples whereas native Storm topologies operate on streams of individual tuples.

Because Trident handles streams as batches of tuples, it falls under the category of micro-batching tools discussed in chapter 1. As you'll recall from that chapter, micro-batching is a hybrid between batch processing and stream processing.

This fundamental difference in how Trident treats streams as a series of batches is why there are operations and not bolts in Trident. We think in terms of the stream and the series of operations we can apply to that stream. The operations discussed in section 9.1.1 will modify either the tuples that flow within the stream or the stream itself. In order to understand Trident, you must understand both streams and operations within Trident.

Next we'll discuss a message queue implementation that's well suited for use with Trident. It matches Trident's needs so closely that it's bundled with Storm to be used with Trident topologies.

9.2   *Kafka and its role with Trident*

Storm maintains a unique relationship with Apache Kafka when it comes to message queues that serve as a source of input. That's not to say that other message queue technologies can't be used. We've been careful throughout the book to point out how Storm can be used with a number of different technologies, such as RabbitMQ and Kestrel. What sets Kafka apart from other message broker implementations? It boils down to the core architectural decisions made during the creation of Kafka. To help you understand what makes Kafka such a good fit with Trident, we're going to briefly discuss Kafka's design and then talk about what characteristics of this design align well with Trident.

9.2.1   *Breaking down Kafka's design*

This section will briefly dive into Kafka's design, but only as far as is necessary for you to understand why it's relevant to Storm and Trident.

> **NOTE** We use some standard Kafka terminology throughout this chapter. Two of the terms more commonly used are 1) *topic*, which is a feed of messages for a particular category and 2) *broker*, which is a server/node that's usually one of many running in a Kafka cluster.

The Kafka website describes itself in two ways, both of which serve as clues to why the design fits well with Trident:

- It's a publish-subscribe message broker, rethought as a *distributed commit log*.
- It's a distributed, partitioned, replicated commit log service that provides the functionality of a messaging system, but with a unique design.

Let's talk about each of these, because understanding these basic design decisions will help you see how Kafka aligns with Trident.

PARTITIONING FOR DISTRIBUTING A KAFKA TOPIC

When a message producer writes to a Kafka topic, it writes a given message to a particular partition of that topic. A *partition* is an ordered, immutable sequence of messages

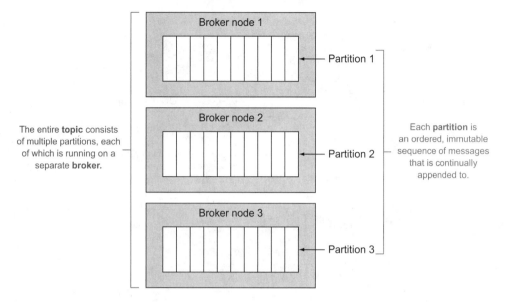

The entire **topic** consists of multiple partitions, each of which is running on a separate **broker**.

Each **partition** is an ordered, immutable sequence of messages that is continually appended to.

Figure 9.2 Distribution of a Kafka topic as group of partitions on many Kafka brokers

that's continually being appended to. A topic can have multiple partitions, and these partitions can be distributed across multiple Kafka brokers. A message consumer will read from each partition in order to see the entire topic. Figure 9.2 illustrates a single topic distributed across multiple partitions.

By partitioning a topic, Kafka gains the ability to scale a single topic beyond a single broker (node) for both reads and writes. Each of the partitions can additionally be replicated to provide resiliency. This means that if you have n replicas for a partition, you can lose up to n - 1 replicas without suffering any data loss.

Having multiple partitions and being able to scale those partitions are important concepts to grasp when it comes to Trident. As you'll see later in this chapter, this maps well with how a Trident topology reads data from a stream. But before we get ahead of ourselves, we should elaborate a bit more on how Kafka stores messages.

MODELING STORAGE AS A COMMIT LOG

The storage model Kafka uses for messages within a topic yields many advantages—in both terms of performance and functional characteristics. We know from the previous section that a partition is an ordered, immutable sequence of messages on the filesystem. This represents a commit log. Each message within the partition is assigned a sequential identifier, called an *offset*, which marks where in the commit log each message is stored.

Kafka also maintains an ordering of messages within a partition, so strong ordering is guaranteed when a single consumer is reading from the partition. A message consumer reading from a particular partition will then maintain its own reference to its

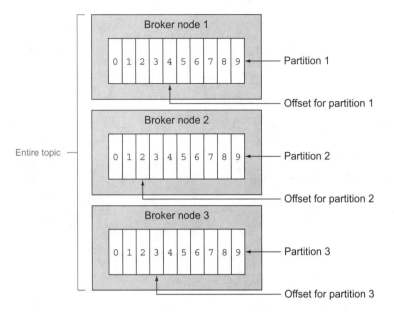

Figure 9.3 A partition contains an immutable, ordered sequence of messages, where the consumers reading these messages maintain offsets for their read positions.

current position, known as that consumer's offset into the commit log. Figure 9.3 illustrates offsets for multiple partitions.

Kafka doesn't discard messages after a consumer advances its offset; they're kept in the log for a configured time period (such as 24 hours or 7 days). Once that time interval elapses, Kafka will compact the log and purge any older entries.

You should now have a general idea of how Kafka's design works. A topic serves as a feed of messages for a particular category. This topic can then be broken into multiple partitions, which are immutable, ordered sequences of messages. These partitions can each be distributed across different brokers in the Kafka cluster. We'll now elaborate on some of the advantages of this design in terms of both functionality and performance.

THE FUNCTIONAL AND PERFORMANCE ADVANTAGES OF KAFKA'S DESIGN

The functional advantages of this design include the following:

- Because messages aren't discarded immediately and the consumer decides when or when not to advance its offset into the commit log, it's easy to replay any messages from Kafka.
- Similarly, if your consumers fall behind for a long time and it no longer makes sense to consume those queued messages due to some consume-by-deadline requirements, it makes it easy to advance the offset by a large number into a new read position to skip all the expired messages.

- If your consumer acts on messages in batches and needs to complete the batch all at once or not at all, this can be accomplished by advancing the offset for a batch of sequential messages from a partition in one go.
- If you have different applications that need to subscribe to the same messages from a topic, consumers can easily read these different applications from that topic's same set of partitions. This is facilitated because a message isn't discarded after one consumer is done with it but rather the consumer controls its own offset into the commit log.
- On the other hand, if you want to ensure that only a single consumer consumes each message, you can do so by pinning a single consumer instance to a particular partition of a topic.

The performance advantages include the following:

- Whether your message bus ends up being bottlenecked by the message producer or the message consumer, that bottleneck can be easily addressed by increasing the number of partitions.
- The sequential and immutable nature of the commit log along with the sequential nature of the consumer's offset advancement pattern (in most cases) buys us many performance advancements:
  - Disk access is often expensive but in most cases this is due to the random access nature that's common among most applications. Because Kafka is designed from the ground up to make use of sequential access to data in the filesystem, modern operating systems will make efficient use of that by way of read-ahead caches and write-behind caching to give you large strides in performance improvements.
  - Kafka makes excellent use of the OS disk cache. This allows Kafka to sidestep maintaining expensive caches in-process and not subject itself to garbage collection pressure.

We have a decent picture of Kafka's general design along with the advantages, both functional and performance-related, that this design provides. It's time to identify how Kafka aligns with Trident, making it such a great choice for Trident that it now comes bundled with Storm.

9.2.2 Kafka's alignment with Trident

You're probably able to imagine how wonderfully Storm would benefit from both the functional and performance advantages of Kafka. Kafka provides a performance advantage that's an order of magnitude over its competition. For that reason alone, Kafka is the message bus of choice for native Storm. But when used with Trident, it's clear why it's such a good choice as the messaging implementation:

- Because Trident performs micro-batching within a stream, it relies on being able to manage a batch of tuples atomically. By allowing Trident to advance its consumer offset, Kafka supports this functionality.

- Messages aren't discarded, so by rewinding the offset, you can replay messages from any point in time (up to Kafka's log expiry time interval). This allows Kafka to behave as a reliable data source on which you can build a reliable spout, both for Trident and native Storm.
- As we'll see later, Trident can use Kafka partitions to serve as a primary means of parallelism within a Trident topology.
- A Storm spout implemented for Kafka can maintain its consumer offsets for the different partitions in Zookeeper, so when your Storm or Trident topology is restarted or redeployed, you can continue processing from the place where you left off.

Let's pause for a moment and see what we've covered so far. By now, you should understand the following:

- Trident provides an abstraction on top of Storm's primitives, allowing you to write code that expresses "what" is being done rather than "how" to do it.
- Trident streams are handled as a series of batches of tuples rather than individual tuples, one at a time.
- Trident has operations, instead of bolts, that you apply to streams. These operations include functions, filters, splits, merges, joins, grouping, aggregation, state updater, state querying, and repartitioning.
- Kafka is the ideal queuing implementation for Trident topologies.

We're finally ready to dive into our use case and apply all of these Trident principles to our design and implementation. As we go through the use case, try to keep in mind Trident's operations and how it handles streams, because this will help steer our design.

9.3   *Problem definition: Internet radio*

Let's say we want to start an internet radio company. We want to be conscientious about paying fair royalties to artists for their music that gets streamed through our internet radio platform. To do this, we decide to keep track of play counts for individual songs by artist. These counts can later be queried for use within reporting and for assigning royalties. In addition to paying royalties, we're fairly ambitious and want to be able to query/report on the types of music our users prefer in order to provide them with the best possible experience when using our application.

Our users will be listening to our internet radio on various devices and on the web. These applications will collect "play logs" and send that information to us to be streamed into our topology from our Trident spout.

With this problem definition in hand, let's take a look at the starting and ending data points, much like we've done in previous chapters.

9.3.1   Defining the data points

For our scenario, each play log will be streamed into our topology as JSON containing the artist, the title of the song, and a list of tags relevant to the song. The next listing provides an example of a single play log.

Listing 9.3   Sample play log entry for the stream of play logs

```
{
  "artist": "The Clash",
  "title": "Clampdown",
  "tags": ["Punk","1979"]
}
```

The play log JSON gives us a starting point for our data. We want to persist three different types of counts: counts by artist, by title, and by tag. Trident provides a `Trident-State` class that we'll use for this. We'll get more into `TridentState` later—what's important now is that you understand the data we start with and where we want to end up.

With the data defined, the next step is to define the series of steps we need to go from a feed of play logs to the counts stored in `TridentState` instances.

9.3.2   Breaking down the problem into a series of steps

We've established that we'll start with a play log and end with counts for artist, title, and tag. In forming a conceptual solution, we need to identify all the steps between our start and end.

Remember earlier when we said to keep in mind the various Trident operations when discussing the design for our use case? This is where we'll look at those operations and see which make sense in our scenario. We end up with the following:

1. A spout that emits a Trident stream. Remember that a Trident stream consists of batches of tuples as opposed to individual tuples.
2. A function that deserializes (splits) incoming play logs into tuple batches for artist, title, and tag.
3. Separate functions to count each of the artists, titles, and tags respectively.
4. Trident state to persist the counts by artist, title, and tag, respectively.

These steps are illustrated in figure 9.4, which illustrates our design goal. Next we need to implement the code for the Trident operations that we'll apply to the stream of tuple batches containing play logs.

9.4   Implementing the internet radio design as a Trident topology

At this point, we're ready to implement a Trident topology that meets our design goal established in figure 9.4. You'll notice as we start to go through the implementation that much of the code for our topology is handled within the topology builder class

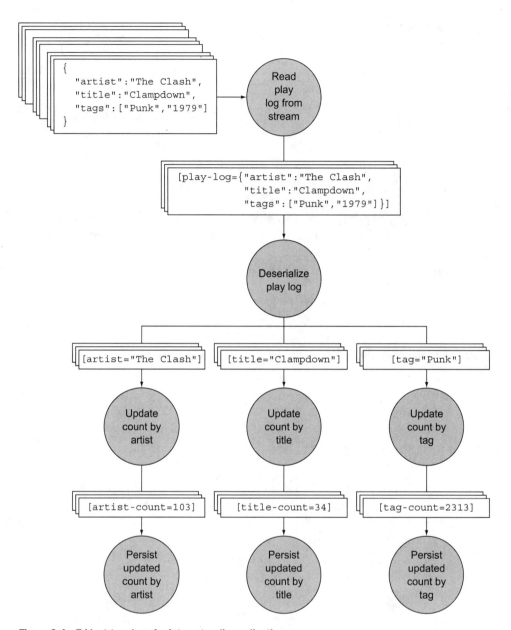

Figure 9.4   Trident topology for internet radio application

(TopologyBuilder). Although we do implement some functions for the operations used, the TopologyBuilder is where you'll see the code expressed in terms of the "what" rather than the "how."

Let's start with the spout for our topology. Fortunately for us, Storm comes with a built-in spout implementation that we can use, saving ourselves some time.

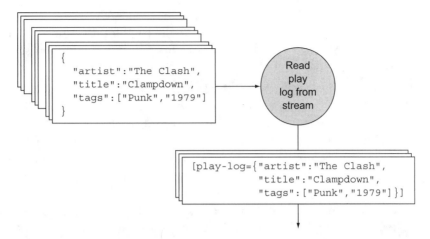

Figure 9.5 The Trident Kafka spout will be used for handling incoming play logs.

9.4.1 Implementing the spout with a Trident Kafka spout

We'll use the Trident Kafka spout that comes with the official Storm distribution. Figure 9.5 shows where this Trident Kafka spout will be used in the topology.

Although the implementation details of this spout are outside the scope of this chapter, we'll show you the code for wiring up this spout in the `TopologyBuilder` class in the next listing.

Listing 9.4 Wiring up a `TransactionalTridentKafkaSpout` in the `TopologyBuilder`

```
public TopologyBuilder {
  public StormTopology build() {
    TridentTopology topology = new TridentTopology();          Instantiate the
    topology.newStream("play-spout", buildSpout());            TridentTopology.
    return topology.build();
  }                                                   Create a new stream
                                                      named play-spout and
                                                      attach the Kafka spout
                                                      instance.
  private TransactionalTridentKafkaSpout buildSpout() {
    BrokerHosts zk = new ZkHosts("localhost");
    TridentKafkaConfig spoutConf = new TridentKafkaConfig(zk, "play-log");
    spoutConf.scheme = new SchemeAsMultiScheme(new StringScheme());
    return new TransactionalTridentKafkaSpout(spoutConf);
  }
}
```

Turn the Trident-Topology into a Storm-Topology.

Use the transactional Trident spout, which provides reliability.

Specify the ZkHosts and Kafka topic name.

Define StringScheme to deserialize a Kafka message into a String.

ZkHosts is used to configure the Zookeeper that Kafka is connected to. This spout will query that to dynamically determine the partition information for this Kafka topic.

We now have a spout implementation that will emit batches of play logs. The next step is to implement our first operation that will take the JSON for each tuple in the batch and transform that JSON into separate tuple batches for artist, title, and tags.

9.4.2 *Deserializing the play log and creating separate streams for each of the fields*

The next step to implement in the design is to take the batches of incoming `play-log` tuples and emit batches of tuples for each of the fields we're interested in counting: artist, title, and tag. Figure 9.6 illustrates the batches of input tuples, our operation, and batches of output tuples, with each batch being emitted on a separate stream.

Looking at the figure, you can see we need to do two things: 1) convert the JSON into separate tuples for the artist, title, and tags fields, and 2) create a separate stream for each of those fields. For the first task, we're going to take a look at the each operation.

Trident provides an `each` operation that can be applied to each tuple, one at a time. The `each` operation can be used with a function or a filter. In our scenario, an each function seems like the appropriate choice, because we're transforming the JSON into Trident tuples for artist, title, and tag. If we needed to filter out any data for some reason, then a filter would be a more appropriate choice.

IMPLEMENTING AN EACH FUNCTION

A function takes in a set of input fields and emits zero or more tuples. If it doesn't emit anything, the original tuple is filtered out. When using an each function, the

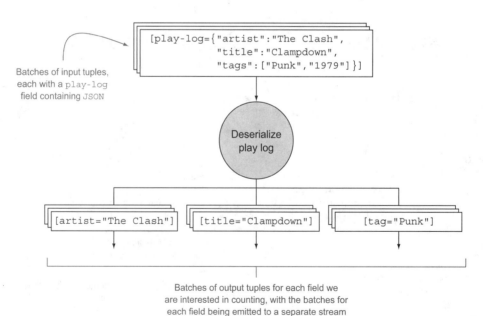

Figure 9.6   Operation for deserializing JSON into Trident tuples for each of the artist, title, and tags fields

fields of the output tuple are appended to the input tuple. The following listing provides the code for implementing an each function for our topology.

> **Listing 9.5** `TopologyBuilder.java` with an each function for deserializing the play logs

Select the fields from the tuple that will be sent to the each function. In this case, we're sending all fields within the stream (play-log is the only field).

The each operation is being applied to the stream emitted from the spout.

```
public TopologyBuilder {
   public StormTopology build() {
      TridentTopology topology = new TridentTopology();

      Stream playStream = topology.newStream("play-spout", buildSpout())
         .each(
               new Fields("play-log"),
               new LogDeserializer(),
               new Fields("artist", "title", "tags")
               );

      return topology.build();
   }

   ...
}
```

LogDeserializer is the each function that will run on all tuples from the stream.

The fields on output tuples from the LogDeserializer are named.

After the each operation, you have a newly transformed stream with this operation applied that you can tack on another operation to.

The new stream will contain the fields play-log, artist, title, and tags. The each function LogDeserializer is built by providing an implementation for the BaseFunction abstract class, and will deserialize the input tuple with a JSON string into the required output. Implementing a BaseFunction is similar to implementing a BaseBasicBolt in native Storm. The following listing shows the implementation.

> **Listing 9.6** `LogDeserializer.java`

Look up the input fields into this function. Observe that only the input fields named in the each method in Topology Builder are accessible here.

```
public class LogDeserializer extends BaseFunction {
   private transient Gson gson;

   @Override
   public void execute(TridentTuple tuple,
                       TridentCollector collector) {
      String logLine = tuple.getString(0);
      LogEntry logEntry = gson.fromJson(logLine, LogEntry.class);
      collector.emit(new Values(logEntry.getArtist(),
                                logEntry.getTitle(),
                                logEntry.getTags())));
   }

   @Override
   public void prepare(Map config,
                       TridentOperationContext context) {
      gson = new Gson();
   }
```

The execute method takes in a tuple and collector just like BaseBasicBolt but in this case they are TridentTuple and TridentCollector instead of Tuple and BasicOutputCollector.

Deserialize a string into a POJO using Google GSON.

Emit the fields that were deserialized using TridentCollector. Within a function, you can emit zero or more tuples for the input tuple. In this case, we're emitting one.

```
@Override
public void cleanup() { }

public static class LogEntry {
    private String artist;
    private String title;
    private List<String> tags = new ArrayList<>();

    public String getArtist() { return artist; }
    public void setArtist(String artist) { this.artist = artist; }

    public String getTitle() { return title; }
    public void setTitle(String title) { this.title = title; }

    public List<String> getTags() { return tags; }
    public void setTags(List<String> tags) { this.tags = tags; }
  }
}
```

Projections

When you define an `each` function as `stream.each(inputFields, function, output-Fields)`, only a subset of fields (represented by `inputFields`) from the original stream is sent into the function (the rest become inaccessible within the function). This is called *projection*. Projections make it extremely easy to avoid issues that people commonly encounter with having sent unnecessary fields into a function.

You can also use the project(..) method on the stream to remove any unnecessary fields that are hanging around after an operation. In our case we have the play-log field as part of the stream after the `LogDeserializer` operation and we don't need the original JSON anymore. It's better to get rid of it; keeping unnecessary data in memory will affect efficiency (particularly in Trident because we're treating a stream as a series of batches and that involves keeping more data in memory within a JVM than a regular Storm topology):

```
playStream = playStream.project(new Fields("artist", "title", "tags"));
```

As we mentioned earlier, we must do two things: 1) convert the JSON into separate tuples, which we've now done, and 2) create a separate stream for each of those fields. Let's take a look at that second task next.

SPLITTING A STREAM AND GROUPING THE FIELDS

If we were to end our implementation right now, we'd have a single stream containing batches of tuples with four values. This is because of the following in `LogDeserializer`:

```
collector.emit(new Values(logEntry.getArtist(),
                          logEntry.getTitle(),
                          logEntry.getTags()));
```

Figure 9.7 illustrates where we currently are versus where we want to be.

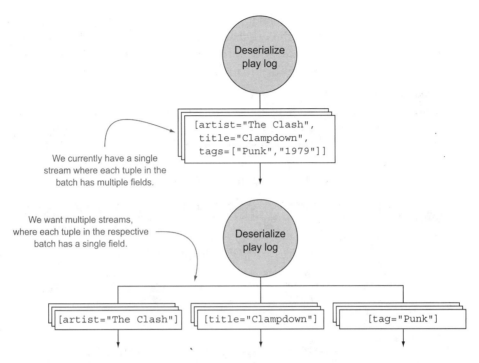

Figure 9.7 We want to move from a stream with tuples containing multiple values to multiple streams with tuples containing single values.

Fortunately for us, splitting a stream is easy. We hold multiple references for the stream from the split origination point and then continue to apply different Trident operations to those references, as shown in the next listing.

Listing 9.7 Splitting the stream originating from `LogDeserializer` into three separate streams

```java
public StormTopology buildTopology() {
    TridentTopology topology = new TridentTopology();

    Stream playStream =
        topology.newStream("play-spout", buildSpout())
        .each(new Fields("play-log"),
            new LogDeserializer(),
            new Fields("artist", "title", "tags"))
        .each(new Fields("artist", "title"),
            new Sanitizer(new Fields("artist", "title")));

    Stream countByTitleStream = playStream;

    Stream countByArtistStream = playStream;

    Stream countByTagStream = playStream;

    return topology.build();
}
```

We have added a filter here, called Sanitizer, that filters out any garbage artist or title values. See the source code for this filter's implementation.

By holding references to the same split point, playStream, in different stream variables, you can continue to apply different operations to each of them starting at the same point going forward.

We have code for creating separate streams, but there isn't anything to those streams. They're just references to the originating `playStream`. We need to associate each of those streams with the fields we're interested in splitting on. This is where grouping the tuples by field name comes into play.

GROUPING TUPLES BY FIELD NAME

Trident provides a `groupBy` operation we can use for grouping together tuples with the same field name. A `groupBy` operation first repartitions the stream so that tuples with the same selected field values fall within the same partition. Within each partition, it then groups the tuples together whose group fields are equal. The code for performing these `groupBy` operations is in the next listing.

Listing 9.8 Grouping by artist, title, and tag in the three split streams

```
public StormTopology buildTopology() {
    TridentTopology topology = new TridentTopology();

    Stream playStream =
        topology.newStream("play-spout", buildSpout())
        .each(new Fields("play-log"),
            new LogDeserializer(),
            new Fields("artist", "title", "tags"))
        .each(new Fields("artist", "title"),
            new Sanitizer(new Fields("artist", "title")));

    GroupedStream countByTitleStream = playStream
        .project(new Fields("artist"))          ← Drop all fields except artist.
        .groupBy(new Fields("artist"));         ← Group by the artist field.

    GroupedStream countByArtistStream = playStream       Drop all fields except title.
        .project(new Fields("title"))
        .groupBy(new Fields("title"));          ← Group by the title field.

    GroupedStream countByTagStream = playStream
        .each(new Fields("tags"),               ← Because tags is a List<String>, use an each function to split that list into multiple tuples and name it tag.
            new ListSplitter(),
            new Fields("tag"))                   Drop all fields except tag.
        .project(new Fields("tag"))
        .groupBy(new Fields("tag"));            ← Group by the tag field.
    return topology.build();
}
```

`ListSplitter` is an each function implemented in a similar manner to `LogDeserializer`. The difference is that `ListSplitter` splits the `tags` list into individual `tag` tuples.

   Now that we've split the streams and performed a grouping on each of the `artist`, `title`, and `tag` fields, we're ready to calculate the counts for each of these fields.

9.4.3 *Calculating and persisting the counts for artist, title, and tag*

The next step is to aggregate the `artist`, `title`, and `tag` tuples in order to calculate the counts for each. Figure 9.8 provides a reminder of where we are in the topology design.

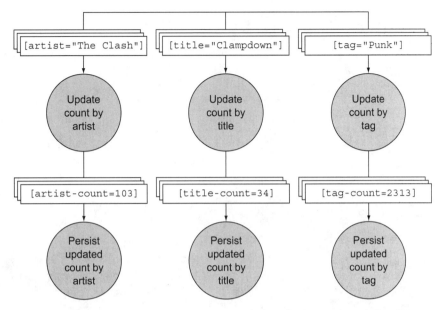

Figure 9.8 Counting each of the `artist`, `title`, and `tag` values and persisting those values to a store

According to figure 9.8, there are basically two steps here: 1) aggregate the tuples by value for each stream to perform the counts, and 2) persist the counts. Let's start by looking at three different ways to aggregate tuples and identify the one that's best for our scenario.

CHOOSING AN AGGREGATOR IMPLEMENTATION FOR PERFORMING THE COUNTS
There are three ways to aggregate tuples, each with its own interface for defining how it should be implemented:

1   CombinerAggregator
```
public interface CombinerAggregator<T> extends Serializable {
    T init(TridentTuple tuple);
    T combine(T val1, T val2);        ❶
    T zero();                          ❷
}                                      ❸
```

A CombinerAggregator calls the init ❶ method for each tuple, and then uses the combine ❷ method to combine each tuple's init value and returns a result. If there are no tuples to aggregate, it returns the zero ❸ value.

2   ReducerAggregator
```
public interface ReducerAggregator<T> extends Serializable {
    T init();
    T reduce(T curr, TridentTuple tuple);    ❶
}                                             ❷
```

A ReducerAggregator calls the init method ❶ just once for the aggregation, and then calls reduce ❷ with each tuple and current value.

```
3  Aggregator
   public interface Aggregator<T> extends Operation {
     T init(Object batchId, TridentCollector collector);
     void aggregate(T state, TridentTuple tuple, TridentCollector collector);
     void complete(T state, TridentCollector collector);
   }
```

An `Aggregator` is a more low-level abstraction interface for implementing more complex aggregations. Please refer to the Storm documentation for more information.

The majority of the time, you'll use `CombinerAggregator` or `ReducerAggregator`. If the initial value for the entire aggregation isn't dependent on any single tuple, then you'll have to use `ReducerAggregator`. Otherwise, we suggest `CombinerAggregator` because it's more performant.

Benefits of CombinerAggregator over ReducerAggregator

When you're running an aggregate operation with a `ReducerAggregator`- or an `Aggregator`-based implementation, a repartitioning of the stream takes place so that all partitions are collapsed into one and the aggregation takes place on that one partition. But if you use a `CombinerAggregator`-based implementation (as we do with `Count`), Trident will perform partial aggregations on the current partitions and then repartition the stream into one stream and complete aggregation by further aggregating the partially aggregated tuples. This is far more efficient because fewer tuples have to cross the wire during the repartition. `CombinerAggregator` should always be preferred because of this reason; the only time you'll have to resort to `ReducerAggregator` is when you need to seed an aggregation with an initial value independent of the tuples.

For our scenario, let's use a built-in aggregator called `Count` that implements `Combiner-Aggregator`. This is a simple implementation that will allow us to count artists, titles, and tags within our groupings. The next listing shows the implementation for `Count`.

Listing 9.9 Built-in `Count.java` that implements `CombinerAggregator.java`

```
public class Count implements CombinerAggregator<Long> {        Aggregated
  @Override                                                      result data
  public Long init(TridentTuple tuple) { return 1L; }            type is a Long

  @Override
  public Long combine(Long val1, Long val2) { return val1 + val2; }   ◁──

  @Override
  public Long zero() { return 0L; }       ◁──
}
```

For each tuple, pick the value from the tuple to be used in the aggregation. We're just counting tuples, so it's always one. Storm also comes with a built-in SumCombinerAggregator that gets the value within the tuple ((Number) tuple.getValue(0)).

If there are zero tuples to aggregate, use this value.

Aggregates two values together. This will be called for each respective tuple and current count value.

We know that we'll be using the Count class to perform the actual counts, but we still need to wire up Count instances somewhere in our TopologyBuilder. Let's look at various ways to do this next.

CHOOSING AN AGGREGATE OPERATION TO WORK WITH OUR AGGREGATOR IMPLEMENTATION

Trident provides three ways to use an aggregator with a stream:

- partitionAggregate—This operation takes on the single responsibility of aggregating tuples and works only within a single partition. This operation results in a Stream containing the aggregate result tuple(s). The code for setting up partitionAggregate is as follows:

```
Stream aggregated = stream.partitionAggregate(new Count(),
                                        new Fields("output"));
```

- aggregate—This operation takes on the single responsibility of aggregating tuples and works across all partitions within a single batch of tuples. The operation results in a Stream containing the aggregate result tuple(s). The code for setting up aggregate is as follows:

```
Stream aggregated = stream.aggregate(new Count(),
                                new Fields("output"));
```

- persistentAggregate—This operation applies across multiple batches and takes on the dual responsibility of aggregating the tuples and persisting the results. It will persist the aggregated results to a datastore managed by a <state-factory>. A state factory is Trident's abstraction for working with a datastore. Because it works with state, persistentAggregate can work across batches. It does this by aggregating the current batch from the stream and then aggregating that value with the current value in the datastore. This operation results in a Trident-State that can be queried against. The code for setting up persistentAggregate is as follows:

```
TridentState aggregated = stream.persistentAggregate(<state-factory>,
                                        new Count(),
                                        new Fields("output"));
```

In this list, the Count aggregator could be replaced with any CombinerAggregator, ReducerAggregator, or Aggregator implementation.

Which of these aggregation operations best suits our needs? Let's start with partitionAggregate. We know that partitionAggregate works within a single partition, so we must figure out if we need to aggregate within a single partition. We've already applied a groupBy operation to group tuples by a field (artist, title, and tag) and then count the number of tuples within that group across the entire batch. This means we're going across partitions, making partitionAggregate not the choice for us.

Next up is aggregate. The aggregate operation works across all partitions within a batch of tuples, which is what we need. But if we decide to use aggregate, we'll need to apply another operation to persist the aggregated results. So aggregate can work if we decide to take on additional work and build more that allows us to aggregate across batches and persist the results.

We have a feeling there's a better choice for our scenario, which brings us to persistentAggregate. The name alone gives us the feeling that it might be the operation we need. We need to both aggregate counts and then persist those aggregated results. Because persistentAggregate works with state and thus works across batches, it feels like the perfect choice for our scenario. In addition, persistentAggregate leaves us with a TridentState object that can be queried against, making it easy for us to build the various reports we discussed earlier in the problem definition.

We've settled on persistentAggregate for our solution, but there's one last piece we need to define before we're done. Let's look at the code for persistent-Aggregate again:

```
TridentState aggregated = stream.persistentAggregate(<state-factory>,
                                            new Count(),
                                            new Fields("output"));
```

We still need a <state-factory>, which we'll discuss next.

WORKING WITH STATE

We need an implementation of StateFactory when dealing with state in Trident. This StateFactory serves as an abstraction that knows both how to query and update a datastore. For our scenario, we're going to choose MemoryMapState.Factory, which is bundled with Trident. MemoryMapState.Factory works with an in-memory Map and will serve our needs fine for now. The code for wiring up this factory can be seen in the following listing.

> **Listing 9.10 Using a persistentAggregate operation to update/persist counts in TopologyBuilder.java**

```
public class TopologyBuilder {
 public StormTopology buildTopology() {
  TridentTopology topology = new TridentTopology();

  Stream playStream =
    topology.newStream("play-spout", buildSpout())
    .each(new Fields("play-log"),
        new LogDeserializer(),
        new Fields("artist", "title", "tags"))
    .each(new Fields("artist", "title"),
        new Sanitizer(new Fields("artist", "title")));

  TridentState countsByTitle =
    playStream
    .project(new Fields("artist"))
    .groupBy(new Fields("artist"))
    .persistentAggregate(new MemoryMapState.Factory(),
                new Count(),
                new Fields("artist-count"));  <—
```

Applying persistentAggregate operation to the GroupedStream with a Count Combiner-Aggregator using a MemoryMapState.Factory gives us a TridentState.

```
TridentState countsByArtist =
  playStream
   .project(new Fields("title"))
   .groupBy(new Fields("title"))
   .persistentAggregate(new MemoryMapState.Factory(),
                    new Count(),
                    new Fields("title-count"));

TridentState countsByTag =
  playStream
   .each(new Fields("tags"),
       new ListSplitter(),
       new Fields("tag"))
   .project(new Fields("tag"))
   .groupBy(new Fields("tag"))
   .persistentAggregate(new MemoryMapState.Factory(),
                    new Count(),
                    new Fields("tag-count"));

   return topology.build();
 }
}
```

Applying persistentAggregate operation to the GroupedStream with a Count Combiner-Aggregator using a MemoryMapState.Factory gives us a TridentState.

That brings the basic implementation of our Trident topology to a close. We're now at a place where we have in-memory counts for all of the fields we're interested in: `artist`, `title`, and `tag`. We're done now; ready to move on, right? Well, not quite. We'd hate to leave you hanging with these in-memory counts that you have no way of accessing. Let's look at a way to implement access to these counts. It will come in the form of Storm's DRPC functionality.

9.5   *Accessing the persisted counts through DRPC*

Now that we have `TridentState` objects with counts by artist, title, and tag, we can query these state objects to build the reports we need. We want our reporting application to be external to Storm, so this reporting application needs to be able to query this topology to get the data it needs. We'll make use of distributed remote procedure calls (DRPC) for this purpose.

In Storm DRPC, the client will invoke a DRPC request with a Storm DRPC server, which will coordinate the request by sending it to the corresponding Storm topology and wait for the response from that topology. Once it receives the response, it will communicate that back to the calling client. This in effect acts as a distributed query by querying for multiple artists or tags in parallel and summing up the results.

This section covers the three parts of Storm DRPC required to implement our solution for querying the counts:

- Creating a DRPC stream
- Applying a DRPC state query to the stream
- Using the DRPC client to make DRPC calls via Storm

We'll start our explanation with the DRPC stream.

9.5.1   *Creating a DRPC stream*

When the Storm DRPC server receives a request, it needs to route it to our topology. For our topology to be able handle this incoming request, it needs a DRPC stream. The Storm DRPC server will route any incoming requests to this stream. The DRPC stream is given a name that's intended to be the name of this distributed query we want to execute. The DRPC server will identify which topology (and which stream within that topology) to route incoming requests based on this name. The next listing shows how to create a DRPC stream.

Listing 9.11   Creating a DRPC stream

```
topology.newDRPCStream("count-request-by-tag")
```

The DRPC server accepts arguments for a DRPC function as text and forwards it along with the request to this DRPC stream. We need to parse the textual arguments into a form that we can make use of within the DRPC stream. The following listing defines the contract for the arguments for our `count-request-by-tag` DRPC stream to be a comma-delimited list of tags we want to query by.

Listing 9.12   Defining the contract for the arguments for the DRPC stream

```
topology.newDRPCStream("count-request-by-tag")
        .each(new Fields("args"),
              new SplitOnDelimiter(","),
              new Fields("tag"));
```

Listing 9.12 references an each function called `SplitOnDelimiter`, so let's take a look at that class's implementation, as shown in the following listing.

Listing 9.13   SplitOnDelimiter.java

```
public class SplitOnDelimiter extends BaseFunction {
  private final String delimiter;

  public SplitOnDelimiter(String delimiter) {
    this.delimiter = delimiter;
  }

  @Override
  public void execute(TridentTuple tuple,
                   TridentCollector collector) {
    for (String part : tuple.getString(0).split(delimiter)) {
      if (part.length() > 0) collector.emit(new Values(part));
    }
  }
}
```

> The implementation is just like the LogDeserializer we built earlier to parse a play log.

This gives us a basic DRPC stream to work with. The next step is to apply a state query to this stream.

9.5.2 Applying a DRPC state query to a stream

The state query we want to execute in response to this DRPC request is to count the number of play logs by given tag arguments. Let's refresh our memory of how we calculated `TridentState` for the tags before we continue, as shown in the next listing.

Listing 9.14 Creating the `counts-by-tag` stream resulting in `TridentState`

```
TridentState countsByTag = playStream
    .each(new Fields("tags"),
          new ListSplitter(),
          new Fields("tag"))
    .project(new Fields("tag"))
    .groupBy(new Fields("tag"))
    .persistentAggregate(new MemoryMapState.Factory(),
                         new Count(),
                         new Fields("tag-count"));
```

We stored the counts by a given tag in an in-memory map with the tag as the key and count as the value. Now all we need to do is look up the counts for the tags we received as arguments for the DRPC query. This is achieved through the `stateQuery` operation on the DRPC stream. An explanation of the `stateQuery` operation can be seen in figure 9.9.

As the figure illustrates, the `QueryFunction` we choose needs to know how to access the data through the `TridentState` object. Fortunately for us, Storm comes with a built-in `MapGet` query function that can work with our `MemoryMapState` implementation.

But implementing this state query isn't as simple as adding the `stateQuery` operation to the end of our DRPC stream. The reason for that is in our original play stream, we repartitioned the stream using a `groupBy` operation on the `tag` field. In order to send `count-request-by-tag` requests from the DRPC stream into the same partition that contains the needed tag in the `TridentState`, we need to apply a

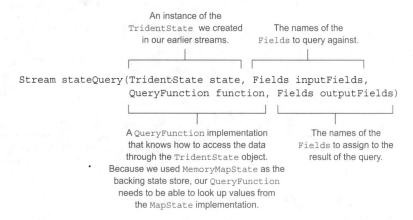

Figure 9.9 Breaking down the `stateQuery` operation

groupBy operation on the DRPC stream as well, on the same tag field. The next listing provides the code for this.

Listing 9.15   Looking up `counts-by-tag` by querying a source of state

```
topology.newDRPCStream("count-request-by-tag")
    .each(new Fields("args"),
        new SplitOnDelimiter(","),
        new Fields("tag"))
    .groupBy(new Fields("tag"))
    .stateQuery(countsByTag,
            new Fields("tag"),
            new MapGet(),
            new Fields("count"));
```

Group the incoming DRPC query request arguments by tag.

Initiate a state query against the countsByTag state object.

Use the tag field value from the grouping.

Use a built-in MapGet operation that will look up a value from a Map by key.

Emit the resulting value from the map as a count field.

Now we have the results of the count for each tag that we wanted. We can stop here in the DRPC stream and be done. Optionally, we can append an additional each operation to filter out null counts (that is, tags that haven't yet been encountered on the play stream), but we'll leave the nulls as something to be handled by the DRPC caller.

This brings us to our final step: being able to communicate with Storm via a DRPC client.

9.5.3   *Making DRPC calls with a DRPC client*

Making a DRPC request to this topology can be done by including Storm as a dependency in your client application and using the DRPC client built into Storm. Once you've done this, you can use something similar to the code in the next listing for making the actual DRPC request.

Listing 9.16   Performing a DRPC request

```
DRPCClient client = new DRPCClient("drpc.server.location", 3772);
try {
    String result = client.execute("count-request-by-tag",
                        "Punk,Post Punk,Hardcore Punk");
    System.out.println(result);
} catch (TException e) {
    // thrift error
} catch (DRPCExecutionException e) {
    // drpc execution error
}
```

Initiate a DRPC Client with the hostname and port of the Storm DRPC server.

Provide the function arguments as a comma-delimited list.

Invoke a DRPC request with the same DRPC function name as used in the topology.

Print the result containing the JSON-encoded tuple

DRPC requests are made over the Thrift protocol, so you'll need to handle the Thrift-related errors (usually connectivity-related) as well as DRPCExecutionException errors (usually feature-related). And that's it. We haven't left you hanging. You now have a topology that maintains state with the counts for various fields of artist, title, and tag, and you're able to query that state. We've built a fully functional topology using Trident and Storm DRPC.

Or is that it? If you've learned anything from earlier chapters, it's that once you've deployed your topology, your job as a developer hasn't ended. The same holds true here. Section 9.6 discusses how Trident operations map to Storm primitives using the Storm UI to identify the spouts and bolts that are created under the covers. Section 9.7 will then touch upon scaling a Trident topology.

9.6   *Mapping Trident operations to Storm primitives*

Recall that in the beginning of the chapter we discussed how Trident topologies are built on top of the Storm primitives that we've become comfortable with over the course of this book. With our use case complete, let's take a look at how Storm turns our Trident topology into bolts and spouts. We'll start by looking at how our topology, sans our DRPC spout, is mapped down to Storm primitives. Why not just look at everything at once? We feel it will be easier to understand what exactly is going on by addressing the core Trident streams first and then tacking on the DRPC stream.

Without our DRPC spout, our TopologyBuilder code can be seen in the following listing.

> **Listing 9.17   TopologyBuilder.java without the DRPC stream**

```java
public TopologyBuilder {
  public StormTopology build() {
    TridentTopology topology = new TridentTopology();

    Stream playStream = topology
      .newStream("play-spout", buildSpout())
      .each(new Fields("play-log"),
            new LogDeserializer(),
            new Fields("artist", "title", "tags"))
      .each(new Fields("artist", "title"),
            new Sanitizer(new Fields("artist", "title")));

    TridentState countByArtist = playStream
      .project(new Fields("artist"))
      .groupBy(new Fields("artist"))
      .persistentAggregate(new MemoryMapState.Factory(),
                      new Count(),
                      new Fields("artist-count"));

    TridentState countsByTitle = playStream
      .project(new Fields("title"))
      .groupBy(new Fields("title"))
      .persistentAggregate(new MemoryMapState.Factory(),
                      new Count(),
                      new Fields("title-count"));
```

```
TridentState countsByTag = playStream
  .each(new Fields("tags"),
        new ListSplitter(),
        new Fields("tag"))
  .project(new Fields("tag"))
  .groupBy(new Fields("tag"))
  .persistentAggregate(new MemoryMapState.Factory(),
                       new Count(),
                       new Fields("tag-count"));

return topology.build();
}


...
}
```

When our Trident topology is being turned into a Storm topology, Storm takes our Trident operations and packages them into bolts in a way that's efficient. Some operations will be grouped together into the same bolts whereas others will be separate. The Storm UI provides a view into how that mapping is being done (figure 9.10).

As you can see, we have one spout and six bolts. Two of the bolts have the name "spout" in them and four others are labeled b-0 to b-3. We can see some components there but we have no idea how they're related to our Trident operations.

Rather than try to figure out the mystery behind the names, we'll show you a way to make it easier to identify the components. Trident has a name operation that assigns a

Spouts (All time)

Id	Executors	Tasks	Emitted
$mastercoord-bg0	1	1	800

Bolts (All time)

Id	Executors	Tasks	Emitted	Transferred
$spoutcoord-spout0	1	1	180	180
b-0	1	1	0	0
b-1	1	1	0	0
b-2	1	1	4440	4440
b-3	1	1	0	0
spout0	1	1	1720	1720

Figure 9.10   Our Trident topology broken down into spouts and bolts in the Storm UI

name we specify to an operation. If we name each collection of operations in our topology, our code ends up like that in the next listing.

Listing 9.18   `TopologyBuilder.java` **with named operations**

```
public TopologyBuilder {
  public StormTopology build() {
    TridentTopology topology = new TridentTopology();

    Stream playStream = topology
      .newStream("play-spout", buildSpout())
      .each(new Fields("play-log"),
            new LogDeserializer(),
            new Fields("artist", "title", "tags"))
      .each(new Fields("artist", "title"),
            new Sanitizer(new Fields("artist", "title")))
      .name("LogDeserializerSanitizer");

    TridentState countByArtist = playStream
      .project(new Fields("artist"))
      .groupBy(new Fields("artist"))
      .name("ArtistCounts")
      .persistentAggregate(new MemoryMapState.Factory(),
                           new Count(),
                           new Fields("artist-count"));

    TridentState countsByTitle = playStream
      .project(new Fields("title"))
      .groupBy(new Fields("title"))
      .name("TitleCounts")
      .persistentAggregate(new MemoryMapState.Factory(),
                           new Count(),
                           new Fields("title-count"));

    TridentState countsByTag = playStream
      .each(new Fields("tags"),
            new ListSplitter(),
            new Fields("tag"))
      .project(new Fields("tag"))
      .groupBy(new Fields("tag"))
      .name("TagCounts")
      .persistentAggregate(new MemoryMapState.Factory(),
                           new Count(),
                           new Fields("tag-count"));

    return topology.build();
  }

  ...
}
```

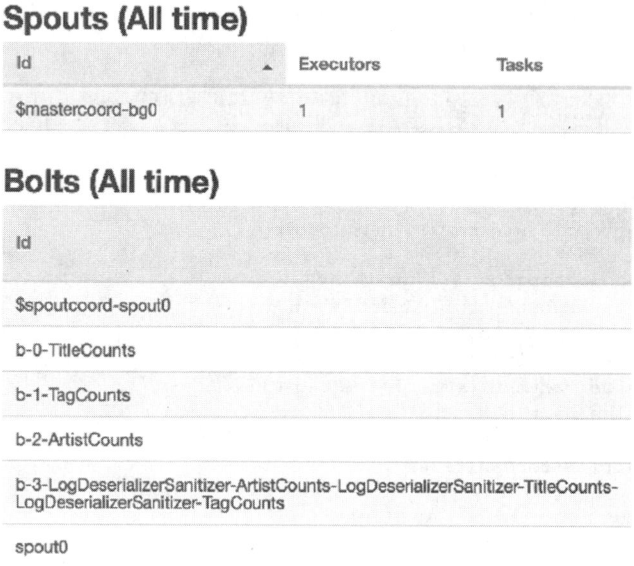

Spouts (All time)

Id	Executors	Tasks
$mastercoord-bg0	1	1

Bolts (All time)

Id
$spoutcoord-spout0
b-0-TitleCounts
b-1-TagCounts
b-2-ArtistCounts
b-3-LogDeserializerSanitizer-ArtistCounts-LogDeserializerSanitizer-TitleCounts-LogDeserializerSanitizer-TagCounts
spout0

Figure 9.11 Our Trident topology displayed on the Storm UI after naming each of the operations

If we take a look at our Storm UI, what's going on becomes much more apparent (figure 9.11).

We can see that our `b-3` bolt was log deserialization and sanitation. And our `b-0`, `b-1`, and `b-2` bolt our title, tag, and artist counting, respectively. Given the amount of clarity that using names provides, we recommend you always name your partitions.

What's up with the name of the log deserialization bolt? `LogDeserializerSanitizer-ArtistCounts-LogDeserializerSanitizer-TitleCounts-LogDeserializerSanitizer-TagCounts`—what a mouthful! But it does provide us with a great deal of information. The name indicates that we're getting our data from the log deserializer and sanitizer and feeding into artist counts, title counts, and tag counts. It's not the most elegant of discovery mechanisms but it beats just b-0 and so on.

With this additional clarity, take a look at figure 9.12, which illustrates how our Trident operations are mapped down into bolts. Now let's add back the DRPC stream with relevant names as well. The code for this appears in the next listing.

Listing 9.19 The DRPC stream with named operations

```
topology.newDRPCStream("count-request-by-tag")
  .name("RequestForTagCounts")
  .each(new Fields("args"),
      new SplitOnDelimiter(","),
      new Fields("tag"))
  .groupBy(new Fields("tag"))
  .name("QueryForRequest")
  .stateQuery(countsByTag,
          new Fields("tag"),
          new MapGet(),
          new Fields("count"));
```

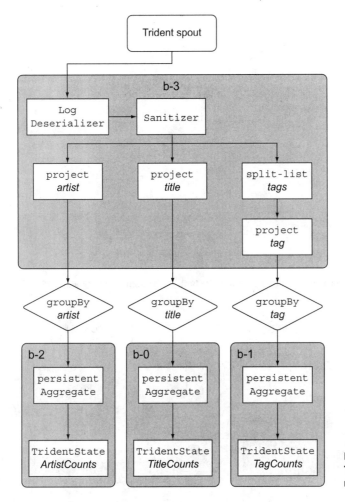

Figure 9.12   How our Trident operations are mapped down into bolts

Adding the DRPC stream with named operations results in the Storm UI seen in figure 9.13.

What has changed? Well…

Our log sanitizer bolt is now b-2 rather than b-3. This is very important. You can't rely on the autogenerated bolt names remaining the same when you make changes to the number of bolts in the topology.

The number of named bolts has increased from 4 to 5 and the names of those bolts have changed.

We have some unnamed bolts. What's going on with the bolt name changes? The addition of our DRPC spout has changed the mapping onto Storm primitives and names have changed accordingly. Figure 9.14 shows the final mapping of Trident/DRPC operations into bolts.

Bolts (All time)

Id	Executors	Tasks
$spoutcoord-spout0	1	1
b-0-TitleCounts	1	1
b-1-LogDeserializerSanitizer-ArtistCounts-LogDeserializerSanitizer-TitleCounts- LogDeserializerSanitizer-TagCounts	1	1
b-2	1	1
b-3-TagCounts-QueryForRequest	1	1
b-4	1	1
b-5-RequestForTagCounts	1	1
b-6-ArtistCounts	1	1
spout0	1	1

Figure 9.13   The Storm UI with named operations for both the Trident topology and DRPC stream

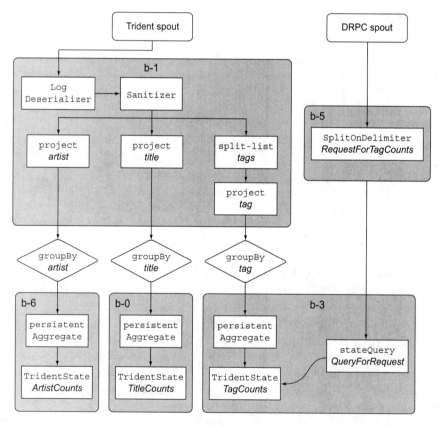

Figure 9.14   How the Trident and DRPC streams and operations are being mapped down into bolts

Note how "Tag Counts" and "Query for Request" are mapped to the same bolt and the name has been adjusted accordingly. Okay, but what about those unnamed bolts? The reason why we saw some components named as spouts in the bolts section of the UI is because Storm runs Trident spouts wrapped in a bolt. Remember that Trident spouts aren't the same as native Storm spouts. Additionally, Trident topologies have other coordinators that allow us to treat an incoming stream as a series of batches. Storm introduced them when we added the DRPC spout to our topology and changed how it was mapped to Storm.

Identifying how Storm maps Trident operations to native Storm components is easy with a few extra lines of code. Adding names is the key and will save you headaches. Now that you have an idea of how to map native Storm components to Trident operations via names and the Storm UI, let's turn our attention to the final topic of this chapter: scaling a Trident topology.

9.7 Scaling a Trident topology

Let's talk units of parallelism. When working with bolts and spouts, we trade in executors and tasks. They form our primary means of parallelism between components. When working with Trident, we still work with them but only tangentially as Trident operations are mapped down to those primitives. When working with Trident, our primary method to achieve parallelism is the partition.

9.7.1 Partitions for parallelism

With Trident, we take a stream of data and work with it across one or more worker processes by partitioning the stream and applying our operations in parallel across each of the partitions. If we had five partitions within our topology and three worker processes, our work would be distributed in a fashion similar to what's shown in figure 9.15.

Unlike Storm, where we imagine our parallelism as spreading executors across a series of worker processes, here we're imagining our parallelism as a series of partitions being spread across a series of worker processes. The way we scale our Trident topology is by adjusting the number of partitions.

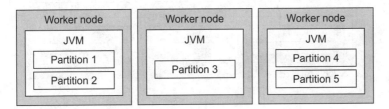

Figure 9.15 Partitions are distributed across storm worker process (JVMs) and operated on in parallel

9.7.2 *Partitions in Trident streams*

Partitions start at the Trident spout. A Trident spout (a much different beast from a Storm spout) will emit a stream, which then has a set of Trident operations applied to it. This stream is partitioned to provide parallelism for the topology. Trident will break down this partitioned stream into a series of small batches containing thousands of tuples to perhaps millions of tuples, depending on your incoming throughput. Figure 9.16 shows the zoomed-in view of what a Trident stream looks like between two Trident operations or between the Trident spout and the first Trident operation.

If parallelism starts at the spout, and we adjust the number of partitions to control parallelism, how do we adjust the number of partitions at the spout? We adjust the number of partitions for the Kafka topic we're subscribed to. If we had one partition for our Kafka topic, then we'd start with one partition in our topology. If we increased our Kafka topic to having three partitions, the number of partitions in our Trident topology would change accordingly (figure 9.17).

From here, our stream with three partitions can be partitioned further by various operations. Let's step back from talking about having three partitions from the spout and go back to having just one; it will make everything else easier to reason about when learning more about parallelism within our Trident topology.

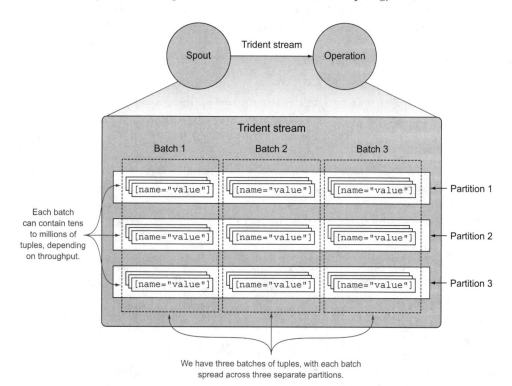

Figure 9.16 Partitioned stream with a series of batches in between two operations

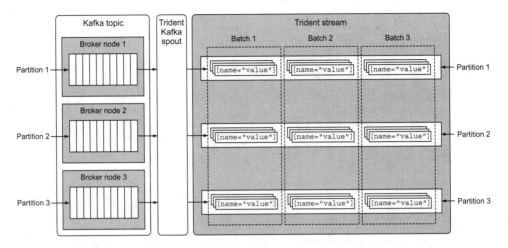

Figure 9.17 Kafka topic partitions and how they relate to the partitions within a Trident stream

Within a Trident topology, natural points of partition will exist. Points where partitioning has to change are based on the operations being applied. At these points, you can adjust the parallelism of each of the resulting partitions. The groupBy operations that we use in our topology result in repartitioning. Each of our groupBy operations resulted in a repartitioning that we could supply a parallelism hint to, as shown in the following listing.

Listing 9.20 Specifying parallelism at the points of repartition

```
public static StormTopology build() {
  TridentTopology topology = new TridentTopology();

  Stream playStream =
    topology.newStream("play-spout", buildSpout())
            .each(new Fields("play-log"),
                  new LogDeserializer(),
                  new Fields("artist", "title", "tags"))
            .each(new Fields("artist", "title"),
                  new Sanitizer(new Fields("artist", "title")))
            .name("LogDeserializerSanitizer");

  TridentState countByArtist = playStream
    .project(new Fields("artist"))
    .groupBy(new Fields("artist"))
    .name("ArtistCounts")
    .persistentAggregate(new MemoryMapState.Factory(),
                    new Count(),
                    new Fields("artist-count"))
    .parallelismHint(4);

  TridentState countsByTitle = playStream
    .project(new Fields("title"))
    .groupBy(new Fields("title"))
    .name("TitleCounts")
```

```
        .persistentAggregate(new MemoryMapState.Factory(),
                            new Count(),
                            new Fields("title-count"))
    .parallelismHint(4);

TridentState countsByTag = playStream
    .each(new Fields("tags"),
        new ListSplitter(),
        new Fields("tag"))
    .project(new Fields("tag"))
    .groupBy(new Fields("tag"))
    .name("TagCounts")
    .persistentAggregate(new MemoryMapState.Factory(),
                        new Count(),
                        new Fields("tag-count"))
    .parallelismHint(4);

topology.newDRPCStream("count-request-by-tag")
        .name("RequestForTagCounts")
        .each(new Fields("args"),
            new SplitOnDelimiter(","),
            new Fields("tag"))
        .groupBy(new Fields("tag"))
        .name("QueryForRequest")
        .stateQuery(countsByTag,
                    new Fields("tag"),
                    new MapGet(),
                    new Fields("count"));

    return topology.build();
}
```

Here we've given each of our final three bolts a parallelism of four. That means they each operate with four partitions. We were able to specify a level of parallelism for those because there's natural repartitioning happening between them and bolts that came before them due to groupBy and persistentAggregate operations. We didn't specify any parallelism hint to our first two bolts because they don't have any inherent repartitioning going on between them and the spouts that came before them. Therefore, they operate at the same number of partitions as the spouts. Figure 9.18 shows what this configuration looks like in the Storm UI.

Forcing a repartition

In addition to natural changes in partitions that happen as a result of groupBy operations, we have the ability to force Trident to repartition operations. Such operations will cause tuples to be transferred across the network as the partitions are changed. This will have a negative impact on performance. You should avoid repartitioning solely for the sake of changing parallelism unless you can verify that your parallelism hints post repartitioning have caused an overall throughput increase.

Bolts (All time)

Id		Executors	Tasks	Emitted	Transferred	Capacity (last 10m)
$spoutcoord-spout0	▲	1	1			0.000
b-0-RequestForTagCounts		1	1			0.000
b-1-TagCounts-QueryForRequest		4	4			0.000
b-2-LogDeserializerSanitizer-ArtistCounts-LogDeserializerSanitizer-TitleCounts-LogDeserializerSanitizer-TagCounts		1	1			0.000
b-3-ArtistCounts		4	4			0.000
b-4		1	1			0.000
b-5		1	1			0.000
b-6-TitleCounts		4	4			0.000
spout0		1	1			0.000

Figure 9.18 **Result of applying a parallelism hint of four to the `groupBy` operations in our Trident topology**

This brings us to the close of Trident. You've learned quite a bit in this chapter, all of which was built on a foundation that was laid in the first eight chapters of this book. Hopefully this foundation is only the beginning of your adventure with Storm, and our goal is for you to continue to refine and tune these skills as you use Storm for any problem you may encounter.

9.8 Summary

In this chapter, you learned that

- Trident allows you to focus on the "what" of solving a problem rather than the "how."
- Trident makes use of operations that operate on batches of tuples, which are different from native Storm bolts that operate on individual tuples.
- Kafka is a distributed message queue implementation that aligns perfectly with how Trident operates on batches of tuples across partitions.
- Trident operations don't map one-to-one to spouts and bolts, so it's important to always name your operations.
- Storm DRPC is a useful way to execute a distributed query against persistent state calculated by a Storm topology.
- Scaling a Trident topology is much different than scaling a native Storm topology and is done across partitions as opposed to setting exact instances of spouts and bolts.

afterword

Congratulations, you've made it to the end of the book. Where do you go from here? The answer depends on how you got here. If you read the book from start to end, we suggest implementing your own topologies while referring back to various chapters until you feel like you're "getting the hang of Storm." We hesitate to say "mastering Storm" as we're not sure you'll ever feel like you're mastering Storm. It's a powerful and complicated beast, and mastery is a tricky thing.

If you took a more iterative approach to the book, working through it slowly and gaining expertise as you went along, then everything else that follows in this afterword is for you. Don't worry if you took the start-to-end approach; this afterword will be waiting for you once you feel like you're getting the hang of Storm. Here are all the things we want you to know as you set off on the rest of your Storm journey without us.

YOU'RE RIGHT, YOU DON'T KNOW THAT

We've been using Storm in production for quite a while now, and we're still learning new things all the time. Don't worry if you feel like you don't know everything. Use what you know to get what you need done. You'll learn more as you go. Analysis paralysis can be a real thing with Storm.

THERE'S SO MUCH TO KNOW

We haven't covered every last nook and cranny of Storm. Dig into the official documentation, join the IRC channel, and join the mailing list. Storm is an evolving project. At the time this book is going to press, it hasn't even reached version 1.0. If you're using Storm for business-critical processes, make sure you know how to stay up to date. Here are a couple of things we think you should keep an eye on:

- Storm on Yarn
- Storm on Mesos

What's Yarn? What's Mesos? That's really a book unto itself. For now, let's just say they're cluster resource managers that can allow you to share Storm cluster resources with other technologies such as Hadoop. That's a gross simplification. We strongly advise you to check out Yarn and Mesos if you are planning on running a large Storm cluster in production. There's a lot of exciting stuff going on in those projects.

METRICS AND REPORTING

The metrics support in Storm is pretty young. We suspect it will grow a lot more robust over time. Additionally, the most recent version of Storm introduced a REST API that allows you to access the information from the Storm UI in a programmatic fashion. That's not particularly exciting outside of a couple of automation or monitoring scenarios. But it creates a path for exposing more information about what's going on inside Storm to the outside world in an easily accessible fashion. We wouldn't be surprised at all if some really cool things were built by exposing still more info via that API.

TRIDENT IS QUITE A BEAST

We spent one chapter on Trident. A lot of debate went into how much we should cover Trident. This ranged from nothing to several chapters. We settled on a single chapter to get you going with Trident. Why? Well, we considered not covering Trident at all. You can happily use Storm without ever needing to touch Trident. We don't consider it a core part of Storm, but one of many abstractions you can build on top of Storm (more on that later). Even if that's true, we were disabused of the notion that we couldn't cover it at all based on feedback where every early reviewer brought up Trident as a must-cover topic.

We considered spending three chapters on Trident much like we had three chapters on core Storm (chapters 2 to 4) and introducing it in the same fashion. If we were writing a book on Trident, we would have taken that approach, but large portions of those chapters would have mirrored the content in chapters 2 to 4. Trident is, after all, an abstraction on top of Storm. We settled on a single chapter intro to Trident because we felt that as long as you understood the basics of Trident, everything else would flow from there. There are many more Trident operations we didn't cover, but they all operate in the same fashion as the ones we did cover. If Trident seems like a better approach than core Storm for your problems, we feel we've given you what you need to dig in and start solving with Trident.

WHEN SHOULD I USE TRIDENT?

Use Trident only when you need to. Trident adds a lot of complexity compared to core Storm. It's easier to debug problems with core Storm because there are fewer layers of abstraction to get through. Core Storm is also considerably faster than Trident. If you are really concerned about speed, favor core Storm. Why might you need to use Trident?

- "What" not "how" is very important to you.
  - The important algorithmic details of your computation are hard to follow using core Storm but are very clear using Trident. If your process is all about the algorithm, and it's hard to see what's going on with core Storm, maintenance is going to be difficult.

- You need exactly once processing.
  - As we discussed in chapter 4, exactly once processing is very hard to achieve; some would say it's impossible. We won't go that far. We will say that there are scenarios where it's impossible. Even when it is possible, getting it right can be hard. Trident can help you build an exactly once processing system. You can do that with core Storm as well but there's more work involved on your part.
- You need to maintain state.
  - Again, you can do this with core Storm, but Trident is good at maintaining state, and DRPC provides a nice way to get at that state. If your workload is less about data pipelines (transforming input to output and feeding that output into another data pipeline) and more about creating queryable pools of data, then Trident state with DRPC can help you get there.

ABSTRACTIONS! ABSTRACTIONS EVERYWHERE!

Trident isn't the only abstraction that runs on Storm. We've seen numerous projects come and go in GitHub that try to build on top of Storm. Honestly, most of them weren't that interesting. If you do the same type of work in topology after topology, perhaps you too will create your own abstraction over Storm to make that particular workflow easier. The most interesting abstraction over Storm that currently exists is Algebird (https://github.com/twitter/algebird) from Twitter.

Algebird is a Scala library that allows you to write abstract algebra code that can be "compiled" to run on either Storm or Hadoop. Why is that interesting? You can code up various algorithms and then reuse them in both batch and streaming contexts. That's pretty damn cool if you ask us. Even if you don't need to write reusable algebras, we suggest you check out the project if you're interested in building abstractions on top of Storm; you can learn a lot from it.

And that really is it from us. Good luck; we're rooting for you! Sean, Matt, and Peter out.

index

Big Data
Principles and best practices of scalable realtime data systems
by Nathan Marz and James Warren

ISBN: 9781617290343
425 pages, $49.99
April 2015

Hadoop in Action, Second Edition
by Chuck P. Lam and Mark W. Davis

ISBN: 9781617912272
525 pages, $49.99
July 2015

Hadoop in Practice, Second Edition
by Alex Holmes

ISBN: 9781617292224
512 pages, $49.99
September 2014

Solr in Action
by Trey Grainger and Timothy Potter

ISBN: 9781617291029
664 pages, $49.99
March 2014

For ordering information go to www.manning.com

YOU MAY ALSO BE INTERESTED IN

Elasticsearch in Action
by Radu Gheorghe, Matthew Lee Hinman, and
   Roy Russo

   ISBN: 9781617291623
   400 pages, $44.99
   June 2015

Clojure in Action, Second Edition
by Amit Rathore

   ISBN: 9781617291524
   400 pages, $49.99
   June 2015

The Joy of Clojure, Second Edition
by Michael Fogus and Chris Houser

   ISBN: 9781617291418
   520 pages, $49.99
   May 2014

Neo4j in Action
by Aleksa Vukotic and Nicki Watt
   with Tareq Abedrabbo, Dominic Fox,
   and Jonas Partner

   ISBN: 9781617290763
   304 pages, $44.99
   December 2014

For ordering information go to www.manning.com